D0299840

The Coincidence File

Ken Anderson

Bounty
Books

First published in 1999 by Blandford, a Cassell imprint

This edition published in 2007 by Bounty Books,
a division of Octopus Publishing Group Ltd
2-4 Heron Quays, London E14 4JP
Reprinted in 2009

Text copyright © Ken Anderson 1999
This volume copyright © Octopus Publishing Group Ltd 2007

All rights reserved. No part of this work may be
reproduced or utilized in any form or by any means,
electronic or mechanical, including photocopying, recording
or by any information storage and retrieval system, without
the prior written permission of the publisher.

ISBN: 978-0-753714-99-7

A CIP catalogue record for this book is available from
the British Library

Printed and bound in Great Britain

Contents

Preface 7

Introduction 13

PART I   chapter one Awareness 20

chapter two Morphic Resonance 43

chapter three Playing with Numbers 54

chapter four Intuition 63

chapter five Jung and Astrology 70

chapter six Time 76

chapter seven Miracles 81

chapter eight Names 92

chapter nine Fancy Meeting You Here 99

chapter ten Diary Keeping 104

PART II   chapter eleven Coincidence File I 122

chapter twelve Coincidence File II 134

chapter thirteen Coincidence File III 146

chapter fourteen Coincidence File IV 158

chapter fifteen Coincidence File V 169

chapter sixteen Coincidence File VI 180

chapter seventeen Coincidence File VII 189

PART III   chapter eighteen The Lincoln–Kennedy Assassinations 199

appendix Psychology and Coincidences 229

Notes to Text 239

Further Reading 247

Index 251

Preface

In many ways this is a people's book – extraordinary stories told by normal people amounting to a body of evidence that shows just how all-pervasive coincidences are in our lives. Many of these stories, from all over the world, were provided by readers of my previous work *Coincidences: Chance or Fate?*. Their generosity in sharing their experiences and the other material they have gathered has contributed greatly to the genesis of *The Coincidence File*. I am most grateful.

In fact, reading *Coincidences: Chance or Fate?* brought about some unusual synchronistic appearances for some. Singaporean psychic counsellor Scarlet Kesavan was fascinated by the coincidence involved with her purchase of the previous book. In 1993 she attended a rally in Singapore conducted by the evangelist C. E. Davies, and was impressed by his brochure, which she placed in the Bible she had bought at the rally. Having looked through its pages briefly, she put it aside.

Two years later, almost to the day that she had attended the Davies rally, she felt an urge to begin reading the Bible. It is a calendar Bible so she started on that day's page, 2 August. The following day she received a copy of *Coincidences: Chance or Fate?* in the mail. The cover illustration shows two bolts of lightning striking one spot. She glanced at the brochure, which depicts an eerily similar scene: in the foreground the evangelist is performing miracle cures, in the background two lightning bolts are striking at one place in a black sky. As she compared the cover with the brochure, Scarlet found herself agreeing with the latter's heading: All Things Are Possible. Scarlet adds:

> I don't know why I chose to read the Bible all of a sudden. Could it be that
> I may find interesting material for myself in both books. Or is it just the
> message on both covers that gives the message?

Coincidences have been a hobby of David Ball of Frinton-on-Sea, Essex, for many years. He stresses that it is a minor hobby because he feels he could easily became obsessed. He read in the 'Diaries' section (Chapter 15) of *Coincidences: Chance or Fate?* several entries that jogged his memory regarding very similar personal experiences. Then another occurred, good enough, in the circumstances, to record. This is his own diary entry for 13 June 1996:

> I had just been reading *Coincidences: Chance or Fate?*, last chapter 'Diaries', when I remembered my neighbour's front door key which he had given me for security reasons while he was away. I went into the next room, found the key and put it on a key ring with my other neighbour's key, given to me earlier for the same reasons. I studied them so as to remember which was which, then I thought, 'That's daft, if one doesn't fit, it's the other.' Having sorted that out I looked up, and there looking back at me was the title of a library book lying on the table, *Philosophy in a New Key* (Langer, Harvard University Press, 1967).
>
> Returning to *Coincidences: Chance or Fate?* I came across, '11 March...had two extra door keys cut...Neither worked. Later today was speaking to a woman about a hall she manages. She said she had just had two new keys cut and neither of them worked...'

Ball goes on to say that a few days later he went to stay for a week in his apartment on the Spanish Mediterranean island of Menorca and was woken on the second day by a carpenter replacing the lock on the front door of the block. He was given a new key by the president of the block's community association and some others which he agreed to distribute to other owners (he being the association secretary).

Wyn Griffiths of Caerphilly, Mid Glamorgan, writes he has many friends who have had coincidence experiences, but he personally could not remember anything like that happening to him. Then one day he was reading *The Celestine Prophecy* by James Redfield, which has a great deal to say about the subject of coincidences. After finishing the first chapter he visited the local library. Wyn goes on:

> The first book I picked off the shelf was yours *(Coincidence: Chance or Fate?)*. I came home, started reading your book, turned on the radio and, as I was reading your bit about Dr Rupert Sheldrake (pp. 42–4), I heard the very man talking on BBC Radio about telepathic dogs. That impressed me greatly and I shall be on the lookout for more.

While Sue Flentjar of Wangaratta, Victoria, also found her thoughts of coincidences changing when she went to her public library and took out my book. That night she was about a third of the way through it, concluding her reading with the anecdote about Tony Hancock, whose life came to an end with his suicide in 1968. In 1992 during filming of his life story, cast and crew were re-creating the famous 'The Blood Donor' scene, when one of the crew pointed out that of all the studios in the vast complex, they had chosen the one that Hancock had used to do the original sketch. At that point Sue put the book aside and went to sleep. 'I read this segment with not a great amount of interest,' she confesses, 'as I had never heard of that particular sketch and didn't really know much about Tony Hancock himself, as he was probably a little before my time.'

Next day, at the retirement hostel where she works, Sue was moved 'for some reason' to flick through a pile of 45 rpm records that had been lying around for at least a year as far as she could remember:

> Believe it or not the second record in the pile was a recording of 'The Blood Donor' by Tony Hancock. Why I chose this particular day to look through those records is a mystery to me, as I have no interest in old records at all and the fact that I did on a day after reading your book is something that absolutely amazes me. It certainly makes me look differently at the mystery of coincidences.

Teresa Holland, of Clearview, South Australia, also has a tale to tell. After reading my book, which she borrowed from the library, she forgot to note my address, which is in the back of the book, so asked a friend, Wendy, who is a librarian, to get the book for her. However, during a busy working day, Wendy forgot the request until she came upon a copy by accident. It was on the floor next to the box where books are put to have the bar-codes replaced. Wendy naturally assumed that it had somehow fallen out of the box. But when she examined the book she found its bar-code was in order. 'So there was no reason at all that the book should have been there,' Teresa writes. 'I had returned the book a week before, so it should have been on the shelf. Spooky!!'

Mrs Suni G. Cabrera of Carolina, Puerto Rico, wrote to say:

> Thank you very much for writing this book…I tend to read rather esoteric books, combined with biographies and art books. This terrific book is my first on the subject and through it I have thought much about the collective unconscious and such…I'm enjoying it.

She goes on to say that two-thirds of the way through reading *Coincidences: Chance or Fate?* she took a break in order to balance her chequebook. Her balance looked like this:

```
        $ 50.00
        $532.01
        $ 68.00
        $ 16.65
Total: $666 .66.
```

She also adds a tip for those who want an above average level of awareness: 'Perceiving one coincidence certainly sets you up for another.'

Tony Mills of Bristol says that before borrowing *Coincidences: Chance
or Fate?* from his local library he took it from the shelf and opened it
part way through the section that talks about G. K. Chesterton. After
deciding to take the book out he made his way to the fiction section
where he came across a new book by one of his favourite authors, Terry
Pratchett, *Good Omens,* which Pratchett co-wrote with Neil Gaiman.
Lifting it from the shelf, he glanced at its cover where there was a dedi-
cation: 'To the memory of G. K. Chesterton, a man who knew what
was going on.' Mills adds:

> I have long been an observer of [coincidences] and many times have thought I
> was alone in this. It's amazing how some people simply switch off from these
> fascinating occurrences, leaving one with the feeling that interest in them must
> be a kind of madness! Anyway, it was a great treat and relief to read your
> book, if only to feel that I'm not alone. Thanks for a stimulating book, and may
> all your synchronicities be favourable!

Greg Carden, of Northport, Alabama, says he had gone to a bookstore
hoping to find a copy of Ira Progoff's *Jung, Synchronicity and Human
Destiny* (Dell, New York, 1973). He failed to do so but did come across
Coincidences: Chance or Fate?. 'I have wondered why there were no published accounts of a large series of synchronicities till I found your
book,' he writes. 'I feel quite blessed. Whatever the theory, they are, I
think, entertaining to read about.'

In *Coincidences: Chance or Fate?* (pp. 66–8) I wrote in some detail
about the connection of Beatle John Lennon with the number 9.
Although the number appeared to have eluded him at his death – he
was shot dead in New York at 11.15 p.m. on 8 December 1980 – a
numerologist has pointed out that in numerology the influence of the
following day begins at 11 p.m. the previous day. Several readers,
including Teresa Holland of South Australia and Wilma Ward of
Middletown, New York, came up with an alternative suggestion: at the
time of his death, it would have been five hours later in his birthplace,
England, and therefore 9 December.

A chill ran through Eileen Greenwood when she read a short anecdote headed 'Butlers did it' in a previous book of mine, *Extraordinary Coincidences* (HarperCollins, Sydney, 1993). The item appeared on page 166 of that book and told how on 1 April 1930 two men, each named Butler, both butchers by occupation, had been found shot dead. One was named Frederick Henry Butler, the other David Henry Butler. They were not related and had not known one another. Both had shot themselves with pistols and were each found by the side of their cars. As she absorbed the facts, Eileen found her memory and emotions stirring as she identified with them. She was born on 1 April 1930 (in Portsmouth, England), their next-door neighbours were named Butler. Her second husband's name is Frederick and her brother's name is Henry. Her only son is named David. Her first husband shot himself and was found by the side of his car on 16 April 1966 (or 16/4/66 – note the page number). Having got over her surprise, Eileen read on and two items later on the same page came across the number 424. Again her memory stirred. She had been among the evacuees from England to Australia in 1940 and had never forgotten her identity number – 424.

The following is a selection of other readers' comments on *Coincidences: Chance or Fate?*:

> I am teaching a course on paranormal experiences, and came across your book *Coincidences: Chance or Fate?*. It was a marvellous find, and has been very helpful to me in this part of my research. It is the first formal study I have ever found on the subject. I also appreciate your effort to discover the 'meaning' of these events. That is quite courageous. Your interpretation of the phenomenon in terms of probability theory is interesting, but I agree that is 'probably' due to some spiritual law which we have yet to discover.
> Rev. John W. Sloat, Edinburg, Pennsylvania, USA

> I checked out *Coincidences: Chance or Fate?* from the local public library and read it completely through in one sitting. That means it's absolutely interesting and very relevant to my life.
> Catherine Cline, Jacksonville, Florida, USA

> I enjoyed your book very much, I read a review about it and ran out and bought it and read it last night, it was great!
> John Drake, Irving, Texas, USA

> I love your book. Not only is it the greatest and most amazing collection of truly extraordinary occurrences and coincidences, you have also done so much far-reaching and diverse research into the meaning of coincidences that I can only marvel. Eye-catching chapter headings make finding favourite passages easy. So, besides being a serious study for those of us who collect them *Coincidences: Chance or Fate?* makes a beautiful coffee-table book. People

will invariably want to share their own amazing experiences, even if at other times they'd be hard pressed to admit them at all.
Ute Kaboolian, Cliffside Park, New Jersey, USA

I have enjoyed reading our book.
Hilary Sumner, Unionville, Connecticut, USA

I have read with pleasure *Coincidences: Chance or Fate?* which hints somehow at an invisible intelligence force beyond. I wish you success.
Peter Suba, The Archimedes Foundation, Toronto, Canada

The subject is very intriguing and the book much enjoyed.
Robert Beame, Milton-Freewater, Oregon, USA

I appreciate and congratulate you for the great pains you have taken to complete this invaluable and treasured book. I sincerely pray the Almighty to bless you with more energy, support and courage for your sincere and dedicated research work on this and whatever new topics/issues you are going to undertake.
S. Hari Haran Iyer, Pimpri, Pune, Maharashtra State, India

I have just finished reading your book and I found it fascinating. Coincidence is something we can all relate to; it probably happens more often than we are even aware of.
Rhonda Russell, Hastings, Victoria, Australia

Thank you for your book. It was fun to read.
Sharon Martens, Milwaukee, Wisconsin, USA

Keep up the good work and may God bless you in all your efforts.
Lilian Mahoney, Coventry, England

I would like to take a few more lines to thank the many people who have contributed not just their own anecdotes, but constructive thoughts, wisdom and professionalism, in particular, my wife Jacqueline Lee Lewes, my agent Fiona Inglis (Curtis Brown), consultant editor Stuart Booth, editor Antonia Maxwell, Martin Cochrane (Australia), Joanne Stead (England) and Jeriann Sharf (USA).

Every effort has been made to contact holders of copyright material used in this book and I am grateful to those authors, academics, publishers, etc. who have willingly consented to the use of such material.

I look forward to hearing from you.

Ken Anderson
PO Box 429, Newtown, NSW, Australia 2042
E-mail: anderson@aisl.com.au
Fax: 02 99 08 20 64

Introduction

Like its predecessor, the main aim of *The Coincidence File* is to entertain, but it does have a secondary aim: to raise, or improve the reader's awareness of this ubiquitous phenomenon.

Coincidences retain an age-old fascination and mystery, no matter what your perspective or how you interpret them. However, with the new millennium approaching, they have, for many people, taken on a special cachet and a mystical aura. The phenomenon has become a 'hot' topic for the New Age followers, many of whom appear to believe they are a recent 'discovery', pointing to a coming higher evolutionary stage and New Age of enlightenment.

The first thing we should understand about this 'discovery' – that coincidences somehow carry more than their intrinsic value – is that for many centuries coincidences were regarded as symbols of our inter-connectedness with the universe, with nature, with one another, and with a higher plane of existence. Non-causal events, such as a miracle recovery from serious illness, a dream or vision of the future, or the unexpected meeting between two or more people, have been regarded since the dawn of civilization as indicators of the common resonances that run through the very existence of life. In brief, coincidences were accepted long ago as natural occurrences and an indivisible part of the spiritual life that dominated society.

Then came the seventeenth century and a mechanistic view of the world, as espoused by the new scientists, Isaac Newton, Johannes Kepler, and Galileo. In this brave new world, the idea of apparently unconnected events joining to create a meaningful incident held no sway. A further blow to this idea came with the development of probability theory (see p. 54). Probability came of age in the twentieth century and mathematicians have enjoyed themselves for years reducing the odds of many seemingly, to the layman at least, 'amazing coincidences' to a statistically probable level. Given a large enough sample number, calculated into a comparison equation, many mathematicians assert that the oddest things are not only possible but likely to happen. Mathematicians allow little room for significant coincidences.

A contrasting view is based on another theory from earlier in the twentieth century. Pioneering psychologist Carl Jung and the physicist Wolfgang Pauli decided that there was, after all, something more than chance behind many coincidences. The two theorized that coincidences could have a *meaningful* quality – that they were *significant*. They used the word 'synchronicity' to describe their theory. However, it is widely agreed that Jung and Pauli did not explain their idea very well, and all sorts of hypotheses and theories have grown from their original abstractions.

Today we find a prevailing view diametrically opposed to that which insists most, if not all, coincidences are chance, or that some coincidences are meaningful and others are certainly not. This view is based on the belief that everything in our lives has been pre-ordained (whether determined by God or some other unnamed universal power is beside the point). A typical holder of this view is Lilian Mahoney of Coventry, who claims to have a vast experience of many 'so-called coincidences'. She explains, 'I now state with full conviction that there is no such thing as "coincidence". Everything that happens is meant to happen.' This philosophy does not deny the occurrence of significant coincidences in our lives – in fact it insists they all must have mystical and spiritual meaning. Chance does not play a part. As Lilian explains, the 'earth plane' is a place of learning for our spirit which then passes over to another plane, and continues its upward progression to an even higher level. Lilian says the one thing we must learn on this plane is to listen to the voice within us, as it is God using us as channels to do his work. Lilian related in a letter to me a 'small example' of this. She had called at a friend's house on a day that she normally did not visit. A postcard had just arrived addressed to a man that her friend had never heard of. But Lilian had, although she had not seen him for many years, since they were teenagers. She also knew the man who had sent the card from the same era, having sung with him in a church choir. The sender, Billy, had put the correct house number on the card, but the wrong street. Lilian knew the correct address and offered to deliver it. She was halfway there when – for the first time in many years – she ran into the man in the street. She handed him the card telling him she had been on the way to his house to deliver it. 'God used me as a channel to get that card delivered,' she insists. 'I was meant to call at my friend's house on that particular day: *no* coincidence. It was spirit-inspired and meant to happen. God moves in mysterious way to help us at all times.'

This deterministic viewpoint is gaining ground rapidly at the turn of the millennium, and the anxious search for new answers to age-old questions renews itself: Who am I? Where does humankind come from? Where is it going? What influences the cosmos? Books that deal with promises of New Age synchronicity have flooded the book-shelves. *The Celestine Prophecy,* despite being dismissed by its critics as New Age propaganda, was on *The New York Times* best-seller list for 98 weeks. Its author, James Redfield, rejects the theory of probability as an explanation for coincidences and argues that people are coming to realize that coincidences are an indication that there is another side of life, and that other processes are at work behind the scenes. He argues that an increasing number of people are becoming conscious of co-incidence as a guiding force in their lives, and that the number of these believers will continue to rise dramatically, so that by early in the twenty-first century a point of 'critical mass' will be reached when some insights into our consciousness will be revealed, leading to a dramatic change for the better. A new millennium full of peace and enlightenment will have dawned. Each of us will have discovered that which is lacking in our lives, in our restless search for meaning. He believes that we should take note and act on the coincidences that occur in our lives They are, apparently, the signposts to the New Age.

I am in full agreement with the suggestion of noting coincidences. Keeping a record helps us to assess objectively their significance. Memory is often unreliable and tainted by natural prejudice. You will see in these pages many anecdotes that may not have survived but for their being noted very shortly after their occurrence.

Psychotherapist and author Robert H. Hopcke, in his recent book *There are No Accidents: Synchronicity and the Stories of Our Lives* (Riverhead Books, 1997), says that we like to think we are in control of our lives, and think we know what is best for ourselves, but the 'random chance' of synchronicity often reminds us that we are not the sole author of our own stories. In the promotional material for his book, Hopcke identifies synchronicities as more than random chance occurrences, claiming they can occur deliberately, for example 'during periods of personal transition, when perhaps we are ready for change, but don't know it ourselves. In such a case it may take synchronicity to wake us up, to point us in the true direction of our lives rather than allowing us to continue on the path we think we are on.' His book, it is claimed, can help us analyse our synchronistic experiences so that we may understand who we really are.

Based on my own observations, I believe that Redfield *et al.* are correct, in that more and more people are becoming aware of the coincidences in their lives. Whether this awareness will lead to some kind of a climax that changes humankind's thought processes for the better is open to question. Indeed, such a philosophy has the potential for a great deal of frustration.

We must keep in mind that such a deterministic viewpoint is not so very different from the spiritual status coincidence enjoyed up until the late Middle Ages. To arrive at today's populist viewpoint we must combine it with the views of those still attempting to analyse Jung's theory that meaningful (synchronistic) coincidences are related not only to unconscious psychological processes but to the workings of a universal mind.

Jeriann Sharf, creator of the synchronistic-based mind games *Fun Runes* and *MAGIspear,* told me how she gets around this apparent paradox:

What we're dealing with is the 'not-really-a-coincidence' coincidence. These non-coincidence coincidences are perfectly intelligible to anyone who understands such things. For those who don't, synchronicity is difficult to explain except by example, because even logic has its limits. Synchronicity happens, for instance, when a car bearing the license plate GOFORIT whizzes by you at the precise moment you were wondering if you should try hot-air ballooning this weekend. Miracle to religionists. Coincidence to rationalists. But synchronicity to those in the know.

Actually it's the Universe's way of reminding us that there is something bigger going on here. And that 'something bigger' is what life is all about. Fortunately somebody else noticed this too and gave it a name, 'synchronicity', so that everybody is satisfied including the rationalists who still can't really account for why it happens, just that it does. (Rationalists I know would tend to respond to that comment by saying if it cannot be explained, why bother to try!)

In any case, hinting is what the Universe does through the form of 'coincidences' to remind us who we are and that we are connected to the greater whole. Through these eerie coincidences we begin to catch sight of the threads in the fabric of the grand overall design as the Universe weaves the fate of one individual into the fate of another in a greater meaning called Destiny. In these moments of synchronicity the people, places and events that we encounter seem to have meaning for us, and we sense that we are where we are for a reason. Suddenly life has meaning and purpose. It is as if we are all participants in The Big Show with the Universe as the Great Choreographer. It is the difference between being *in* the movies instead of *at* the movies. And the Oneness of the Universe is the Ultimate show.

Despite the differing perspectives of the rationalists and those who believe in meaningful occurrences, their definitions of coincidence are but a matter of degree. The rational definition holds that 'A coincidence may be defined as a surprising concurrence of events, perceived as meaningfully related with no apparent causal connection.'[1] The Jungian definition asserts that 'Coincidences involve the significant coming together of two lines of events, each of which has its own causal background while neither is causally related to the other.'[2]

To summarize, what we are facing in the new millennium is a new-found interest in, not to say fascination with, an ancient phenomenon. To avoid being caught up in this enthusiasm with all its unfounded promises of enlightenment through coincidence, we should approach the subject with as much objectivity as possible, remembering all the time that many of those who argue the case for causal coincidences are too often sceptics with fixed perspectives.

There are non-sceptical 'experts' on the subject. Their opinions and experiences won't make the academic papers and their findings arise from personal and empirical evidence and anecdote. We will meet some of them in these pages. However, in this field, we are all experts – after all, very few people have not experienced at least one 'amazing' coincidence, and most of us have more than one which we analyse and discuss. What makes us experts is the fact that each coincidence is a unique event, never to be repeated in exactly the same way. We own that experience to do with what we like, to analyse how we may.

A good starting point for our exploration of coincidences is the acceptance that many coincidences do have a basis in chance – *accidents do happen*! Acceptance of a chance element by no means restricts us in our view of the possibilities of coincidence. We are left with many examples that manifest themselves as miracles, intuitive decisions, clustering effects, morphic resonances, mystic experiences. However, in both categories, chance and meaningful, we find anecdotes that are fascinating, mysterious, amusing, and intriguing.

We must keep in mind that personal perspective is not immutable. It changes according to circumstances. For example, preparing this book required me to collect, organize and analyse a vast amount of material. It was a practical job and required the left, practical, reasoning side of my brain. However, when I consider many of the anecdotes, as individual unique occurrences, my imagination is stirred, activating the right, creative, intuitive hemisphere. To function in society, we need to use both left and right hemispheres. Work and lifestyle may mean we use one more than the other, and this affects our perspective towards a great many things.

About the Book

I have organized *The Coincidence File* into three parts:

Part I This contains general chapters aimed at raising or increasing our awareness of the nature of coincidence and related topics. Chapter One details the personal stories of people who have changed their outlook on life as a result of varying processes they experienced while coming to the conclusion that coincidence did have meaning in their lives. It also includes advice from objective observers about how we might go about raising our own awareness and how this could lead us to a richer life. This is reinforced by Chapter Ten: Diary Keeping, which will hopefully lead the reader to start keeping a diary. Many coincidences escape unnoted unless we have fallen into the habit of recording them. A record enables us to reflect on the meaning – the personal significance of a coincidence can take a long time to become apparent.

Part I also includes chapters on intuition, morphic resonance, probability, numinous numbers, the clustering effect, astrology, time, miracles, same names, chance encounters and other related matters.

Part II This comprises several chapters which offer a wide range of coincidence anecdotes from people all around the world. This is probably one of the largest selections to be gathered in one book since *Coincidence: Chance or Fate?*. Many of them have left me deeply impressed and amazed. I am sure the reader will feel the same way.

Part III I present here what I believe to be the most thorough examination yet of the similarities between the Lincoln and Kennedy assassinations, the most important historical coincidence case of modern times. This is perhaps the perfect case history for examining the interweaving of types of coincidences. The links between the two men and the events surrounding their assassinations are well documented and present us with a perfect case study. I have often suggested it, when asked in interviews to nominate the most intriguing coincidence of all. Initially I knew only the basic details. For this book I went exploring further, and can now present an exhaustive examination of those links, including a number that had not before come to light.

A final word on the exploration of coincidences from Dr Caroline Watt, who has written an appraisal of the phenomena in the Appendix (see p. 229):

Just as a person who is open to the idea that coincidences may have paranormal interpretations may selectively interpret events so as to strengthen this belief, so can a person who is closed to the possible paranormal interpretations of coincidences selectively interpret events so as to strengthen this belief. All too often I find in the so-called 'sceptical' literature (sceptical should mean questioning, not counter-advocacy) examples of passionately held beliefs (in the non-existence of paranormal phenomena) that are dressed up as objective and rationally held positions. Hence I find myself just as cautious when considering 'anti-paranormal' arguments and rhetoric as I am when considering 'pro-paranormal' positions. There is no substitute for careful scientific inquiry on this matter, and a familiarity with the literature is essential before passing judgement.

To conclude, the essence of coincidences lies in the fact they are largely personal – *and unique* – and deeply impressive to those experiencing them. Nevertheless, they can also be fascinating and compelling for the rest of us. Through the sense of wonder they so often invoke, we find ourselves taking a fresh look at the world around us. Perhaps it is not, after all, as dull and ordered as many appear to believe, or as others would have us believe it is.

PART ONE

chapter one

Awareness

It would be a contradiction in terms to say, as some New Age gurus do, that we can 'create' our own coincidences. The very essence of a coincidence is, of course, in its non-causal nature and, to a degree, its spontaneity. We must also keep in mind that each coincidence experience is unique to an individual. It has never happened before and will not happen again. If something similar does happen, it will not be in quite the same way.

On the other hand, we can build an awareness of meaningful co-incidences. In this chapter we will consider the experiences of a number of men and women and their stories of finding a greater awareness through synchronistic events.

First we need to examine the question of 'awareness'. I am uneasy when I read sweeping statements that tell us that coincidences should be a major guiding force of our lives. Certainly, a developed sense of awareness gives our lives a deeper, richer resonance – too many people live a mechanistic existence, guided only by surface stimulus. If used wisely coincidences can be a useful tool in dealing with life's problems, and can make us aware of an inner existence and an interconnection with nature and the universe.

Victor Mansfield, Professor of Physics and Astronomy at Colgate University, Hamilton, New York State, has been a student of Jungian psychology for more than twenty-five years. In his book *Synchronicity, Science and Soul-making* (Open Court, Chicago, 1995), a comprehensive exploration of the psychological, spiritual and philosophical implica-tions of Jung's concept of synchronicity, he argues that synchronicity plays an important role in our psychological development:

> If the world and my ego are an unfolding of the soul then in principle it's
> possible to intuit symbolic meaning in all experience. All life is teaching me if
> I can cultivate the sensitivity to its meanings, properly interpret its promptings.

Since waking life is an unfolding of the self, we can symbolically interpret important waking experiences like a numinous dream.

However, reading meaning from experiences in the outer world, cultivating symbolic intuition, or developing a sensitivity to synchronicity experiences, is treading on slippery ground, especially when we are first trying to differentiate these talents. It's all too easy to turn trivia into cosmic occasion of meaning. Divine revelations and epiphanies then become a dime-a-dozen – a typical syndrome in mental hospitals. There the mad are always receiving divine revelations from the most trivial and inane occurrences.

Mansfield goes on to argue that, since our capacity for self-delusion and ego aggrandizement is endless, we need to proceed with the utmost rationality and balance, which, he says, are the character traits in shortest supply:

Unfortunately, almost no guidelines exist here, except perhaps the cultivation of humility, but even that can be turned into a source of pride. Where are we to turn?

The problem is still more complex, because interpreting synchronistic experience is at least as difficult as interpreting a big dream. Interpreting our own dreams is difficult because they are often expressing a major unconscious compensation and therefore the interpreter, the ego that needs the compensation, is in the worst position to make the interpretation. Even if the interpretation is simple and straightforward our lopsidedness prevents us from seeing the truth and instead we often fashion an incorrect interpretation based on our psychological problems. All these dangers and difficulties apply at least as much to interpreting synchronistic experiences, to extracting the acausal meaning of the connections between the inner and outer. Not only can we impose meaning on events when none exists, but we are predisposed to make the wrong interpretations even when genuine meaning is manifesting in a synchronistic experience.

Added to all these dangers is that even one powerful synchronicity experience can be an inflating experience. The little voice says, 'Surely I must be a very advanced and chosen person if the world is meaningfully arranging itself for my benefit, my education.' Rather than the ego becoming a servant of the higher, integrally related to the world, the world becomes assimilated by the ego. Nearly identical problems also appear at the spiritual level, since our own ego is the unsurpassed master of self-delusion.'[1]

In brief, Mansfield shows us one of the first steps to building awareness is learning both to suppress the involvement of the ego in the process, and to sort the simple coincidences from those that are meaningful.

There are other steps that should be taken to build awareness. Another research scientist, Lou Caracciolo, offers some general guidelines, among them: learn to expect the unexpected at all times; develop the habit of dropping into waking meditation; develop open sensory channels so that useful coincidental information is not filtered out as a result of 'dogmatic linguistic memory'; and accept the fact that 'discontinuous and unpredictable' events do happen.

I have often read, and even come to believe, that creative people experience more than the average number of coincidences. Caracciolo questions whether 'creative' is the right word here, claiming 'a mind that is constantly poised on the edge of inquiry, expansion or learning will tend to have synchronistic events happen more readily'. The anecdotes told in this chapter would tend to back up that claim.

Caracciolo claims that people with a very strong, presupposed internal mental image tend to 'mutilate and alter' experiences until they fit their own internal mental image:

While in some areas of human endeavour this is useful, for the studying or creation of synchronistic events, it is not.

For a person to recognize synchronistic events they must be completely submerged in sensory experiences, not letting a loud voice-over, internal pictures, or feelings mutilate direct awareness. This is quite different from the way human beings usually interact with the world.

Now let us consider some examples of how people have built an awareness of synchronistic meaning in their lives, and whether or not they follow the guidelines outlined by these two academic experts.

The Staff of Life

Since her teens, Karen Setlowe, of Kirland, Washington State, has been aware of certain phenomena surrounding her which she attributes to coincidence, fate or psychic awareness. In January 1977 she became poignantly aware that she had been gradually tapping into a form of spiritual awareness when several events occurred that led up to a major life transition. It began with the death of her father in July 1976.

Because Karen also believes in a soul which outlives the body, she continued to ask him for guidance in certain matters. That autumn she asked him for direction in her acting career, a profession about which he knew a great deal. Within a few days, Karen was asked to take a part she had been wanting to do. She believed this was her father's response to her request for guidance. Several weeks into the run, after a matinee performance, she had a strong desire to drive the two hours to her parents' home to make sure her mother was handling life without her husband. As Karen walked into the house, she announced half-jokingly that the phone was about to ring and it would be for her. She was not expecting a call from anyone in particular, but within minutes the phone did ring; it was friend hoping she was in town because she wanted to invite her to a party. After her bold and unexpected prediction Karen knew she had to go. At the party that evening she met a government official from Inverness, Scotland, who suggested that she perform in his city some day, in the beautiful, new regional theatre. From that innocent gesture, she was commissioned, in part, by the USA Bicentennial Committee, to write and perform a one-woman show she had been researching on Annie Sullivan – Helen Keller's teacher and companion. She spent the next few weeks writing and memorizing the script in order to fly to Scotland at the beginning of January 1977. Despite the natural obstacles she faced – she had never written a play nor performed a one-person show before, and she had never travelled overseas – she 'knew' the project would be a success.

A couple of days before she flew to Scotland, she was preparing to return some of her research material to the library. But before doing so, Karen decided to browse through it one last time and see if there might be some little, overlooked titbit connecting Annie and Helen to Scotland. As she picked up the material one of the books fell open to a page and her eyes immediately focused on a particular paragraph. Days before Annie died she had asked to return to her favourite place on Earth, a small farmhouse she had visited in Scotland. 'I know my soul will be at peace there', she had written.

That farmhouse was in Muir-of-Ord 15 miles (25 kilometres) from where Karen was performing. Annie had died before she could return, but with that fortunate find, Karen was able to add to her script.

After arriving in Scotland, Karen was told the farmhouse had been boarded up and declared derelict years earlier. Despite this bad news, she resolved that somehow she must go to the house. The very next day she received a phone call telling her that a young couple had just bought the house and would welcome her as a visitor. They wanted to hear about Annie and Helen because they felt the house was haunted with loving spirits and knew that the two women had spent some time in it.

A few days later she received a call from a woman who had read about her in the local newspaper. She too wanted to meet her; her mother had been Annie Sullivan's nurse during Annie's final days in New York.

In the following years Karen has been asked to perform the play many times throughout America, but, due to various complications, she has only managed a few performances – and each time, by coincidence, on a key anniversary date in Annie's life. Later she discovered that the initial contact at the party in 1976 she had felt so compelled to attend – and which resulted in her writing her first play, performing her first one-person show, travelling overseas for the first time and obtaining her fellowship for the project – *all* occurred on key anniversaries in Annie Sullivan's life.

More frequently, in recent years, events have occurred to remind Karen of the universal synchronicity in which she believes. 'Either the process is speeding up, or I'm just more aware,' she says. 'Other plays of mine have been produced with interesting synchronicities, but none with the impact of that first project.'

However, another of her works did come close: a one-woman show about Golda Meir, the former Prime Minister of Israel. While researching and writing that play, she secretly wished and visualized that it would premiere at the time of a declaration of peace – to fulfil Meir's wish that she could be around at such an auspicious time. The play premiered in January 1994 – just after the historic Peace Accord was signed. An acknowledgement of that event became a part of Golda's opening remarks in the play.

> I believe we each are on a unique journey – a spiritual one. If we allow ourselves to tap into the collective consciousness protected by God's love, wonderful synchronistic experiences await us. The universe knows what we need and where we can contribute our special gifts. I feel honoured that somehow I connected to Annie and Golda's wishes. With their help, and that of the universe, I look forward to more, wonderful, synchronistic adventures.

An Observant Life

After many years of careful observation, Ute Kaboolian of New Jersey has come to some unique conclusions and beliefs about the presence of synchronistic events in her life:

> The more coincidences I collect, the more I see life as the stage on which they coincide. I see my fellow humans as co-actors on that stage. I suspect that we are writing the script as we go along, moment to moment. I also suspect that there is continuity across time barriers shown to us clearly and consistently in numbers – like a thread in a pattern, here you see it, there you don't. But it's there all the time.

Late in the evening of 27 May 1988, Ute found herself wide awake and with an urge to tune in to the radio. She expected to hear one of two stations, one playing soft rock, the other classical music:

I was surprised to hear sounds that obviously came from neither. They seemed to soar out of a long-forgotten past, sounds that had been waiting in my mind and heart and were now set free to envelope my being all over again. Instantly I was young once more, listening to Glen Miller's orchestra. It was right after World War II, and I was still in Germany where I was born.

How had it happened? Had I, without realizing it, touched the dial so that it had wandered off to what turned out to be station WEVD where Danny Stiles was on the air from eleven o'clock to five o'clock each night for seven nights a week?

Upon hearing Danny Stiles, I pushed the record button just as he was saying, '*Hör zu*, listen very closely, dear hearts…' Here I perked up. *Hör zu* appealed to me as a German. 'Dear hearts' went straight to my heart. That's what my father had always called me. Danny went on, 'I'm all excited – I suppose you can detect that in the sound of my vocal cords – because three weeks from now on *17 June* (here my thoughts and emotions made several somersaults, 17 June just happens to be my birthday) I'll be hosting another of our monthly big band dance parties at the Holiday Inn North.' My parents took me with them on holidays to the North Sea. There were other great revelations or specials associations to me in the broadcast. I wrote to Danny and [on 2 June] he read my whole letter on air. After he had finished he commented on the fact that, since listening to American music was *verboten* by the Wehrmacht this was the reason the United States had short-wave radio broadcasts from London featuring the Glen Miller orchestra. Without pausing he went into a commercial with the words, 'How would you like to visit Portugal?' while I was staring at *Der Rundbrief*, a German publication. On its cover in big letters 'Bilder aus Portugal' [Pictures from Portugal]. I had come across *Der Rundbrief* only an hour before the broadcast while going through some of my papers.

The time element is so important in coincidences. That's why the most unusual coincidence of this episode with Stiles may be the fact that, out of Stiles's six hours of air-time each day, I had picked the precise moment to press the record button as he said '*Hör zu*, listen very closely, dear hearts…'

I have long since ceased to believe in coincidences as chance happenings. Lately, more and more, my family and friends have noticed and told me about them. We compare notes. Some 'coincidences' cannot be shared without going into too many associations that have to be taken on faith by others. Thus, sometimes the game has to be played like Solitaire. But that is fun too. This way, one can prove to oneself the simply astounding fact there seems to be purpose everywhere in everything.

Echoing Lou Caracciolo's words that for a person to recognize synchronistic events they must be completely submerged in sensory experiences, Ute goes on:

> However, one has to be in a certain frame of mind to play this game where coincidences are purposeful. I usually know or feel when this might happen and it never fails to put me in an adventurous mood, where anything can happen, where the unexpected could be expected and where time would magically coalesce so that mere sounds of words, or syllables and the associations they provoke, glide into each other effortlessly, almost predictably, while there is always an element of surprise remaining.

Ute goes on to relate that on 12 May 1989, almost a year – and many coincidences – later, a letter arrived, on the 31st anniversary of her arrival in the United States in 1958. It was the only letter in the post:

> An only letter cannot be overlooked. It was the Greenpeace whale campaign letter. Its timely arrival made my head spin. Only the previous evening, 11 May 1989, our friend, Wayne Thiel, had surprised us with a visit and was himself surprised when he heard me play his song of whales and men, entitled *Always One*, on tape. Wayne's tape also contained the song *Egypt*.

> Right after he had given me the initial tape, a penfriend, Peter Danison, who knew nothing of the tape, suggested we play a game to find coincidences and I started off with the word Egypt. On hearing of this coincidence from me, he followed up with yet another one. He wrote, 'I too am a musician, and have written a piece of music, *From Egypt*.' In the same letter he said, 'I've been playing with the idea that coincidences are like symbolic echoes of one's beliefs at work in framework two. There would be a central issue of focus in framework one, then 'little coincidences' like seeing something going on in your life portrayed the same day on a television show.

Here Peter is referring to a Seth concept. Seth concepts are based on a 22-volume work written by the late Jane Roberts and her husband Robert Butts as a consequence of trance communications which they made with an entity named Seth. Followers say its main concepts are that humans create their own reality, that we are multi-dimensional beings who exist throughout eternity, developing into more fulfilling individuals, that evil and destruction do not exist and that the purpose of our lives is to enjoy ourselves spiritually, mentally and physically. Framework one pertains to officially accepted events, framework two to events usually considered unimportant, occurring at random and not worthy of our attention generally and in particular. Our coincidences go under framework two.[2]

On 11 March 1988, Ute wrote to her penfriend Peter:

I told him that my daughter had received her *Banana Republic* spring catalogue in today's mail. Title page? 'Egypt'. Page 31 sports the *Traveller's Eye* T-shirt which is a special rendition of the cover. I was born in the year 31, and there has been much recently surrounding that number. Peter replied that on 11 March he had put on his Banana Republic vest for the first time this year – the same date as our letter. Peter tells me that every time he hears from me by letter or phone he has come across a reference to [President] Lincoln in a book or on a television show, a day or two before.

Ute goes on to look at the numinosity of numbers more closely and recalls their significant role in her life:

If we do have a hand in making our reality according to what we think is important to us, then maybe anniversaries and other dates stress this importance in ways that cannot be overlooked. They also show us how we, as individuals, are connected to the greater experience of our universe. When my husband and I were married in 1958 I was 27 years old. On 15 July 1989, we celebrated our 31st wedding anniversary. I was born in 1931. My husband has a 31 in his social security number. I have a 58. In 1958 he was twice my age. As he tells it, first he had to wait 27 years for me to be born, then another 27 years before he was able to meet and marry me. In 1958 our ages added up to 9 (2+7=9 and 5+4=9). In 1989 our ages were reversed, my husband was 85, I 58, which is the year I got married and started a new life. In 1989, both our ages totalled 13, the reverse of 31, the year I was born. In some ways we seemed to have come full cycle.

Art as a medium is a veritable treasure trove of coincidence. I have made a few personal associations with some of the paintings of surrealist René Magritte. On 23 February 1989, I wrote in my diary that my son's friend John Celidoniko had brought over the book *Magritte* by A.M. Hammacher a few days before. His painting *The Pleasure Principle* threw me for a loop. Magritte painted it in 1937 to depict Edward James, author of *The Gardener who Saw God*.

The book was also written in 1937, the same year in which I had a rather strange experience, when I was six years old, that was synchronistic with the painting. While standing on my garden path [address: Berlin 37, of all places] my mind suddenly merged with that of the universal mind in an explosion of white light. I had no awareness of my physical or non-physical body, or of the world. In this timeless experience I was one with everyone and all there is. To me everything was suddenly all so simple, like turning on a light switch, a click in the mind. Questions were inconceivable. For the first and only time in my life everything made sense. I tried to hold onto this state for as long as I could. But before I knew it, the familiar sun was back. There must be two suns, the six-year-old thought, one white, one golden. I told no one, then I forgot about it. Had I set myself the task of painting the experience I could not have done justice to it the way Magritte did with his portrait of James, who is shown sitting at a table while his head has been absorbed by a ball of radiant white light. On the table lies a stone remarkably similar to one I have in my possession and which I cherish for some unaccountable reason. Another of Magritte's paintings, *The Fountain of Youth*, shows as its centre of focus a tombstone that appears to be made of marble – also known as the stone of light – with the word COBLENZ etched into it in big bold letters. Protruding from the middle of the stone's upper rim is an eagle's head, its profile the stone's only ornament. My father, Albert Herbig, was born and grew up near Koblenz, Germany. Like Magritte, he lived in Paris for well over two years. Next to the tombstone, a leaf grows out of the ground like a tree, its little stem its trunk. Another of my father's endearments for me was 'Stämmche', his little stem. There is a huge stone yo-yo in the background of Magritte's painting. Stones and rocks are strewn all about. Could my father have stepped into the painting he would have tried to pick them all up. When my parents came for a visit in 1961, Papa had to be persuaded not to cart the whole of the United States back to Germany. He took three boxes of stones. Magritte painted it in the year 1957 and it was in that year my mother and I were invited to come to the United States to meet my aunt. The two sisters had not seen each other in some 60 years. We arrived in New York at Pier 57. As we went through Customs, the officer said, 'Young lady, may I ask if you are married?' When I told him I wasn't, he said, 'Maybe you'll get married here and stay in this country.' We all laughed. Who could have guessed that exactly two months and three days later I would be married and that my newly found cousin, my future husband, was standing right next to me when the officer made this quite innocent, yet prophetic remark?

Greg's Spiritual Path

Greg Carden, a university student of Northport, Alabama, created a fictional character for a guru, a tradition in Discordianism (a religion started in the 1950s and influenced by Zen and Taoism) by which he is heavily influenced. This is obvious from the zine (small self-published magazine) *Tsujigiri* he produces. He called his new character Coyote, a pun on two of his heroes, Don Quixote and the Native American Trickster Figure Coyote. He made him an amputee, one-legged like himself. One night when he had been working late on an issue of *Tsujigiri*, he took a break and switched on his television set.

Before the picture even appeared the words blasting out at him were, 'Don Coyote will be right back!' Greg was amazed: 'I just about fainted when I realized there was a kids' cartoon by that name, titled *The Adventures of Don Coyote and Sancho Panda*.'

His next encounter with Don Coyote in the real world occurred when he asked his mother, who was going to a book shop, to bring him home any books on coyotes. The store had only one such book, entitled *Don Coyote* by Dayton O. Hyde. Greg started to read it with some interest, thinking that it wasn't really that much of a coincidence: it was not as though this Don Coyote was missing a leg. Then, about half way through, the author describes an incident in which he witnesses a hunter shoot Don Coyote, who survives but loses one of his hind legs in the process. 'I thought I had totally fabricated an amputee by the name of Don Coyote, but it seems someone else had already written a book about a *real* Don Coyote amputee.'

Some time later he came across a book, *Rainbow Nation Without Borders* by Alberto Ruz Buenfil, which contained a reference to Huehuecoyotl, an Aztec deity whose name means basically Old Man Coyote. A few days later he discovered that Huehuecoyotl was one of the many manifestations of the deity Tezcatlipoca, who lost his foot to a Chaos Monster (a deity in Meso-American mythology) when he created the world. This last discovery led him to carry out some interesting research that resulted in an article showing there are many gods, deities and sages in various myths and religions who are amputees:

> I experienced a slew of amputee synchronicities while writing that article. Once when I was stuck, my professor started talking about Zen (this was not during the Taoist part of the course, he just got off the subject). He told a story of one Zen monk to show the drastic nature of Zen. He achieved mystical realization after getting his leg chopped off in an accident. I went up to ask him about that example after class, hoping that by some miracle he'd know of a source for it I could follow up. As it turned out, he had just used that story in a paper he was writing so could tell me the exact page and book in question.

In fascinating detail, Greg relates how his research led him by synchronicities from one amputee in religion to another:

> One-legged figures in mythology are often meant to symbolize the *Axis mundi*; the link between this plane and heaven. I've certainly gained spiritual lessons from my amputation. For example, that you should have one foot in the physical and one foot in the spiritual.

The synchronicity that shook his ideas of reality happened in his first semester at St Mary's College, Maryland. The night before his 'Introduction to Psychology' class, he was reading (instead of his psychology homework) a book on philosophy, *Labyrinths of Reason* by William Poundstone. The section that particularly intrigued him was Poundstone's discussion of the 'brain in the vat' theory: that our brains are floating in the vat of a mad scientist, who is zapping our neurones with electrodes so that everything we seem to be perceiving is just an illusion.

Next day in class he found the lecturer rather boring and began sketching a human brain floating in a clear liquid in a vat. As he was finishing the sketch, the professor said he had something to show the class. He reached beneath his desk and brought out an actual human brain floating in a clear vat. As if that wasn't enough, Greg found the story of how he got hold of the vat even more implausible than the coincidence he had just been involved with. The lecturer said that another professor on campus found it in the closet of his new house when he had moved in.

Greg's most amazing coincidence has to with his survival as a child from a cancer:

> For the past two years I've been going once a month to the Pain Clinic of Kirkland Hospital due to the nerve problem in my residual limb to get the narcotics I have to take for chronic pain. One visit, early on, after I'd moved down to Alabama from Virginia, I found myself in the pharmacy with a long wait. I had forgotten to bring a book to read, so picked up the magazine that was on the table next to me. It was published by a local cancer research group. I noticed there was an article on a survivor of childhood cancer. I immediately turned to that story, curious to see whether this person was very religious or not, as I had noticed that other survivors of cancer from such a young age often share that interest with me.

> It turned out this individual was, indeed, religious (a Methodist minister, in fact). But the parallels did not end here, by any means. The article talked about how in 1976, when this person was around five years old, he was hit in the knee with a basketball, or football (my memory is sketchy as to the precise details, I know it was one of the two). His knee was very swollen and painful later that night and he was soon taken to hospital. They eventually diagnosed him as having Ewing's Sarcoma. This is basically my same medical history. In 1976 when I was five I slipped on a bunk-bed ladder and hit my knee very hard. Later that day my knee was very swollen and painful. I was taken to hospital where I too was eventually diagnosed with Ewing's Sarcoma (although a mutant form). Both of us were living in Alabama at the time as well. Ewing's Sarcoma is a very rare form of bone cancer and,

statistically, bone cancer is one of the rarer forms of that disease. Furthermore, it usually affects people in their mid to late teens. Both of us were uncharacteristically young in developing it. When I was first diagnosed a doctor told my parents, quite matter-of-factly, that I was going to die. We both beat the odds though. And there I was reading about him by sheer luck due to the fact that I'd forgotten to take a book with me and had a longer than usual wait, that this magazine was sitting next to my chair, that they'd done a story on this particular person. I wrote down the issue number and so forth, resolved to get a copy of my own. I also wanted to try and track down the person somehow (I had no idea where the guy lived, even if he was still in Alabama or not) and tell him about the coincidences. Unfortunately I was not able to locate a copy, not even in the campus library, so I eventually put the whole thing on the backburner of my mind,

Many months later, I was taking a class in the University of Alabama religious studies department – an upper-level course on Buddhism and Western Nihilism. When the time came for the mid-term test, a friend, actually the only person in the class I knew, asked if I would like to be in his study group. I said yes, and he introduced me to another student who would also be in the group who was a pastor. During the first study session, we got to chatting about religion in general, and I discovered the minister and I had many common interests. Changing the subject he asked me how I had lost my leg. I told him a bit of my medical history (without being specific) and he told me that he'd had cancer too, in his knee. He was pretty vague and I figured he did not want to talk about it, so did not press him. After that we met a few more times and I learned more about him. Then it clicked. I asked him if he'd had Ewing's. He had. Yep, he was the guy in the article I'd wanted to track down. That we were both in the same college let alone the same class is astounding. Shortly after my diagnosis our family had moved out of Alabama and lived mainly in Northern Virginia. When my father had retired a few years before we had moved back to Alabama. The fact we shared so many common interests, the medical history and the incredible odds against my seeing the article about him let alone having a chance meeting with him afterwards still perplex me. The term 'mere coincidence' just seems laughable at this point.

I have read that when one begins to journey along a spiritual path synchronicities often become the signposts that one is heading in the right direction. As my fictional guru (Don Coyote) says, 'The connection density ratio increases as one approaches the Centre of the Web.' Another possibility is that the nature of the subjects I explore is inducive of synchronicity – a playful attitude, non-linear thinking, an appreciation of an underlying order beneath seemingly chaotic phenomena.

Woman of Substance

A unnamed woman friend of Victor Mansfield writes:

My first lesson in value that I can remember came when I was about six or seven years old. I traded rings with a girl in my Sunday School class. Although mine was a genuine pearl ring in a 30-carat gold band, I didn't much care for it. I much preferred my friend's pretty shiny red ring (that I realize now was most likely from a ten-cent bubble gum machine).

When we both got home our parents were shocked and I remember the girl's parents coming to the door, apologizing profusely, and the dramatic exchange of the appropriate rings took place. It was almost ceremonial. Obviously I had done something quite wrong. But I had no idea what it was since I had no conception of collective value at the time. All I knew was that hers was shiny, red and in my opinion much prettier than my dull white one with the thick gold band. This event had a huge impact on me. After it I only wore the ring a very few times as a little girl, kept it in my jewellery box most of time, and never thought much about it again.

As a young adult in my twenties I was involved in a serious love relationship. It had reached a stagnant point where I knew that if things didn't change, it wasn't going to last. Another man arrived on the scene. He was foreign, quite exotic, and very attractive. I absolutely delighted in the excitement of being around him and started wondering if I should abandon my long-term relationship for an exciting fling.

One afternoon I was thinking about the coming evening and a possible date with the new person. I had left the evening open just in case something would arise. I started actively entertaining this possibility. I got out of my car, reached into my pocketbook for parking meter money, and pulled out the very pearl ring from my childhood. As I retrieved the ring it was instantaneously clear to me that if I were to have this affair, I was going to once again trade my pearl for the flashy imitation. This time, however, I had a very meaningful relationship to lose in the process. I knew somewhere deep inside that the benefits gained from sticking with my meaningful relationship (although not totally apparent to me then) were ultimately more valuable than possibly losing it to a whirlwind short-lived passion. How did the ring get there? I have no idea. I must have gone to my parents' apartment sometime before this event and brought back several items from my past – or then again it may have been the trolls.

This lesson of seeing deeper value in life has been a continual theme for me. I am continually placed in situations where I have to be very aware of the flash and glitter of appearances. It seems to require an inner self-reflection to discern the deeper meanings in experience. Often in my life, I have learned about deeper meanings from choosing the flashy red bubble gum rings and have been terribly disappointed. My experience of pulling out the pearl ring 15 years later also had a profound message for me. I recognized at that moment of holding the ring in my hand that I was at a turning point and that I could no longer be naive about the choice I was making. By the way, I did choose the long-term relationship.[3]

Seeing Coincidences

The writer William Burroughs suggests another way for us to build an awareness of coincidences, and therefore a deeper awareness of our lives. Put simply, he advises his students to be observant:

> Take a walk around the block. Come back and write down precisely what happened, with particular attention to what you were thinking when you noticed a street sign, or passing car, or stranger or whatever caught your attention. You will observe that what you were thinking just before you saw the sign relates to the sign. The sign may even complete a sentence in your mind. You are getting messages. Everything is talking to you. At this point some students become paranoid. I tell them that of course they are getting messages. Your surroundings are your surroundings. They relate to you.[4]

Dulce Pombeiro of Southampton is an unwitting follower of Burroughs's advice. She lives in a high state of awareness by relating to her surroundings in exactly the way the veteran writer advises. In the course of her everyday tasks she notes the constant stream of coincidences that flows over her. Hanging out the washing, she notices when the plastic pegs exactly match the colour of the garment being hung on the line. Such observations she calls the lowest form of coincidence, but even so she does not allow them to escape into oblivion.

The day after Dulce made her first appointment with a chiropractor, *The Times* carried an article with the headline: 'Princess endorses chiropractor's help'. She then boarded a bus and saw a former neighbour, Mrs Carpenter, whom she had seen for many years. They only had time for a brief chat before Dulce's stop. As she alighted, on an impulse she decided to call on a jeweller's to ask about a silver salt spoon. The jeweller's at which she stopped: Carpenter's. Glancing across the road her eye caught a sign above a kitchen shop. Another Carpenter's.

When Briton Terry Waite was released from a long captivity in the Middle East, Dulce and her husband, David, were on a short holiday at Chagford on Dartmoor. Excited at the news they dashed to the newsagent to buy a newspaper for more details. Just by the counter, she noticed some bars of chocolate on a display stand, their name – Terry's.

On a wet, cold April day a friend, Isabel Walker, and her husband came to tea. It was a rare and warm occasion enjoyed by all. Although she seldom buys magazines at the supermarket checkout, shortly after Isabel's visit Dulce found herself buying one. Within its pages she found an article by a regular contributor, also called Isabel Walker.

For some time she had been thinking of tracing some distant relatives in Guatemala. In a move unrelated to that, Dulce joined Amnesty International. One of the first magazines she received from the human rights organization contained the address of the Guatemalan embassy in London, plus an address to contact local authorities of that country. That same summer she met by chance, through friends, a Spanish teacher with whom she began to correspond and whose home is in Caceres, Spain. The names of her relatives in Guatemala – Caceres de Lacerda.

One day, at random she opened Virginia Woolf's biography by Quentin Bell. She read that the birthday of Woolf's nephew, Julian, was 4 February and realized she was reading the book on 4 February.

Once, about to enter the booksellers Dillons, two redheads passed by. Both were youngish, clad in rusty tones and presented a striking appearance. A second later, after stepping into the shop, the first publication that caught her eye was titled: *The Soldier and the Redheaded Woman.*

While waiting for Heavenly Sent, her dry-cleaners, to arrive, she picked up a piece of mail she would not normally bother to open and the words staring at her – Heavenly Comfort.

Dulce and her husband had been trying to buy a house owned by a John Harrison. During this time she received a business letter from another John Harrison. A third mention of the name came as she was listening to the radio. Finally, when they received their copy of *The Sunday Times*, the name Harrison was written across the front page – they had been given his copy of the paper that day. Dulce claims:

Coincidences occur frequently when I am attuned or tuned in. When housework prevails, the mind switches off in a manner of speaking. Then coincidences simply switch off too. At one point I noted they occur more frequently in winter, when I am indoors, more dependent on books and radio for mind feed. Not all minor coincidences are recorded by me for they are at times too frequent or perhaps too insignificant…little dots in everyday life. Yet I perceive an uncanny element somewhere.

Between my actions and thoughts, there seems to be a connection, if only fleeting. For example David came in from work one day saying, 'Did you miss me?' David never asks this question. The magazine in front of me had the sentence: 'What the Dutch are missing.'

Just as I started reading a novel called *A Pair of Spoons*, my friend Jennie called and chatted on in her lively manner. Then she mentioned those large Portuguese spoons, a metre high, to stir or mix something really large.

On the eve of travelling to Cornwall we watched on television a programme about a sea monster which showed up at Portscatho, the very place we were travelling to next day.

A programme of Majorcan music was on air. David visited neighbours and returned to tell me they are flying to Majorca the week after next. Lots of people fly to that island these days, yet there is always that subtle link, somewhere twixt facts and words and thoughts...

I decided to cook scrambled eggs for David, something I never do during the week and very seldom on any other occasion. David did not know of my culinary plans when he told me of a television programme that night, about Lady Montague. I quote: 'And she is quite happy to eat scrambled eggs when her husband goes off to these functions on his own.'

Anyone with the slightest interest in coincidences (and that excludes very few people) would recognize these incidents. 'Oh, sure, things like that happen to me,' I can hear the reader say. 'They're pretty trivial, why bother to take a note of them?' Trivial they may be, especially when taken in isolation and when they concern another person, but in total they amount to compelling proof of the way coincidences interweave themselves into the fabric of our everyday life, covering us like a rainmist. Furthermore, the events that trigger Dulce Pombeiro's incidents appear to somehow indicate, as Burroughs asserts, the immediate future. After meeting Mrs Carpenter, she is overcome by an 'impulse' to go to a jeweller's named Carpenter's and, as if to reinforce that decision, she spies the name a third time – three instances of the name, all within a minute or so. For no particular reason other than the obvious, altruism, she joins Amnesty International and finds it provides her with an address that spurs her long-delayed decision to locate her relatives. Dulce feels her mind is often anticipating or reading ahead of time and space, that there is a definite link between her stream of consciousness and the outside world. She concludes by relating two coincidences that are anything but trivial.

On 11 February 1993, she was attempting to solve *The Times* crossword while listening to music on the radio. 'What is this music?' she asked her husband. Neither of them knew. She returned her attention to the puzzle. Coming to 23 across, the clue was: *The Creation* composer. She asked David if he knew the answer, but before he had time to reply the piece of music on the radio came to an end and the announcer clearly said: '*The Creation* by Haydn.'

In another significant incident her family searched through copies of old newspapers for an article on earthquakes, to help their granddaughter Charlie with her homework. When they were unsuccessful, her husband suggested they try the Internet, and there they found some text on the subject. Charlie also needed a picture and they could not find one on the Internet. Then, on the hall bookcase, she spotted an old copy of *Reader's Digest*, the only one that Dulce had ever bought. It had been sitting behind some books for years. She had come across it a few days before and removed it from its hiding place. Glancing at the cover she found its heading leaping out at her: 'Earthquakes in LA'. Charlie used the article and the coloured illustration that went with it for her homework.

Would these coincidences have come about had she not prepared herself by dutifully noting the 'trivial' matters? Both examples are indicative of a foreknowledge provided by no known source. When she asked the question, 'Who was composer of *The Creation*?', how could she have possibly consciously known it was about to be answered for her? What led her to hunt out the old *Reader's Digest* from its hiding place after so many years, and then, instead of putting it in the rubbish, leave it in a position that provided the answer to the problem of her granddaughter's homework, without being consciously aware the answer to that problem lay within the pages of the magazine? Dulce, it appears, has developed a faculty that offers her extraordinary insights and intuition, a knowing that began with her decision to observe and note the 'trivial' incidents, and that, she says, has led her to believe there is 'a mysterious mechanism at work behind the scenes of everyday routine'.

I asked Dulce whether she had somehow tuned in to a level of consciousness that made her receptive to greater coincidences as a result of noting the minor coincidences. Her response:

I cannot answer straightforwardly. What I do know is that there is something out there within reach of the mind that works in conjunction with coincidence. The more you tune in, the more you connect. So ultimately the answer may well be 'yes'.

The Links of Life

Suzanne Venecek, of Downers Grove, Illinois, is one of those who believe that coincidences ebb and flow through a person's life, appearing when needed:

> My life is such a well-spring of synchronicity, so much so that I feel like I'm in a play that has already been scripted. Over the past several years, my life has been very traumatic, and based on the corresponding synchronistic events that have been occurring prior to and through this period, I have come to believe that they are cosmic clues that define the people and events that are supposed to be part of our lives – all part of the script.

She goes on to give extensive details of how the same names have occurred among her husbands, friends and relatives to such an extent that they form a pattern. Adopted as a child, she began a search for her birth mother when she was 28 years old. Suzanne (or Sue as she is also known) finally succeeded in locating her real mother – on her 30th birthday, 10 February 1976. 'On the morning of my birthday I was no closer to finding her than finding a needle in a haystack,' she says. Then, in the post, came an unexpected letter with the details she had been seeking for two years. By 3 p.m. that day she was talking to her mother, Shirley Davis, for the first time in her life – and on her birthday. As they got to know one another a pattern of synchronicity in their separate lives began to reveal itself. Shirley's birthday and that of Sue's eldest son, Bill, are 9 May and 5 May respectively. Sue's youngest daughter, Jenny, and her eldest son, John, have birthdays on 9 May and 5 May respectively. Both Shirley and Sue had four children and one miscarriage, and both had two boys and two girls. Shirley had her children in the order girl, boy, girl, boy. Sue had her four in reverse order. Shirley had been divorced twice, as had both Sue and her sister, Terry. Shirley and Terry are both married for a third time, leading Sue to wonder whether a third marriage is in her cosmic script.

Shirley's children are called Sue, Bill, Terry and Gary, and Sue realized that the names of her newly discovered brothers and sisters, and of her first husband, Mike, and second husband, Robert (Bob) White, have cropped up throughout her life, and continue to do so in significant relationships, and in business and social contacts. Her birth-father was also named Bill, as is Shirley's third husband.

One intriguing example came shortly after she and her husband Bob White had split up. On an impulse she took on some voluntary work at the local Veterans' hospital. Her first assignment was to turn the pages and highlight text for a quadriplegic who was doing a college psychology course. At her first session she highlighted for him the name Robert White. Some time after this she was browsing through the religious section of the library, looking for something inspirational, when she came across a book of essays by famous people. Something told her that within its pages she would find the inspiration or guidance she so badly needed at a particularly traumatic moment in her life. At home she had no sooner opened the book when she found herself reading that when the writer felt depressed or unhappy, he would go to the local Veterans' hospital and visit the paraplegics and quadriplegics. At that point she searched for the name of the author who had given her the reassurance she needed about her decision to put aside her own cares and devote her time to the needs of others. His name was White:

> I couldn't believe my eyes. I came upon this book so randomly that I was just astonished at the author's name and his reference to the Veterans' hospital for that is just what I had done – and, of course, highlighting Robert White in my guy's psych book the first day I helped him.

While going through her divorce from Bob, Sue had driven into a McDonald's for lunch at Downer Grove township. She noticed the car in front of her in the drive-through had the licence plate: BOB AND SUE. Some months after her divorce from Bob in September 1995, Sue was again on the lunch-time drive-through queue and noticed the same car, only this time its plate had been changed to: JUZ ME.

Both Sue's ex-mothers-in-law were named Lorraine, and both were born on 10 April. Furthermore, Sue says that after reading *Coincidences: Chance or Fate?* she realized that the number 10, or a combination of numbers adding up to 10, is a significant number 'invading my life'. She was born on 10 February 1946 (10/2/46). On her 30th birthday she found and spoke for the first time to her mother. The digits in each of her wedding dates add up to 10: 16 March (16/3) and 22 June (22/6). The birthday of her second husband, Bob, is 27 October (27/10).

Sue's first husband's birthday is 10/10. She lived in house number 1027 before her first marriage and rented apartment number 46. She chose at random a number for her banking and other security codes that amounts to 10. Significant events have also happened to her friends and relatives on dates that amount to the number 10. 'I really don't know what the number stands for in terms of numerology,' she writes, 'but it certainly seems to play a role in my life, hinting at some other important crossroads.'

Sue found herself finally deciding to divorce Bob, after prevaricating for a long time, on his birthday. 'At times I believe we are held back from taking action until the perfect moment in time, or until the appropriate circumstances are in place to make a move,' she says. As it turned out, her timing was, for a number of complex reasons, perfect. In her own words:

> I really believe that I have been experiencing exactly what I was supposed to experience. I think each of us comes into this life with a lesson plan. I guess we have free will to follow through with the plan or not…to follow our intuition and guidance, or not. I'm familiar with the theories of Carl Jung concerning coincidence, but it also appears to me that a lot of the events and synchronicities that have occurred in my life seemed destined to play out the way they did and were independent of what I was doing or thinking at the time. It certainly appears to me that the coincidences linking all of us [that is, her friends, relatives and business associates] came with us into this life and certainly, and quite obviously, pre-date by years our meeting and being involved with each other. It's like a cosmic web has been spun in our particular lives linking all of the players together and drawing all of us towards a certain point in time…From what I have observed in my own life, there certainly appears to be an obvious orchestration of events that seems to challenge our basic understanding and concepts of reality.

In summary, the people cited in this chapter are all proof that an awareness of coincidence can be cultivated, although individuals each have their own experience of them.

Exposing the Myth

A final note on creating awareness of coincidences: beware of the myth that becomes legend. In *Coincidences: Chance or Fate?* I told the legendary story of actor Charles Coghlan, who became ill and died in Galveston, Texas, during a tour of the American state in 1899. He was buried in a lead coffin inside a vault. In September of the following year, so the story goes, a hurricane hit Galveston, flooding the cemetery, and Coghlan's coffin floated out into the Gulf of Mexico. The coffin drifted from there into the Atlantic. In 1908 some fishermen on Prince Edward Island, Canada, found the coffin and hauled it ashore and Coghlan was reburied in the graveyard in the church in which he had been baptized. I based this story on at least two credible sources.[5] It has also been used in a number of major television documentaries, and is a legend of some substance.

When an extract of *Coincidences: Chance or Fate?* featuring this story appeared in December 1995 in America's largest-selling newspaper, the *National Enquirer*, it piqued the interest of a journalist, Mary Mackay, on Prince Edward Island itself. She set out to track down the truth of the strange and persistent coincidence that has linked Prince Edward Island and Galveston Island in Texas for 100 years. Her report appeared in the Prince Edward Island newspaper the *Guardian Weekend* in October 1996. She began by exposing the myth that Prince Edward Island was Coghlan's birth-place. He was in fact born in 1841 somewhere on the opposite side of the Atlantic, most likely in England. It was in London that Coghlan's talents as a fine Shakespearean actor blossomed, as did his other talents as a hypnotizer of women and a practical joker of robust proportions. Legend has it that he offended royal sensibilities by dropping a piece of ice down the cleavage of Lillie Langtry, actress and mistress of the party host, the Prince of Wales.

By the mid-1880s Coghlan had migrated across the Atlantic. After finishing a successful but strenuous season in New York City he rented a cottage at Abell's Cape in Bay Fortune, Prince Edward Island. The area was fraught with legends of Captain Kidd's treasure. Even the cottage itself was said to be the haunting ground of the ghost of Edward Abell, an English landlord's agent murdered during a monetary dispute in 1819.

Intrigued by the serenity and tales of the area, Coghlan purchased the property for a summer residence. This, in turn, attracted other performers and Bay Fortune became a veritable actors' colony. Most notable of all actor arrivals was performer Charles P. Flockton, who, in a strange twist of fable and fate, is probably the inspiration for the enduring Coghlan legend.

After more than a decade of summers on Prince Edward Island, Coghlan embarked on a theatrical tour of Galveston with one of his most successful plays, *The Royal Box*, said to have been written during his island visits.

Coghlan did not see the turn of the century. He died of heart failure on 27 November 1899 and was buried at Lakeview Cemetery by the Levy Brothers' funeral home. There, Coghlan's remains and his memory rested in peace until a torrential hurricane struck Galveston Island on 9 September 1900. In less than 24 hours 7,000 of Galveston's 37,000 residents, and another 2,000 in the bay area, were killed. Some victims were buried in mass graves, others were dumped at sea but floated back to shore. Apparently, many among Galveston's cemetery population were washed out to sea. An article in the Charlottetown *Daily Examiner* newspaper, a year after the hurricane, stated that Coghlan's body was recovered not far from Lakeview Cemetery and reburied. However, within a few years, the story of Coghlan and his floating coffin was born and soon took on a life of its own. In the late 1920s a cartoon in Ripley's *Believe It or Not* series, entitled 'Charles Coghlan Comes Home', featured the performer's floating coffin journey to Prince Edward Island. This sketchy scenario piqued international attention and that of Coghlan's daughter, Gertrude Pitou, in New York, who tried to pinpoint the source of her father's fabulous story.

Ripley attributed his sources as none other than the infamous ice-cube-down-the-cleavage actress Lillie Langtry and author Sir Johnston Forbes-Robertson. Robertson's book *A Player Under Three Reigns* introduced the Coghlan-coffin tale as 'a curious fact [that] was told me about the end of this fine actor which I must set down'. After years of searching, Coghlan's daughter was unable to establish any truth to the theory.

Meanwhile on Prince Edward Island, Bay Fortune residents, many of whom had known the former summertime resident, were bewildered by the persistent legend. Time and time again they dismissed the floating-coffin saga and Coghlan's reburial in the local cemetery as a 'fairy tale' and 'pure nonsense'.

A search by Mackay of the Bay Fortune United Church cemetery did unearth a headstone dated 17 November 1905 commemorating actor and colony member Cuthbert Cooper, a friend of performer Charles Flockton. But Charles Coghlan is not buried there, or in any other cemetery on Prince Edward Island. Mackay writes:

> As the cod swims, it's a lengthy float from Galveston to Prince Edward Island. Although it is theoretically possible that Charles Coghlan made this coffin trek, Allyn Clarke, head of ocean circulation at Nova Scotia's Bedford Institute of Oceanography, said it is unlikely. A ship wrecked off the Carolinas once drifted this same course, but came ashore on the shore of Saint-Pierre and Miquelon [islands] near Newfoundland. However, Clarke said Coghlan's coffin would have to detour through the Cabot Strait into the Gulf of St Lawrence, then backwash onto the shores of PEI, rather than New Brunswick or the Iles de la Madeleine.

(Author's note: Newfoundland is northeast of Prince Edward Island and Nova Scotia is immediately to its southeast; they form a barrier, broken by the Cabot Strait, between it and the Atlantic.)

Mackay found Coghlan's first, if not final, resting site at the Lakeview Cemetery, and this still exists today, albeit under a few extra metres of earth after the height of the entire island was increased following the storm of 1900. After checking the cemetery records for 1899, Bill Bond, owner of Lakeview Cemetery, spied Coghlan's name and date of demise and interment. However, a search of the cemetery failed to find a monument or marker bearing Coghlan's name.

Once again the window of opportunity for the floating-coffin theory slides open. The very storm that provides the *modus operandi* also makes it impossible to prove whether it happened or not. Shortly after Coghlan's death, another Bay Fortune actors' colony member died during a tour of San Francisco. His wish was that his body be cremated and returned to the island he loved so much. So, on a bluff overlooking Bay Fortune and beneath a sundial bearing the words 'the creeping shadow marks another hour of absence' lie the ashes of Charles P. Flockton.

In all fairness, Mackay leaves the possibility of the legend being fact open, because she has not been able to conclusively prove it is not so. On the balance of her findings, though, the legend must be consigned to the 'very doubtful' file.

chapter two

Morphic Resonance

One October day in 1997, for no apparent reason, the line about 'do not go gentle into that something-or-other-night' popped into my mind. I wrestled with it, trying to remember the full quotation and its sources. After trying for some moments to recall the missing word, or words, I dismissed it from my mind, although for the rest of the day it niggled occasionally as random thoughts can do...

That night, I settled down rather late to read one of that morning's newspapers. Just as I was about to put it aside, feeling that I had caught up with the latest events, my eyes fell on a small item about a national poll in Britain that had been held to select the country's favourite post-war poem. The winning poem was 'Warning: Not Waving but Drowning' by Stevie Smith. I had never heard of either the poem or its writer, but second on the list was 'Do Not Go Gentle Into That *Good* Night' (my emphasis) by Dylan Thomas.

As I realized that this coincidence had led me to find the answer to the pestering thought from earlier in the day, I felt myself being absorbed into a sudden wave of affinity. It was as though I had joined thousands of people whose memory (faulty or otherwise) had been stirred once again by the words of the outstanding Welsh writer. In my late night musings, I imagined Thomas's well-loved work crackling over the cosmic airwaves – for all I know others' minds may have been filled inexplicably that day with the words of Stevie Smith, although I rather thought not. Thomas may have come second in that particular poll, but he was undoubtedly the better-known poet. In any case, my mind, seeking some rationale for these imaginings, brought me to Rupert Sheldrake's morphic resonance theory, the idea that we draw our thoughts from a collective memory rather than our own minds. The item in the newspaper was, as it turned out, particularly relevant. Sheldrake illustrates his theory with an example of what he means by a morphic field, or collective memory, by citing an experiment

43

conducted at Nottingham University that showed how people found a crossword in a newspaper significantly easier to solve when it had already appeared the day before. According to Sheldrake they were helped by the fact that possibly millions of others had already gone through the mental processes of puzzle-solving the previous day.

A rather perverse example of the morphic resonance effect on crossword puzzles is to be found in issues of *Crozworld*, the monthly magazine of the Australian Crossword Club. The magazine comprises puzzles set and adjudicated by members. Regularly eerie coincidence connections occur between different puzzles in the same issue. For example in one issue, the setters of two puzzles both used former British Prime Minister North as all or part of a solution. Club officials could not remember the little-known Prime Minister being mentioned before. In the same issue, a solution in one puzzle was 'suspender belt', and a clue in another puzzle 'garter belt'. The answer to a clue in a third crossword was 'orthoptera' (the cockroach order of insects) and the solution in a different puzzle of the same issue was 'cockroach'.

Still awake, and beginning to wonder just how many of our random thoughts were our own, I recalled that just the previous day Jackie, my wife, was speaking to a colleague she had not been in touch with for some time. During the conversation she asked whether he had heard any news of another mutual colleague. Neither of them had heard from her for nearly a year following her traumatic dismissal from a magazine. That evening the colleague rang back. He had arrived home to find a new free magazine in the post. Opening it he noticed its editor was the 'missing' friend. The first issue had been posted that day to thousands of homes – when Jackie checked she found one had arrived in our mail that day. Was its 'presence' in the minds of so many what triggered the inquiry from Jackie?

When Sheldrake first postulated his theory in 1981 that nature has a kind of collective memory and the experience of one group of animals (including, of course, the human animal) can influence the way others in the same group behave thousands of kilometres away, the respected journal *Nature* proclaimed it 'a book for burning'. (Shades of Kammerer and his book on series coincidences – see p. 58.)

However, subsequent experiments in reputable universities have since supported his theory. It is similar in some ways to Jung's ideas of a universal memory. Sheldrake postulates an evolutionary progression of nature, rather than the static view of immutable natural laws that has for so long been accepted as scientific fact.

The British biologist finds support for his theories in the fact that when a new organic chemical is crystallized, on the first occasion it may not do so all that easily; but on subsequent occasions crystallization should occur more and more easily, as though the substances remember the process.

Further arguing his case for collective memory, Sheldrake says the conventional theory that everything we can remember is somehow stored inside our brain in the form of material patterns is just speculative. He believes we remember because of the resonance of ourselves in the past.[1] The following story from my files is, perhaps, a dramatic example of this effect.

Return to the Past

An English woman, who uses the pen name Eugenie, told me how she spent an uneasy night and early morning debating the wisdom of having enrolled by post for a one-year course in poetry. She had already successfully completed two years of the course. She kept reminding herself that her real aim in life was to achieve a shift in her level of consciousness. Would further study of poetry help her in this aim? Suddenly a crystal clear thought came to her with such force it appeared to resolve her dilemma: 'It's putting Ossian on Pelleas,' she said speaking the thought out loud. Eugenie went on:

> This meant absolutely nothing to me so I looked in my *Golden Age of Myth and Legend* which I had recently bought second-hand and hadn't had time to read. I was startled to see:
>
> **Ossa**: Mountain in Thessaly, which the Titans piled upon Pelion.
> **Pelion**: A high mountain in Thessaly, upon which Ossa is piled by the giants to reach Olympus.
>
> I immediately cancelled the enrolment and they are returning my cheque. And suddenly I feel a lot younger.

Eugenie, a woman of integrity, was grappling with a problem. Her mind, seeking a solution, reached back into the past, into mythology, and found in words that, when uttered so spontaneously, were meaningless to her. Greek mythology is not her field of expertise. How then, we may ask, did those names (or in one case a close enough version of the name) come into her mind?

In the early 1980s Eugenie was working on a sculpture while attending a summer art school, and was using another student as a model. As the face took shape she said to herself 'Arcadius Maximus'. Later, in the twilight following supper, she retreated to her room and lay on her bed by a window overlooking the walled garden. Suddenly and quite unexpectedly she heard the murmur of voices, and saw the reflection of some glimmering lights accompanied by the tread of feet on gravel under the window. She goes on:

> I immediately said to myself, 'It's the [Roman] Legion changing the guard.' Then I realized what I had said and was overcome with genuine anguish and thought, 'I shall never see the Legion again,' and I felt myself straining into the past as if by wanting I could recover the centuries.

Eugenie was inspired into poetry to record the emotional and completely unexpected experience. Here is an extract of her poem:

> They're changing guard
> at Hadrian's wall
> The Emperor Arcadius East
> had a great fall
> How do I know?
> Well I'll tell 'ee
> m'dear
> I was there. Yes I was –
> Over many a year...

(Author's note: some hours after reading Eugenie's letter, I was watching the British television series *Oliver's Travels*. In this particular episode Oliver, the hero (played by Alan Bates), and heroine, Diane (Sinead Cusack), visit Hadrian's Wall (built between Newcastle and Carlisle in AD 121) and book in at a nearby guest house. That night Diane is awoken by the ghostly sound of marching feet and at breakfast the next morning she is told, tongue-in-cheek, by the proprietress that she had heard the sound of the Legion marching. Two days later, 24 January 1997, I saw that it was the birthday of the Roman emperor Publius Aelius Hadrian, the builder of the wall named after him.)

A few years after this incident Eugenie took a coach tour to some historic sites in England. They were driving along a Roman road and as the coach turned the corner she 'saw' (with her inner eye) a column of marching men just ahead of the coach to their left. She instantly recognized them as being from the Legion. But they were bare-headed. Roman legionaries on the march without helmets? That was not the way history depicted them. For some time she held out from mentioning her sighting to their guide, a historian of some expertise. But finally her curiosity got the better of her. He was taken aback at Eugenie's tale of a reported sighting. She, however, pressed on, 'I nearly didn't ask you as they weren't wearing helmets.' At this a look of confidence returned to his face: ghosts he could not handle, but as for historic details . . . He replied, 'They wore their helmets in battle but not on other duties . . .'

Eugenie later came across a reference to a British soldier who, some years ago, was on manoeuvres on England's Salisbury Plain. Surrounded by his twentieth-century companions, he suddenly became aware of being attached to what seemed like an electric dynamo. The next thing he knew he was in the middle of a battle in seventeenth-century England, lying on a hillock with another soldier in a ragged uniform who, growing suspicious at his appearance, accused him of being a spy. The soldier from the twentieth century knew that if he did not get up and run, he would never see his companions again. As he did so, he was just as suddenly back on Salisbury Plain in the present time. Eugenie says she too has experienced similar electric-dynamo sensations. At times they nearly drove her mad. Although she did not go into a time warp, she would awaken in the early hours with words pouring through her head which she later found to be those of early Romans, Plotinus, Aeneas etc.

She also found the well-known references to US General George Patton's belief that he had been a Roman warrior in a previous life. When he took over his first command in France in World War I at Langres, he knew the place well because he had been there as a Roman legionary. He pointed out a Roman amphitheatre, the legionaries' drill ground, and even the spot where Caesar had pitched his tent. Patton's views are absorbing, coming as they did in an age when few Americans could accept the idea of reincarnation.

While working in a busy London office in Old Street, London EC1, Eugenie found herself taking time out from work to make tiny figures out of silver aluminium foil and wire. She put them around the niche in its large entrance hall. She could not at first understand her compulsion, she was not a craftsperson at all, but a very busy executive and had little time to spare, certainly not for such a time-consuming activity completely unrelated to the business in hand. It was utterly pointless. Much later she happened to read that a few doors away in Old Street there had existed in the 1800s a shop, Pollock's Toy Theatre, that had sold tiny silver figures costing one half-pence each. 'I must have caught that encapsulated memory somehow,' she says.

Pecking Order

Sheldrake's most quoted example concerns the behaviour of bluetits. Some time after foil tops arrived on milk bottles, the birds got the hang of pecking through them and drinking the cream. The habit spread rapidly among unrelated bluetits. Milk bottles almost disappeared during World War II and it was only several years after the war that they were used again. Only a few, if any, of the tits who learned the habit before the war could have survived, but, nevertheless, attacks on bottles began again rapidly.[2]

A more gruesome example of birds behaving as though they were driven by some collective memory concerns a flock of vultures who have lived for generations in a gorge near Segovia, Spain. They left the gorge in 1940, flying north to the battlefields of France, and did not return again until 1946, when the locals noted they were 'fully gorged'. Had their predecessors made the same trip in earlier great battles, and were the vultures now driven by no other impulse than a species memory?

In further research Sheldrake was able to show that pet dogs know when their owners are coming home. He found 46 per cent of dogs start preparing to welcome their owners up to an hour before they return home from work, even if their hours are irregular. The animals usually become agitated and go to the window to watch out. Some cats and other pets also showed the same psychic bonding. To many owners this is perfectly normal behaviour. Our own two dogs were always waiting in the hall by the front door to greet us. As they grew older, they would sit there howling, according to our neighbours. When first told this, we found it upsetting news – how long would the neighbours be prepared to put up with it? They reassured us that the dogs would only begin howling shortly before one of us was due to appear. Our neighbours did not express any surprise at this apparent psychic behaviour, even though one admitted the dogs could start howling up to an hour before our return.

When living in Spain, on the windy isle of Menorca, I was constantly amazed at our cat's ability to know when my wife was due to arrive home. The first indication that Jackie's arrival was imminent came with Poca showing signs of restlessness, before walking to the door where she would settle with an expectant air. Nothing would induce her to leave until it was opened by Jackie. I would tell myself time and again that Poca had got it wrong this time…the sound I listened for was Jackie's small but noisy mobilette that could be heard from some distance. But Poca was never wrong. One particular night a howling wind was sweeping across the island. The shutters were rattling and I could hear the sound of planes landing regularly at the airport not far from us. I noted all these sounds as I eyed Poca going into her preparation for her greeting routine. Time ticked by, then I heard the first faint sound of the small motorbike. A minute later it drew up outside the door. I believe that it would have been impossible for Poca to detect the noise until it was very close, that she must have used some other sense.

Some humans also appear to have the ability to see a short way into the future. It is more than a sense of anticipation, of expectancy. It is rather a visualization of what is about to happen often together with a certainty that it will occur.

Kerstin Fischer, of Stockholm, has experienced this phenomenon of 'knowing' the immediate future for much of her life. Here are some of her experiences.

In 1952, she was at a dinner with some older people, when one of the women said of her husband, a retired vicar, that he had recently been expressing a wish to return to Uppsala where he had studied and lived many years before. Kerstin thought to herself, 'Oh my, Uppsala is very windy and cold in the winter' (the town is situated on a plain north of Stockholm). The vicar's wife turned to her and said, 'But there it is windy and cold in the winter – isn't it, Miss Fischer?' Kerstin was left feeling quite perplexed.

Kerstin writes the occasional article which she signs KFR. One day it suddenly occurred to her she had never seen that letter combination on a car number plate. A moment later, a car overtook her and she noticed its plate: KFR.

One summer Kerstin was sitting with her mother in the square between the Royal Theatre and the Foreign Department in Stockholm. Many cars and tourist buses were passing through the square and the two were playing a game, trying to guess what type of vehicle would appear around the corner next, a yellow bus, two blue cars, etc. At last Kerstin said, 'We must see three green buses in a row before we leave.' A moment later three green buses in a row came into sight.

On her way to take part in a music quiz, Kerstin thought the Marine Music Corps would open with *Harlequin's Millions* – they did. Kerstin also lists other incidents that show she has a highly developed intuitive faculty. Meeting a man briefly for the first time in the street, she says as he departed he reminded her of a reporter she knew on the village newspaper – he turned out to be a journalist. On another occasion, a friend began to describe a dress somebody wore to a dinner and Kerstin asked what shade of green it was. In response to his query about how she knew it was green, all Kerstin can offer is that she had 'seen' it as that colour. Again, when she was preparing to visit her mother in hospital, she suddenly found herself in 'empty space under a very bright light'. A moment later the phone rang: it was the hospital to say her mother had died. Years later, the same feeling of light and space engulfed her in the street. When she returned home the phone was ringing – her aunt had just died.

Yet, Kerstin denies she is psychic. 'Nor do I believe the stones in the woods are my ancestors,' she goes on. 'But I do know there are a lot of things between Heaven and Earth.' Kerstin, now in her seventies, contracted polio when she was 24, and she believes that may have made her more observant. (See also Dulce Pombeiro, p. 33; Maurice Haywood, p. 76; 'Impatient Patient', p. 175; 'Night Thoughts', p. 175.)

Academic researchers Combs and Holland see a linkage between morphic fields and synchronicity in the often-celebrated fact that two or more scientists or mathematicians may make very similar and independent discoveries at almost the same time. They cite as an excellent example the calculus developed by Sir Isaac Newton in England and almost simultaneously in Germany by the philosopher, scientist and mathematician G. W. Leibniz. Newton knew nothing of Leibniz's work.

They also point out that in 1981 three theories, including Sheldrake's, were each published independently, each postulating a tendency for patterns, once created, to reproduce themselves.[3]

Sheldrake himself points out that British scientist Charles Darwin's theory of evolution was first announced in a paper presented in 1858 *at the same time* as a paper by Alfred Russel Wallace, a young naturalist who had come independently to the theory of natural selection. Sheldrake explains that Wallace's discovery had come in a sudden illumination while he was suffering from a severe attack of malarial fever in the Dutch East Indies. Sheldrake postulates that behaviour patterns are first set in a mythic time and these are continually repeated and can be traced back to that first time.[4]

This phenomenon is not only confined to synchronistic discoveries. I am constantly amazed by the fact that an incident occurring in one location will result in an unrelated but copycat incident in another location. For example:

On 9 November 1997, a mother in her thirties was murdered in Australia in her Melbourne suburban home; the act was witnessed by her three young children. There appeared to be no motive for the murder and police were, as the cliché goes, baffled. She was the classic 1950s-style mother with strong family values. The murder appeared to be motiveless and police were faced with what veteran detectives said was the hardest case they had ever come across. Just two days before in America a mother, also in her thirties, had been murdered in her home in Sarasota, a quiet coastal town in Florida; the act was apparently witnessed by her children, 23-month-old quads. Again this was an apparently motiveless attack.

The first thought that springs to mind is a 'copycat killing'. But does it sound feasible that a person hearing of the murder of a housewife and mother on another side of the world would set out to do the same thing, simply for the purpose of imitation? However, if we can accept the basic fact that a thought or action by one person in one place can produce the same thought or action in another place, then we can see how the two might have been linked, whatever other differences there may have been in the motives.

A further example occurred on 2 November 1997. Three women died violently in cemeteries within a few hours of one another. In Adelaide, South Australia, a mother and daughter who were visiting a relative's grave at the West Terrace cemetery were shot dead. On the afternoon of the previous day, hundreds of kilometres from the first killings, across the border in Melbourne, a woman tending the grave of her relative was stabbed to death in what police believe was a random killing. Again there was no possible link between the deaths in two widely separated cemeteries. Murders are not uncommon in large cities, but three in a matter of hours, *all* in cemeteries! Any regular reader of newspapers comes across similar non-causally related events more often than others may suppose.

Combs and Holland say that other examples of meaningful coincidences, which may explain the existence of morphic fields, include relatively frequent situations in which two or more persons are thinking or doing similar things at the same time, but with no knowledge of each other. For example, receiving a call from a friend just when you are thinking of calling her, both of you were contemplating the conversation prior to the call. Similarly, you might find yourself thinking of something just as a person nearby starts to talk about it. (Personally, whenever I am moved to write a letter to the editor on some subject, I find that by waiting a day or so one will invariably appear saying exactly what I would have said.) The American academics say that in instances such as these synchronicity may overlap with what we normally think of as telepathy.[5]

Sheldrake argues that telepathy, although from the conventional scientific point of view theoretically impossible, is in theory possible in the context of morphic resonance.[6] Sheldrake, Combs and Holland appear to be postulating the 'accepted' method of telepathy, that is a kind of mental telephone where thought exchange takes place in the here and now, regardless of distance. But the following two anecdotes, similar in content, suggest another aspect of such communication in which the initiating thoughts of the communicators which lead to the 'morphic coincidence' arise at different times.

Late Gift

One day in March 1966, Jenny Grant, on her daily two-hour commuter journey from her home at Avoca to Sydney, was reading the British journal *Countryman* to which she subscribes. The copy was the previous year's Christmas issue that had arrived the previous evening by second-class mail. She chanced upon an advertisement for a calendar which featured Impressionist paintings of cats. A long-time cat lover, Jenny felt an immediate urge to send off for a copy from London.

However, she reasoned that as the magazine was three months old, the chance of the calendar still being in stock must be slight. Despite this, thoughts of the calendar preoccupied her throughout the day and, by the time she was ready to return home, she had determined to place an order, even though she expected to be disappointed.

That evening when she reached home, she found a long cylinder-shaped object sticking from her letter box. 'I just knew without touching it that it was the calendar,' said Jenny. It was. Her friends Barry and Margaret Lello of The Wirral, Merseyside, had seen the calendar advertised at Christmas and knowing Jenny's love for cats decided it would be a suitable, if belated, Christmas present. The calendar and magazine had arrived within a day of one another by second-class mail.

Seeking Faust

Scott D. Malcolm described to me the events which took place in the summer of 1995:

> I was 'at the 'deepest' point of my studies to date. I was reading quantum physics, Schopenhauer, Nietzsche, psychology as well as Buddhist and Hindu texts, Taoism, the Sufi's mythology and so on. I would often disappear for a week at a time, reading entire books in a single sitting, and absorbing the information they contained.
>
> One day, while reading Jung, I came upon a reference to Goethe's *Faust*, so decided to go and find a copy of the title referenced. I went to the same book store as usual, and quickly realized there were several translations from the original German, and each differed to some degree more or less from one another. Not only that, but the particular translation I sought was not at this store. So I went to another, then another, until I had searched every book store I knew of within a 50-mile radius. I could not find it. Not even at the public libraries. I was forced to abandon my search. I'd call around the next day, and see if anyone had a copy.
>
> When I got home, I discovered a small package waiting in the mailbox, addressed to myself, from my oldest sister. This was strange as my sister had

never, in my entire life, sent me so much as a birthday card. It wasn't personal, that's just the way she was. She'd call (collect to be sure) once in a while, but that was it. Well, quite curious to discover the impetus of this ground-breaking event, I opened the package as I was walking through my front door. Inside was an old paperback book, *Faust*, by Goethe and it was the exact translation.

Needless to say, when I discovered the book in the mail, my mind was blown. I had to tell a good friend who's into these sorts of occurrences about what had happened, so I went over to his house. He lives in a 'retirement community' trailer park. While I was relating the day's happenings to him, we heard some sirens close by, and I made the comment, 'it's probably the fire department coming down to the park to put out a trailer fire'. The sirens passed the park and continued on somewhere else, and I finished my story. About ten minutes later, we could hear some commotion outside, and in the distance some new sirens. So we went outside to see what it was all about. There was a trailer, three spots away from my friend's, engulfed in flames, and the fire department was just arriving. While the 'fire' incident wasn't quite as mind-blowing as the book, it did cap off a very peculiar day.[7]

chapter three
Playing with Numbers

It seems to me that mathematicians – working apparently in idle moments – have made an art out of reducing what many of us consider to be 'amazing' coincidences to the point where they triumphantly proclaim that the improbable odds we imagined must have been overcome for such events to occur are, in reality, much less.

For example, race commentators dubbed as 'an amazing coincidence' the fact that in the 1997 Jerez Grand Prix, Michael Schumacher, Jacques Villeneuve and Heinz-Harold Frentzen all lapped in 1 minute 21.072 seconds exactly. There are few Grand Prix fans who would disagree with this accolade.

However, the coincidence caught the eye of academics Jack Cohen and Ian Stewart. They analysed the anecdote in a *New Scientist* article.[1] Cohen is identified as a reproductive biologist and deputy director of the Mathematics Awareness Centre at Warwick University and co-writer with Stewart of *Figments of Reality* (Cambridge University Press, 1997). They explain that the method by which probability theorists are able to cut such rare occurrences down to size is known as sample spaces. For example, top drivers all lap at roughly the same speed, so it can be assumed that the three fastest times would all fall inside the same tenth-of-a-second period. At intervals of a thousandth of a second there are 100 possible lap times for each to chose from; this list determines the sample space. Assume that each time in that range is equally likely. Then there is a 1 in 100 chance that the second driver laps in the same time as the first, and a 1 in 100 chance that the third driver laps in the same time as the other two. This leads to an estimate of 1 in 10,000 as the probability of the coincidence. The authors agree this is low enough to be striking, as likely as a hole-in-one, but not so low that we ought to feel 'amazed'. But, one is tempted to ask, would it not be 'amazing' if the same three drivers recorded the same times twice? (See whist players on p. 55.)

This mathematicians' sport of reducing the improbable to the probable appears to have been largely popularized by Professor Warren Weaver, who, in the 1960s, asserted:

> One of the most striking and fundamental things about probability theory is that it leads to an understanding of the otherwise strange fact that events which are individually capricious and unpredictable can, when treated *en masse*, lead to a very stable average performance.[2]

The professor, who liked a good coincidence himself, is remembered – at least in coincidence circles – for his finding that with 23 people in a room the chances are better than 50/50 that two of them will share the same birthday. One anecdote has it that a mathematically informed guest on *The Johnny Carson Show* raised this point, but when Carson threw it open to his studio audience of more than 200, by asking whether anyone shared his birthday, he could not find one match. The guest, unfortunately, was at a loss to explain the distinction. Perhaps he should have cited the Golden Rule: there is always an exception to the rule.

When I tried the birthday match before an audience of about 130 on a national Australian television show, there were two matching pairs, including two who shared Christmas Day as their birthday.[3]

John Allen Paulos, Professor of Mathematics at Temple University, Philadelphia, puts Weaver's proposition another way. He says that if we imagine a school with thousands of classrooms, each of which contains 23 students, then approximately half of these classrooms will contain two students who share a birthday. He adds that time should not be wasted in trying to explain the meaning of these or other coincidences of a similar type. They just happen.[4]

Despite their analyses, neither Paulos nor Weaver suggests we should simply dismiss *all* coincidences as being of no import on the basis of mathematical probability. 'Coincidences are...sometimes significant,' Paulos concedes.[5] Weaver gives us permission to wonder about them. 'If the occurrence of [a] rare event interests you, go ahead and be interested. This is your personal privilege.'[6] Very noble of them.

While preparing this book I was contacted for comment by some British national newspapers over a baffling event where all four players in a whist drive were dealt a complete suit. Odds of trillions to one against were being quoted. I was able to pull from my files a similar anecdote. A group of card players used to meet regularly at Pilltown, a small village in Northern Ireland, to play whist. One night in the autumn of 1992, a pack of cards was opened, shuffled by two players and dealt by the fourth player. Each of the four was dealt a complete suit. In the autumn of 1994 the same thing happened, a complete set dealt to each player. Each time the same four players were involved.[7] Are the odds here so high that they become an impossibility, and, therefore, beyond probability?

Metascientist Martin Cochrane told me:

> What we must keep in mind when standing before the awesome might of mathematics is that it is only another language, constructed to explain the reality of the physical world. In other words, another social construction by man.

Combs and Holland, like researcher Emile Borel, point out that the probabilistic interpretation of synchronicity – that it is all due to the vicissitudes of mere chance – shows that probability itself has its limits. Borel observes, 'The calculus of probabilities is an exact science whose results are as reliable as those of arithmetic or algebra as long as it confines itself to the *numerical* evaluation of probabilities.' (My emphasis)[8]

Borel's comments were made to counter the argument that we remember coincidences because they stand out in a world where so many 'normal' events occur each day. Statisticians Persi Diaconis and Frederick Mosteller seek to bring this down to some sort of equation. They ask us to imagine that, daily, an incredible coincidence happens to only one person in a million. This appears quite rare, but with a population in Britain of 55 million, each day there are likely to be 55 amazing coincidences. That makes 20,075 incredible coincidences per year. Therefore with a large enough sample any number of outrageous things is likely to happen.[9]

Astronomer Michael Shallis contends that to dismiss coincidences as merely chance, or 'one of those things', is to ignore the real problem of randomness, to appeal inappropriately to probability theory, and to discount the idea of a purposeful universe.[10]

Combs and Holland say that, according to the most common theory of probability, the frequency theory, the likelihood of any event is based upon how often it has occurred in the past. In fact, statistical probabilities may be calculated in the real world in only very few types of situations. One is in the laboratory, where the scientist or engineer has a high degree of control over all conditions. Another is in relating mass studies concerning large numbers of similar events, such as how many Big Macs will be sold in the United States on a particular 4th of July. Exactly who will buy the burgers is not known. Still another situation in which probability can be highly specified involves quantum statistics. Combs and Holland argue that none of these situations applies to most synchronistic coincidences which are never under control and are always unique to the individual:

It has been the strong prejudice of the scientific intelligentsia for the past 300 years to favour reductionistic interpretations. The situation is changing but much of the inertia is still with us. The point here, however, is that the issue of probability is one of choice and not of evidence, there is no hard evidence in the matter of synchronicity...[11]

To illustrate this theory, an old story: Mrs Atlay, wife of a former Bishop of Hereford, dreamed one night that there was a pig in the dining room of the Palace. She came downstairs and in the hall told her governess and children of the dream before family prayers. When the prayers were finished, and no one who had been told the story having left the hall in the interval, she went into the dining room and there was a pig. It was found to have escaped from the sty after Mrs Atlay had arisen. A pig had never been seen in the dining room before, so how can we state the probability of the event, to say nothing of the probability of the dream itself?

A final word on the subject comes from Joseph A. Reif, an American teaching at the Bar-Ilan University, Israel. He tells the story of the man who would not go by plane anywhere because he was afraid that there might be a terrorist on board with a bomb to blow it up. No amount of persuasion could change his apprehension until one day he asked what the possibility was of there being *two* separate bomb holders on board the same flight. When they showed him that the odds of such a coincidence were astronomically squared, he then started flying. But he always took his own bomb with him.

Jung and Numbers

Carl Jung observed that both numbers and synchronicity have always been connected and that both 'possess numinosity and mystery as their common characteristics'. He goes on:

It is generally believed that numbers were invented or thought out by man, and are therefore nothing but concepts of quantities, containing nothing that was not previously put into them by human intellect. But it is equally possible that numbers were found or discovered...they might easily be endowed with qualities that have still to be discovered.[12]

Most people feel they are in some way attached to a particular number or numbers, whether it be their birthday or some other digit or set of digits. The same number crops up throughout their life resulting both in good and bad news, happy and sad experiences, good and bad luck.

Audrey Austin of Kariong, New South Wales, believes her 'number' is 3. She was born at a house whose number was 3. Her last address was also a 3. She has often lived – in Australia and in Britain – at number 6 addresses. At present her address is 24 (2+4=6). She has married 3 times, has 3 daughters and 6 grandchildren. There had been 3 grandchildren for 12 years then, in the space of 18 months, 3 more came along. Her two eldest girls have 3 children each. She migrated to Australia in 1966 when she was aged 33. Her birthday is 6 September 1933 (6/9/33). A member of British Mensa, she joined Australian Mensa and was given membership card number 63. Her local video store gave her card number 693 – she is not going to reveal her PIN number. In fact, according to numerology analyses her number *is* 3 if we take her birthday: 6+9+3+3=21, 1+2=3. (Numerology is a system where sequences of numbers are brought down to a single number as illustrated above. Numerologists use the final number to assess the character and future of the subject.)

The Clustering Effect

Kere Fleming of the Gold Coast, Queensland, tells an anecdote which would have pleased Paul Kammerer, the Austrian biologist who for much of his life was fascinated by serial coincidences.

If Kere had not been such an 'aware' person it may have slipped by without her noting it, as these things so often do. One day, she went to an auction to buy her daughter a twin stroller. It was item number 112. When she registered she was given ticket 112, and 112 is also her house number. Her daughter was admitted to hospital later that day and next day signed herself out – on 12 January (1/12).

Earlier this century Kammerer wrote a book about such effects, *The Law of the Series* (*Das Gesetz der Serie*; Deutsche Verlage-Anstalt, Stuggart-Berlin, 1919), in which he showed evidence of coincidental cases that cluster or converge in manners that are meaningfully related but causally unrelated – events that repeat themselves in time or space too frequently to be passed off as mere chance. In simple words, it never rains but it pours. He held that sequences were proof of a previously undiscovered objective principle of nature – they were visible peaks of hidden cyclic events. His book was greeted with such disdain by his colleagues that it put an end to his academic career and he committed suicide in 1926 on an Austrian mountain path. Generally mathematicians regard examples of the clustering effect as no more than occurrences that can be found in any random system: i.e. they amount to no more than proof of randomness.

It is true that today Kammerer's research has the appearance of curiosity, because much of it consists of recording trivial events. But it can be said that it amounted to the first detailed investigation of synchronicity.

Furthermore, people are more than a random collection of numbers, and when they are interpolated into the serial coincidence equation, one is left wondering whether our fates are indeed decided not so much by our own actions and known forces as by 'hidden' principles as proposed by Kammerer. Finding evidence of such a possibility is not hard, as in the following cases, which generally make grim reading.

On the night of Thursday 27 November 1997, there were three separate bus accidents in India, claiming a total of 77 lives. Among those killed were 34 wedding guests on board a bus that plunged into a canal in southern India. Meanwhile, in Himachjal Pradesh State, 17 people were killed when their bus fell into a gorge. Another 26 died when a bus and truck collided in Maharashtra State.

In the space of a week in August 1997, in three unrelated cases in Sydney, three people charged with murder were found not guilty by juries because of extenuating circumstances.

Within the space of 12 days in 1997, five planes from the former Soviet Union crashed. The cluster of crashes began on 6 December when a giant military cargo plane slammed into an apartment building in Siberia shortly after takeoff, killing nearly 70 people. Russian civil aviation officials blamed the 'run' of disasters on poor maintenance, lack of money and lax controls among the dozens of small airlincs that emerged in the former Soviet republics when the monopoly carrier Aeroflot broke up. These explanations do not, however, explain the cluster effect of the crashes. Given the defects in the Russian-built planes, and the way the industry is run, accidents should be expected to occur on a regular, rather than a clustering, basis. There had been a long period when there were few if any crashes going back to 1994, when there was again a rash of disasters involving planes from the former Soviet Union.

In mid-1997, a hospital on the shores of Lake Burley Griffin, Canberra, the Australian Federal capital, was 'imploded' to demolish it, but something went wrong and a piece of masonry flew outwards from the crumbling building across the lake and killed a girl who had been among the spectators standing at a supposedly safe distance. A few days later in Israel the bridge over which the Australian team was marching at the start of the Maccabiah Games collapsed and four members of the team were killed. The two incidents, both unusual, were enough for observers of the clustering effect to predict there was going to be another fatal accident involving a man-made structure. (See *Coincidences: Chance or Fate?*, pp. 37–44.) There was: a few days later a landslide swept away two ski-lodges in the Austrian Alps killing 18 occupants of one of the lodges.

In ten days over the 1997–8 Christmas/New Year period, four New South Wales farmers died in tractor-related accidents.

In August 1997, five male friends committed suicide in the Bundanoon district of New South Wales. An official report said it was 'almost impossible' to draw a link between the suicide cluster. The following December three more men from the same district killed themselves in three consecutive days. Again there was no apparent link. It was the district's worst year for suicides on record.

In June 1996, a Blackhawk helicopter crashed in Queensland killing 18 men from the defence forces. A week later two Blackhawks collided in the United States killing six and injuring 16. It was the US military's second fatal helicopter collision in just over a month. On 10 May, two Marine helicopters had collided killing 14 soldiers and injuring two – these helicopters were not Blackhawks.

A week before INXS lead singer Michael Hutchence died unexpectedly some time in the early hours of Saturday 22 November 1997 in a Sydney hotel room, another Australian singer, Gordon Wilcock, also died. Both men were stars in their respective fields of entertainment, Hutchence for rock 'n' roll, Wilcock for opera.

The death of Michael Hutchence eerily mirrored that of another pop idol, Kurt Cobain, lead singer of Nirvana, in April 1994. Shortly before his death, Hutchence was presenting a cheery face to the world – as was Cobain. Like Hutchence, Cobain was also confirming his exterior appearance by telling everyone he had never been happier. Also like Hutchence, Cobain had also recently become a father, for the first time, of a baby girl. Following Cobain's suicide – he put a gun to his head – the reaction from his fans was a mixture of sadness and anger that their idol had committed what they saw as a selfish act. Following Hutchence's death – his death was also found to be suicide – his fans too expressed mixed emotions. INXS had just released their latest album, *Elegantly Wasted*.

In the field of pop music, there is a cluster of stars who have met their deaths in light aircraft crashes: Glen Miller, Buddy Holly, John Denver and three members of Lynyrd Skynyrd.

In January 1998, Sonny Bono, the 1960s pop star turned US politician, died in a skiing accident at the Heavenly Valley ski resort in California – a few days after Michael Kennedy, one of the American political dynasty, died in a skiing accident at Aspen, Colorado. Michael became the latest in the cluster of tragedies haunting America's best-known family. Joseph Kennedy died in World War II, his sister Kathleen died in a plane crash aged 28, his brother, the American president, was assassinated as was another brother and presidential candidate, Robert. Michael was the son of Robert, another of whose sons, David, died of a drug overdose.

As with so many coincidence anecdotes, other aspects are also present in the death of Michael Kennedy. Words that were uttered apparently in jest became in retrospect ill-omened coincidences. The Kennedy clan had begun their annual downhill football game the day before the accident. The game is dangerous involving high-speed skiing without poles, tossing a football through an improvised goal. Senior officials of the Aspen Skiing Company had tried to halt the traditional family game. It had, in fact, been suspended the day before with scores tied. As they had left the field, bickering amicably among themselves, one of the Kennedys had vowed, 'We'll play tomorrow, death to the loser.' Next day, with Michael the captain of one team, and his sister, Rory, captain of the other, the game had just begun when Michael caught the ball and rammed face-first into a tree. Couri Hay, a New York publicist who was at the scene, said Michael had encouraged the group to wait until all others had cleared the mountain, 'so that we won't kill anybody'. Hay said they may have been the last words he had spoken. A final coincidence. After their father, Robert, had been assassinated in 1968, their mother, Ethel, asked each of the older children to act as a guardian angel to a younger child. Michael was asked to look after his sister Rory, who had been born six months after their father had died. But as Michael lay badly injured on the ski slope it was Rory who came to his aid, turning him on his side so that he would not choke, applying mouth-to-mouth resuscitation, pounding on his chest and encouraging him with words to fight for his life.

Oversized American comedian Chris Farley died in 1997 at the age of 33 of a suspected heart attack. One of the country's most popular comedians, he first came to prominence on the comedy programme *Saturday Night Live*. His death was eerily similar to that of his idol John Belushi, who also died at 33 in 1982. Farley decided on a career in comedy after watching Belushi perform. Like Belushi, Farley was a highly physical comic who revelled in his size and became renowned for his frenetic characters. In 1990 he gained national prominence when he joined *Saturday Night Live*, which had also launched Belushi on the national stage. Both men had an appetite for food, drink and drugs.

Are we to view such events as mere randomness? Or was Kammerer on to something when he talked of events we notice, because of their newsworthy prominence, giving us glimpses of a hidden principle that may govern our lives? At the end of his book, Kammerer expresses his belief that seriality is 'ubiquitous and continuous in life, nature and the cosmos. It is the umbilical cord that connects thought, feeling, science and art with the womb of the universe which gave birth to them.'[13]

Combs and Holland, who have studied Kammerer's work, are of the view that we should perhaps not be too dismissive of it, claiming 'the very presence of Kammerer's intense fascination strongly suggests the proximity of unconscious activity – activity that may have been more than casually related to the coincidences themselves'.[14]

Kammerer's theories are, like Jung's, difficult to pin down. For example, Jung's whole theory of synchronicity is bound up intrinsically with his theory of the collective unconscious and of archetypes. Yet when we search for some clear definition of either we find incongruities. British psychiatrist Frieda Fordham says:

> To attempt to define the collective unconscious is to attempt the impossible, for we can have no knowledge either of its boundaries or its true nature; all that we can do is to observe its manifestations, describe them, and try to understand them so far as is possible...[15]

When it comes to archetypes, Jung himself says that 'not even our thoughts can clearly grasp them, for [they] never invented them'.[16]

Kammerer must have had no hint of the troubles that lay ahead for him when he first set foot on what turned out to be the perilous (for him) road of synchronicity. His mistake, as far as his professional reputation was concerned, was to say – like Jung – that the coincidence series he had so diligently noted over many years was meaningful.

chapter four

Intuition

As a summer storm whipped up in early 1998, a sudden gust of squally wind slammed our back door, setting off our house security alarm. (Quite why I do not know, as a slamming door had never set it off before.) Once I had managed to turn it off, I realized that the cover plate on the small alarm box mounted on the door had disappeared. I searched outside in the rain, then around the door inside, and found no sign of the cover.

Suddenly my intuition told me where I would find it. After working late a few nights before I had switched on the television and found myself in the middle of a French film (I later found out it was *A Tale of Springtime*). A central theme in the plot involved the loss of a precious necklace, its last known whereabouts in the trouser pocket of a man just before he had changed in front of a wardrobe. In the denouement (apologies for giving it away to those who have not seen the film) the necklace is discovered in a shoe. The man had slipped the shoes off before removing his trousers and the necklace had fallen silently into one of them without his realizing. He put the shoes in a box which he placed on a top cupboard shelf. In true coincidence style of many plots, the necklace is recovered when the box accidentally falls from its shelf while the man is looking for something else. As I stood in the kitchen gazing in frustration around for the cover, my eyes fell on an old pair of shoes I keep by the door for use when working in the garden – and the film's plot rushed into my mind. I picked up one of them, tilted it back and the cover plate slid into view.

Intuition is, as one writer describes it, the 'journey from A to Z without stopping at any other letter along the way'. Australian psychologist Dr Karen Tilker says when men use intuition they often are able to disguise it because they have a greater ability to articulate more logically how they came to a conclusion or decision: 'Women are less skilled at being able to show how they went from point A to point B,' she says.

Intuition is, therefore, a knowing without knowing why; a certainty that 'yes, this is it!' In other words, it is non-causal events – unrelated happenings – coming together to form an intuitive coincidence. In my case these were the French film I happened to glimpse and my search for the cover plate, which brought about a result out of unlikely connections. Often intuition comes in the form of intuitive premonition-like flashes, a certainty about the outcome of an event or the right action to take based on no known information. Intuition is, therefore, illogical and eschews the use of data. However, we should also keep in mind that intuition operates at a real, not abstract level – Einstein said his theories were initiated not by any logical reasoning but by an inner certainty of the beauty and harmony at their core. In other words they were intuitively formulated.

According to Masami Saionji, chairperson of the World Peace Prayer Society, intuition is also a spiritual power with which everyone has been endowed from their very beginning. She says that 'what ultimately decides our fate is whether or not we can make full use of it'.[1]

Lucky Stars

Tony Awad, a 23-year-old Leo, experienced an intuitive coincidence. He read the prediction of *Daily Telegraph* astrologer Arthur Bowman that lucky stars were shining that day for Leos and bought a $A1 scratch Lottery ticket on the strength of that prediction. The young plumber won the instant prize of $A50,000.

At first glance Tony's story would appear to provide ammunition for sceptics: how many times has someone read their daily horoscope telling them it was their lucky day – and it turned out to be a day full of bad fortune? The opposite question might also be asked: how many times has a person under a 'lucky' star, not bought a Lottery ticket? However, the element that came into play in Tony's case was intuition, which told him that the prediction had meaning for him, and he followed it through. For most people astrological guides are a form of amusement; if the prediction or advice given comes true, all well and good. A reading seldom arouses that strong almost indefinable urge within us, that intuitive instinct that we should act on what the stars or other intangible messages surrounding us foretell. Bowman, a veteran astrologer, has been credited by many a grateful reader with inducing them to buy a winning Lottery ticket.

Intuition is also defined as a knowing beyond the realms of any learned knowledge, the direct perception of truth and facts independent of any reasoning process. A simple example is a variation of the incident often quoted in discussions on coincidence: the telephone rings and you know who the caller is before you answer it.

More specifically psychologists say intuition is a function of the right hemisphere of our brains, the side that controls our imagination and gives us insights into other aspects of reality. The left hemisphere is the practical side, and is often seen as more dominant in the male than female.

But in recent years women have been setting a trap for themselves in this field. In their battle for equality they have been forsaking this 'natural' intuitive gift of theirs in favour of logical thought processes – while many men have been going in the opposite direction. Dr Tilker says the reason women have been suppressing, if not abandoning altogether, much of their innate intuitive instincts is in order to compete in the data-oriented world.

The ability of women to discern certain aspects of people's character or certain outcomes of situations is not used as much now because women are adapting more traditional masculine ways of relating in the workplace and at home.

Traditionally men in many professions have been called upon to rely upon specific objective data as the basis for their conclusions. Women are being called upon in the same way. If people are being given information, they want to know what the information is based on and want that to be objective rather than subjective, something external rather than from the person relying on their intuition.

A leading businessman confided to me that in recent times he had come to be guided in most aspects of his life by a 'balanced' use of intuition. He insists the 'tool', as he calls it, has improved his decision-making markedly. He feels more creative, able to come up with fresh ideas and always seems to be in the right place at the right time. A recent survey showed that business people who profess a belief in intuition are better all-round performers, including decision-makers. Scientist Lou Caracciolo, a Jungian student, points out in an unpublished manuscript that many books have been written in recent times about economic forecasters or great minds of industry and their relationships to their gut feelings, hunches or intuitions. A common thread that runs through their lives is the ability to use these instinctive urges for successful decision-making. Caracciolo says, 'Human beings who walk around with everything figured out, as if they have all the answers, or were somehow taught all the answers, are overwhelmed by too many preconceived notions.'

Paper Money

Isaac Gilman, an illiterate immigrant, landed in New York in 1884. As he left the ship, he noticed a stray piece of paper caught in a gap in the wharf. Stooping to retrieve it, he decided it was a symbolic indication of where he could make his fortune in the new country. He began by selling recycled newspaper and soon was running his own highly profitable business. His son and grandson went into the business and today the Gilman Paper Company is the largest privately owned company of its type, supplying virtually all of the non-newsprint paper in the United States. Many people have benefited as a result of Gilman's intuitive decision that day more than a century ago. Until his death in 1997, his grandson was one of America's foremost benefactors. His generosity to the arts and conservation causes was legendary.

Trend spotters are forecasting that it will soon be impossible to manage businesses on the basis of sequential progress, of identifying a challenge, seeking information and forming plans. Intuition, they assert, will become more important than experience – the new millennium will see an Age of Intuition replace the Age of Logic. If so, then we will most certainly need to develop our intuitive faculties to cope, and awareness of coincidence could help us here, if we are to take seriously Philip Slater's comments, that a 'coincidence is a trend we've decided not to take seriously'.[2]

So, rather than abandon it as a means of success in career or personal relationships, women should redevelop their natural ability. Women who spot this trend will start with a natural advantage because men have not had the same emotional and social relationships. Dr Tilker, whose patients include career women in the computer, engineering, advertising and corporate worlds, says:

> For example, you won't find the average man rapping on the phone to his friend or mother for an hour or so. Communications of this type lead one to an exposure of people's emotional nuances in relationships which in turn lead to the development of unconscious sensitivities and give women certain perceptions about people and situations that are lacking in people who are focused upon tangible external objectives alone. Men are capable of internal reflection, but because this personality characteristic is not socially fostered, it is more difficult to harness in adult stages of life. It is for this reason that women, at least until recently, have been the emotional 'monitors' in relationships. This may shift as women become more competitive in the workforce.

> People gather experiences through life and those accumulated experiences

66

can be used in a practical work sense and in order to make predictions about the future. In this sense what we are talking about is experience, subjective thinking, another way of saying intuition.[3]

Psychologists and self-development counsellors say that other ways of developing intuition include turning problems over to our subconscious and allowing it to come up with solutions, paying more attention to our feelings and emotions (gut instincts), allowing our imagination a fuller rein, developing a more creative approach to life, including our careers. We should nevertheless accept that intuition is not infallible, and it may cause us to make a mistake, but we should not rule out its use – we all make mistakes no matter how we approach life's problems.

As noted earlier, intuition is not all about business and career. There is another dimension – a spiritual dimension. Masami Saionji is descended from the Royal Ryuku family of Okinawa (Japan). Educated in the United States and Japan, she is the author of several books and advice columns. She is widely recognized as a guiding voice in the areas of personal happiness and international harmony.

She says intuition refers to the functioning of an unseen power originating at the source of our life:

People with highly developed intuition never experience misery or discord in their lives, because they are living and expressing the will of the Universe itself.

There are people who lead worthy lives relying on neither practical nor factual knowledge. These people are fully aware of the wonders of intuition and they understand it. As they rely entirely on their intuition, they are never led astray by outside influences. They have a strong will to follow their conscience, and they live with confidence.

It is because people's intuition is dim or inactive, or because they are unaware of their intuition, that they have diverted from their true path in life. They have placed themselves in a state of delusion and suffering, experiencing the same needless miseries over and over again.

If each member of humanity were to awaken to his or her intuition, I feel the world would immediately be led to peace.

People who have lost their intuition lack true understanding. They believe whatever is generally believed by the majority and have built their lives around those beliefs having lost track of their inner power and purpose in this world. The majority of today's people are living this way. In living without their intuition they have created a world of illusion, the world of the ego.

> When our actions are guided by our intuition, there is no emotional
> complication, no conflict, or tension.

Saionji says that the essential condition for developing our intuitive
power is always to have our minds attuned to our true Self. She adds:

> You must also be aware that, if thoughts and ideas flash into your mind or
> flicker through your thoughts when you are not attuned to your true Self,
> these thoughts and ideas do not come from your true Self.[4]

A final word on intuition from Arthur Koestler, scientist and well-known
writer on coincidences. He urges us to use our intuition by saying we
should act on impulse rather than logic. 'If you have a sudden overwhelming impulse to take some action, do it, provided, of course, it is
legal. You may well be putting yourself in tune with the natural forces.'[5]

The following anecdote is an example of what can happen if
Koestler's advice is taken.

Intuitive Prediction

Glenn Cooper had just bought Victor Mansfield's *Synchronicity, Science
and Soul-making* and was walking away from the book shop when he
found himself confidentially predicting that before the day was over
he would experience a synchronistic event. For the next four hours as
he strolled the city streets, no such event occurred (at least of which he
was aware). When it came time to catch his train, he began walking
towards the station, at which point he was confronted by a derelict
demanding ten cents to buy a sandwich. For the first time in his life,
Glenn found himself complying with a beggar's request. In fact he gave
him 50 cents. The man thanked him profusely and departed. Glenn
took another six or seven steps when a car turned the corner and
pulled up directly beside him. He looked down at the licence plate and
it read: BEG. Smiling he congratulated himself on having predicted a
coincidence and thought little more about it. However, three days
later, reading Mansfield's book while on another train journey, he
came across a passage which describes beggars wandering the streets as
projections of our own homelessness, abandonment and poverty
rather than someone with an equal right to a quality life – a symbol of
one's own deficiencies.[6]

Cooper explained the point of the coincidence as he saw it:

> It was not until I read Mansfield's sentence that the true meaning of the event
> became apparent to me. The other important part, I believe, is the fact this
> was the first time in my life I had given money to a beggar. So it all begins to
> make sense, particularly within a Jungian context.

A few more points can be made about this incident. The simple act of purchasing the book and dwelling on its contents – an analysis of synchronicity – inspired Cooper's consciousness to a level where his intuitive instincts came into play, whether he was aware of it or not. As he offered no explanation himself for making his prediction, I can only assume he was not consciously aware of a cause behind his seemingly illogical prediction. Furthermore, his faculties remained alert as he wandered the city streets so that when he met the beggar his intuition was telling him that here was his inspired coincidence or at least the beginning of it. This was reinforced by the number plate, and prepared him for the reading of what many might regard as a too-difficult paragraph and promptly forget its message. Cooper found in it insights that brought him a new awareness.

Proper use of our intuitive instincts can give us an awareness of coincidences when they happen, so that they do not slip away into the back recesses of our mind. This instinct, as it develops, can also give us a sense of a pending coincidence, preparing us more fully to deal with it. Initially we have to judge whether or not it is meaningful. If it is, then we may go on to decide if it has a personal and immediate application, possibly in solving a pressing problem, or may be of some help in the future – an indication of a trend! As with any technique, awareness of intuitive coincidence takes time to develop, but when we have mastered it we will have further insights into our world, both the inner and the outer, which are unavailable to those whose views are locked away in a frozen mind set of presumptions.

chapter five

Jung and Astrology

It is claimed that at one stage astrologers abandoned their attempts at proving a causal link between the stars and human destiny in favour of Jung's theory of synchronicity. This is hotly denied by authors West and Toonder, who argue that sophisticated astrologers attributed the operation of astrology to 'synchronicity' long before Jung applied that particular name to it.[1]

The origins of astrology can be traced to the early Egyptians. Scholars point to the astrological symbols in Egyptian monuments, such as the Sphinx, and to ancient myths which show a belief that every part of the universe is related to every other part and is thereby nothing but consciousness, a belief which is similar to Jung's theories.

Jung did show an interest in astrology based on his initial belief that it 'presupposes a meaningful coincidence of planetary aspects and positions with the character of the existing psychic state of the questioner'.[2] He went so far as to express the opinion in 1931 (about the time he first spoke of synchronicity as an acausal principle):

> The cultural philistines believed until recently that astrology had been disposed of long since and was something that could be safely laughed at. But today, rising out of the social deeps, it knocks at the doors of the universities from which it was banished some three hundred years ago.[3]

However, Jung appears to have quickly lost interest the subject after making an interesting but, in the eyes of astrologers, elementary attempt to look for astrological significance in the horoscopes of married couples. The results were inconclusive and Jung decided that astrology was not a matter of synchronicity, but very largely of a causal relationship. (Author's note: in *Coincidences: Chance or Fate?*, pp. 44–54, I gave details of some personal research which appears to show a link between the stars signs and the professions people choose. Earlier more sophisticated research came up with the same correlation that appears to be inexplicable by any means other than astrology.)

Since Jung's rejection of the ancient craft, the relationship between coincidence and astrology has been decidedly ambiguous – a state in which we find much of Jung's work – in which the question is still argued whether astrology is a causal or non-causal phenomenon. If your horoscope tells you it is your lucky day and you buy a Lottery ticket and have a big win, what forces do you conclude were at work? Was there some causal link between yourself and the planetary movements, or an intuitive impulse which would make the action a non-causal synchronistic event?

For many the question is irrelevant. Astrology has been proven not to work over and over again. But the fact remains that astrology, as Jung once observed, did not have its heyday in the benighted Middle Ages, but in this enlightened twentieth century and there are no indications that its influence is waning. It was particularly strong in Germany in the post-World War I era, which may be one reason why it caught the attention of Jung and had him speaking so positively about its resurgence as a subject for academic study. The trauma of war had been the obvious catalyst for the German interest. Suffering military, psychological and economic defeat, they were desperately seeking assurances and signs of hope. Faith in the pre-war systems and methods had gone. In the stars many sought a better future not only for themselves but for the country as well.[4] So one important reason why we should not dismiss the subject lightly is that in times of future crises, people will almost certainly turn to the stars for hope and guidance – as they have done for many millennia, unconcerned what force lies behind astrology.

Millions of people around the world still read the horoscopes offered by newspapers and magazines. At this level astrology is far from dead. Most of us identify with the subject through these star guides. But these were a later invention, introduced by the Greeks around AD 200. Many professional astrologers see horoscopes as the bottom line of the subject, diverting attention from its more traditional uses in medicine, character assessment, psychology, astronomy, myth and tradition.

The following anecdote shows us how one skilled practitioner puts his astrological charts to personal use. In his hands astrology becomes a tool of self-awareness and a confirmation of intuitive synchronicity, which may be where the solution to astrology's ambiguity lies. The story is told in his own words:

The weekend started innocently enough. Al and Rose, their two-year-old son, my close friend Catherine and I were going to fly in Al's single-engine plane to visit friends in Massachusetts for Thanksgiving.

On the morning we were set to leave, I felt the urge to look at my astrological transits (the daily motion of the planets relative to the planetary positions when I was born). Having studied astrology for the past eight years, I thought I had developed a good sense of when to use and not misuse this ancient art. While my prime motivation in studying astrology has always been to use it as a tool of self-understanding, I had also found it useful at certain times for choosing propitious moments for action and inaction.

As I opened the ephemeris to check my transits I was chagrined to find myself in the midst of a particularly difficult aspect – transiting Uranus conjunct my natal Mars – traditionally known for unexpected happenings, accidents, etc. I quickly told Catherine. Her response was, 'I'm not flying with you with that aspect! It's too dangerous. Perhaps I'll drive but no flying.' Intuitively knowing she was right I called Al and Rose, to tell them of our findings and decision. I spoke with Rose, who had studied astrology as long as I had. She said, 'Are you going to let astrology run your life? This aspect doesn't necessarily mean something negative is going to happen. Ultimately each individual creates his own circumstances.'

Naturally, Rose knew just how to push my buttons. I had always struggled with the issues of free will and determinism and prided myself in using astrology to help me live a good life and yet not have it run my life.

On one hand, there is the intuitive knowledge and feeling that there is an ordered cosmos in which patterns and events are to some extent determined by our past actions and guided by an intelligence that includes both our ego and the world it inhabits. On the other hand, I experience myself as a free individual, with the power to create and choose my own life experiences. How can these be reconciled? Most critics of astrology say people use it as a crutch so as not to take responsibility for their actions. But I venture to say that if those people honestly and openly look at their experience, they would see that their lives are more ordered and determined than they would like to admit.

I told Rose I'd think about it and call her back. Rose's reasoning did not impress Catherine, but Catherine came up with a good suggestion. Look at everyone's chart who was going. If everyone else looked free of trouble, most likely whatever would befall me in terms of my aspects might happen internally or psychologically and not manifest in external events. I dutifully looked at everyone's horoscope including Al and Rose's two-year-old son. Surprisingly everyone had either a square or an opposition involving Uranus,

Mars or Venus. Sometimes, it was transiting Mars or transiting Uranus, but in each case, including my own, Uranus or Mars was involved. It was no coincidence. Flying was out of the question – four charts all with problematic aspects to Uranus was too much to ignore. If this was a test of free will or determinism, here I would side with determinism. In fact, when Catherine saw the astrology, she even withdrew her offer to drive.

Confident in my findings I quickly called Rose back to tell her. While she agreed that all of us having these aspects was troubling, she was still not going to let some outside agency ruin her life. I still don't exactly know what happened then. For whatever reason, I gave up all my knowledge, all my intuition and agreed to fly.

I said goodbye to Catherine and left in the single-engine plane for Massachusetts. As we ascended, my misgivings were clear, but I decided I would live with it the best way possible.

The first part of the flight was fine but as we got closer to the Massachusetts coast the turbulence got increasingly intense. Al, the pilot, didn't seem concerned, but when we hit a big air pocket and all our heads butted up against the ceiling I could see him becoming a little unglued. In fact, after we landed, Al admitted that it was the most turbulent flight he'd ever had. As I left the plane, I thought the gods had taught us a lesson. They terrorized us for going against their will, but had spared us with just a really bad flight.

The weekend went smoothly enough as we all had a great time seeing our dear friends. Sunday morning we visited the nearby Vedanta Centre to see Gayatri Devi, a saintly woman, who leads the community there.

Oddly enough, her whole talk was on learning to cope with natural disasters. Her other centre in California had just experienced a devastating fire. As she spoke, I felt her gaze penetrate me – as if she were trying to convey something important to me. I asked Al afterwards if he had felt her staring directly at me. He confirmed my feeling. Only later would the full impact of this experience come home to me.

We said goodbye to our friends, boarded our little plane and took off. As we climbed to about 4,000 feet (12,200 metres), this question just popped out of my mouth: 'Al, if we had an emergency and you had to land the plane where would you land?' Al looked around and said, 'Probably in that lake over there. There's no strip of land around long enough for a landing.' Nothing more was said for about 20 minutes until the following popped out of my mouth: 'Al, what does it sound like when the engine conks out?'

Before he could answer, I learned first-hand. Within 20 seconds of asking the question the engine started sputtering, and then finally nothing. Silence. Five thousand feet (15,000 metres), total cloud cover, Berkshire Mountains in every direction…Silence. We couldn't make radio contact with any airport.

When we broke through the clouds, we had about 60 seconds before hitting the ground. Like a flashback from 20 minutes before a lake miraculously appeared in front of us. Al told us that our only chance was to land on the lake.

Sixty seconds were left to contemplate my fate. Why did I do it? I obviously knew not to go. All these passing thoughts became meaningless as I prepared to die – and to my mind deservedly so. I got as quiet as possible and started meditating and getting ready for I knew not what.

As we glided towards the lake, Al's first pass was somehow not right and he turned the plane sharply to make one last attempt. This time we glided over the shoreline and Al put the plane down 30 feet (9 metres) from land in what was the smoothest landing of my life.

Al told us to get out on the wing, jump in the water and swim to shore. Being a very poor swimmer, the idea of jumping into a cold lake was almost scarier for me than the engine conking out in the first place. What choice did I have? So I jumped in and started swimming. I was wearing a sheepskin coat and forgot to take it off. I almost drowned on the way. As it turned out if I had just stood up, I would have realized I could have walked. We were only in four feet (1.2 metres) of water! Not only that, but we could have stayed on the wing and been rescued by a boat that had heard our engine sputtering.

While getting warm in a cottage by the lake, having been given dry clothes by an extraordinarily helpful man, I was already trying to distil the meaning of these experiences. Fourteen years later, I still ponder the experience and wonder how much meaning there was for me in that cold lake.

For me there were four synchronistic events within this experience:

1. The experience at the Vedanta Centre where Gayatri Devi spoke of natural disasters and pierced me with her gaze.

2. Asking where we would land in an emergency, 20 minutes before the crash.

3. Asking 20 seconds before the engine died what it was like when the engine stopped.

4. The entire astrological scenario, my denial and the unfolding events, which had by far the most lasting impact.

Both before and after the crash, I have had experiences similar to the first three, but I had never before experienced the immediate consequences of wilfully ignoring my knowledge, feeling and intuition. The immediacy and power of the events, especially given the astrological warning, have deeply influenced the use of my will ever since. Now, when a voice in me says wait, or don't, I step back and try to feel and understand what that voice is trying to say. I often consult my astrological indicators to verify my feelings and intuitions. I am always asking the question: 'Is there something objective I should be listening to?' Astrology often helps point to the answer.

I still believe we must exercise basic existential freedom in life. But I equally know that we are so intimately related to the cosmos that we must heed the symbols embedded in the cosmos, i.e. the astrological mandala and others, when they speak to us. This speaking is a gift, a way in which the intelligence guiding both our inner and our outer lives tries to help us – grace, if you will. I learned that to turn my back on it is to turn from life itself.[5]

chapter six

Time

Michael Shallis asserts coincidences can jolt us out of the familiar view of time as linear and causal. Time's reality, he goes on, is multifaceted, enigmatic and complex. Experiencing it through coincidence points to a much more complex, bewildering and awesome aspect of nature, overlooked in the more familiar descriptions of the apparently explicable and seemingly controllable world that is the scientific view of time.[1]

It would be difficult to find a more enigmatic and complex example of time's strange nature than the following anecdote.

Maurice Haywood, of Archway, London, was asleep at home, when he believed he had been awoken by the sound of his wife and son discussing the possible identity of the writer of a letter that had just arrived addressed to him. He called out irritably 'Anderson', hoping they would stop disturbing him. As they ignored him and continued to discuss the letter he became angry. 'ANDERSON!' he called again.

Some time later his wife woke him and said she had been tidying the room adjoining the one in which he was asleep. She heard him call out, went into the room and gently asked him what he had been saying. Haywood had mumbled 'Anderson'. She asked, 'Anderson who?' but he did not reply. A few minutes later she had gone downstairs to take out some rubbish. At the front door she met the postman, who handed her a letter. On the back was a name: 'Ken'.

The letter, posted in South Africa, was from a Ken Anderson (not the author) whom Haywood had known in London and not heard from for some months.

It could be argued that there may be some rationale, some probability, to the incident, if Maurice had been dreaming of his friend. But he had not. His dream was of a conversation that had never taken place in reality which foretold something that was about to happen over which he could not possibly have had any control, or awareness

– the arrival of the postman with a completely unexpected letter from his friend. Maurice was so shaken by the experience he sent the details to the Society for Psychical Research in London.

Naturally, when he came across my book and saw that it was written by another Ken Anderson, he felt compelled to write to me with the details. After I had replied to his letter asking for permission to use the story, he sent me some further information that more firmly places his experience into the realms of the Shallis 'time duality'. He says that when the incident occurred, he was searching for some explanation of 'the mystery of life' (his quotes). He was reading widely in all manner of subjects which might help him understand the fact of 'being'. He was particularly impressed by the writings of Raja Yoga and by Thomas Jay Hudson's *The Law of Psychic Phenomena*.[2] Haywood writes:

> From an ordinary psychological point of view, I had read that it is useful to have someone record any words spoken by a sleeping person, as this would give access to what may be troubling them. I had, therefore, asked my wife to record anything I might say while asleep. This explains why she made the effort to take note of what I had said.

> I did find this precognitive experience very upsetting as it seemed to challenge conventional psychological theory and indicate that Hudson's 'subjective mind' was a high probability.

> I have since then had a number of remarkable 'psychic experiences' which I now accept as another level of reality available to those who wish to follow such a course of study.

Maurice's experience can be compared with the famous account of J. W. Dunne's in which he found his watch, that he had placed on a chest of drawers away from his bed, had stopped at the exact moment he dreamed it had.

In both Dunne's and Maurice's cases we are faced with occurrences that, by any scrutiny, transcend the boundaries of probability and time. Dunne's experience occurred in 1899 and no one in the ensuing century appears to have volunteered a rational explanation.

The writer and pioneer of aviation J. W. Dunne relates how, staying at a hotel in Sussex in 1899, he dreamed he had an argument with one of the waiters about what time it was. Dunne insisted it was 4.30 in the afternoon, while the waiter maintained it was 4.30 in the morning. In the dream Dunne realized the point behind the argument was that his watch must have stopped. He took it from his waistcoat pocket and it had stopped – with the hands at 4.30. At this point he awoke and searched for the timepiece. He found it lying on a chest of drawers and, sure enough, it had stopped and the hands stood at 4.30. Dunne explains:

> The solution seemed perfectly obvious. The watch must have stopped during the previous afternoon. I must have noticed this, forgotten it, and remembered it in my dream. Satisfied on that point, I rewound the instrument, but not knowing the real time, I left the hands as they were.

The next morning, he went downstairs and found a clock so he could reset the watch. 'To my absolute amazement,' he later wrote, 'I found that the hand had lost only some two or three minutes, about the amount of time which had elapsed between my waking from the dream and rewinding the watch.' In other words his watch had stopped at the actual moment of the dream.[3]

Is it possible for us somehow to step out of the bounds of time, to 'see' into the future, not just in the sense of a disembodied psychic message, but actually to see events in these dimensions played out before our eyes?

Seeing the Future

The widely quoted account by journalist J. Bernard Hutton of 'seeing' a Hamburg shipyard under air attack in 1932, ten years before it actually happened in World War II, would appear to be verification of this. He and another witness, photographer Joachim Brandt, clearly heard the loud droning of heavy aircraft engines, followed a short time later by concentrated fire from anti-aircraft guns stationed in the neighbourhood surrounding the yards. This was followed almost immediately by bright flashes in the dark sky as the shots were discharged and the explosions of the shells. Although it was not a dark night and they could not see the heavy bombers that were above them, it was obvious they comprised a large formation.

Hutton managed to reach England before the outbreak of war. In the middle of Hitler's Blitzkrieg, he saw an article in a British newspaper about the successful RAF raid on the same Hamburg shipyards he and Brandt had visited. Eyewitnesses described almost in detail what they had seen happening all those years before.[4]

Most people's reaction to Hutton's story would be much the same as that of their Hamburg news editor at the time – unbridled scepticism. Told in isolation it hardly sounds credible. Hutton, in his book, however, relates a number of other incredible psychic incidents in which he was personally involved, including the miraculous curing by a psychic healer of his deplorably bad eyesight, as attested to by work colleagues. To dismiss his story of the air raid out of hand would be to reject a whole body of personal psychic experience. A further reason for giving it some credibility is the fact that Hutton is not alone in seeing the future acted out before him.

Among Mary Fraser's collection of Nova Scotian folklore are two stories that tell of the future appearing as a physical presence in the present. In c. 1888, a young man at Mule River, Inverness County, Nova Scotia, was taking a message to a neighbour's house after dark, when he saw moving before him on the road an object whose appearance terrified him. It was large and black and had its back turned to him. It had a huge red eye in the centre of its back and a stream of light came from its two eyes in front, so bright that they lit up the shingles on the houses. The monster went up to the neighbour's house, passed around it and then came back down the road towards him, moving so swiftly that he had to jump aside to let it pass. It was only 25 years later that he discovered what he had seen was not a natural monster, but, as some would call it in these polluted days, a man-made one – a motor car.

Fraser's second story is set in the same era. It begins with two woman walking one evening along the main highway that skirts the high cliffs above the waters of the Straits of Canos, at Port Hawkesbury, Cape Breton. At that time the lines of the Canadian National Railways, which years later were to run alongside the road, had not been built. As the two women made their way along the road they heard behind them a loud rushing noise accompanied by a metallic clatter. They looked around and saw a 'huge, awful black thing with one eye in the centre of its face' apparently chasing them. But the monster sped past them with a tremendous rattle and went right through a fish house that stood nearby. The woman ran into the nearest house and hid in it, pale and breathless and scared to death. Years later, one of them heard and saw for the first time in her life a railway train on the mainland of Nova Scotia and recognized it as the one she had seen and heard that night. She died, however, before the Inverness Railway was built. When it was, the line passed right through the fish house as the women had seen.[5]

Perhaps the most compelling account of this strange phenomenon comes from Air Marshal Sir Robert Goddard. In 1934, Goddard, then a young RAF pilot, was caught in a storm while flying over Scotland. In the thick clouds he soon lost his bearings and headed his Hawker biplane down looking for Drem airport. Although he knew from an inspection of it the previous day that it was deserted, he hoped he could use it for an emergency landing until the storm cleared. Just as the airport appeared about half a kilometre ahead of him, the clouds suddenly vanished and he saw the airport abuzz with what seemed urgent activity. Mechanics in blue overalls were working on strange yellow-painted, single-engine aircraft which stood out clearly in the sunlight. Goddard could not identify the type of plane he was now flying over at a low altitude. He also found unusual the fact his flyover failed to attract anyone's attention.

Then, just as suddenly, he was back in the storm, but the sighting of Drem had given him his bearings and he continued on his way home. Some four years later, as war grew nearer, the Royal Air Force re-commissioned Drem as a flying school. It also changed the colour of its training aircraft from silver to yellow and its ground mechanics were issued with blue overalls to replace the orange ones they had always worn. When Goddard visited the re-activated and frantically busy school in 1938, he recognized it as the one he had glimpsed some years before.[6] Goddard was a highly intelligent man, a graduate of both Cambridge and the Imperial Science College, and an ace pilot.

Like Hutton, he was to experience other psychic phenomena in his long life. In one uncanny episode, a fellow officer had a vision of him dying in an air crash. The following day his plane did crash, but he survived. That story became the plot for the film *The Night My Number Came Up*.

The incidents outlined here serve to jolt us out of a mechanized view of linear time, flowing from past to future.

Many people do have precognitive visions or flashes. But they are often suppressed. Why? One reason may be that they are so far out of our normal mind set that they cause some alarm, or worse. Dr Larry Dossey writes of a woman with such a 'gift' who had suffered both physically and mentally as a result. He writes: 'Jane's experience of space and time were extraordinary. For her neither space nor time was bounded...she could violate the presumed unidirectional flow of a linear time at will. Time for her was no river...'[7] After she had been taught some techniques through biofeedback she quickly learned to accept her psychic experiences.

As we learn to raise our own awareness, coincidences may occur that do indeed jolt us out of our complacency regarding the generally accepted view of time and other accepted realities. We should remember that what is being disturbed is not nature's law but our own mind set. Linear time is the psychological illusion.

chapter seven

Miracles

MaryEllen of Seattle, Washington State, writes of a Christmas to remember:

It was not going to be the usual Christmas that year. My mother's husband, Jim, had just been diagnosed with terminal cancer and she was in bed with a gallstone attack.

I was not looking forward to leaving the comfort of my home and friends on Vancouver Island and driving an hour to the British Columbia Ferry Terminal, waiting for a couple of ferries in the Christmas rush and then the lonesome hour and a half trip over the grey waters to Vancouver.

Before leaving the island, I telephoned my best friend, Rita, and wished her a happy and joyful holiday. We usually talked on the telephone several times a day as we were involved in a business together.

The huge ferry boat finally docked in Vancouver, in the dark of the evening. I drove through the torrential rain, with my two cats howling in the back seat of my car. We arrived at our destination and I felt trepidation stepping into the house of my childhood where I had spent so many happy Christmases.

It was as gloomy inside the house as the weather was outside. No one was talking; my mother and Jim were both resting and thinking their own sad thoughts. The weight of their health was everywhere. It seemed the spirit of Christmas had been left behind on the island with the joyful voices of my friends and neighbours.

We all went to bed early that Christmas Eve, almost dreading to wake in the morning, thinking that the spirit of the holiday season had long since evaporated with the diagnosis of Jim's cancer.

I was the first one awake on Christmas morning. Everyone else was sleeping peacefully. I knew that Rita would be up. It was Christmas morning and her two young children would have had her up for hours by now. I dialled Rita's long-since memorized phone number. First the area code, then her number. When she picked up the telephone and said, 'Hello', in a weak, crackly voice, I thought, 'Oh, no! What now! What else could possibly go wrong? Where was her sweet lyrical voice?'

I asked Rita if she was all right and this total stranger says, 'Who is this?' I thought, 'Who is she? It seemed I had just woken up a total stranger on Christmas morning. I apologized and she said it was okay as she had no reason to get up and it was nice to talk to someone.

My heart went out to this woman, and we started to chat. After all, everyone in my house was sleeping, and this woman had no one to talk to and was obviously very alone. I had telephoned my friend long-distance, in Duncan, so I was curious to know where this woman lived. To this day I cannot comprehend how this happened! This woman said that she lived in Burnaby. It was a local calling number! How had this phone call been re-routed to a total stranger like that? Their phone numbers were not even similar. It was as mysterious then as it is now.

Her name was Faith. She was in her late 70s. Faith's husband had died seven years earlier. Her neighbour, a young man in his 20s who always visited her, had left for the holiday to be with his fiancée. Faith had no reason to get up on Christmas morning. She had no one to share Christmas with. I thought her Christmas Day was unfolding worse than ours for we had each other, and that is what Christmas is truly about, love for one another.

Faith and I talked for an hour. We were laughing and sharing. I heard all about her wonderful husband and their years together. I asked her to hold on a minute, as my mother was now stirring in her bedroom. I asked my mother if Faith could come and share Christmas dinner with us. My mother was not feeling well, but she had an understanding and kind heart. She said yes, Faith would be welcome. Faith was so excited to come. Initially, Faith had a long and lonely day looming ahead of her and now it was one to look forward to.

I told Faith how to come on the bus. She then had to hang up and contact the bus station to see if the buses were running that day. I hung up from Faith wondering what kind of woman was coming to dinner.

Faith later shared with us that while she was on the bus coming through town, she was the only passenger, wondering if she had made a good decision to leave the safety of her home and venture out to a total stranger's house.

Faith had to catch three different buses. She left Burnaby behind, wound through Vancouver, had to cross over the Second Narrows Bridge into North Vancouver, and then the bus climbed the mountainside to our home. She passed an hour and a half's worth of homes on Christmas morning. She saw slums, poor homes, apartments, middle-class homes, and then she started to get nervous. She told the bus driver of her mystery morning phone call that had led her out on her adventure. She showed him our address and he turned to her and said, 'You will be fine in that neighbourhood.' But she was still concerned.

Our formerly dreary home changed. My mum dressed up, and Jim mustered enough strength to put on a bright red shirt. To this day, I still remember how good he looked that last Christmas. The whole atmosphere of our home had become one of joy. We awaited the arrival of our mystery guest. Soon, the aroma of the traditional Christmas turkey cooking wafted throughout the house. The time arrived for me to drive to the bottom of the hill and pick up our guest. And there she was, slowly climbing off the bus. What a sweet face she had. She looked at me and visibly relaxed. We smiled at each other and I took the gift of her home to my mother and Jim. We had the nicest time. We had a great meal.

When it was late I drove Faith home to Burnaby. But I want to share some-thing miraculous with you; something so unexplainable that even to this day I cannot believe it happened. I am not making this up. I could not have thought of something so incredible. This is what happens when you expect miracles in your life. As Faith was talking to my mother, they realized they had not shared their last names. They then did so and had the shock of their lives. They had the same last name, Holden, spelled the exact same way! Usually, Holden is spelled with an 'o' but both of theirs was with an 'e'. It is a very rare spelling. Faith had been married to a man from England, as my mum currently was. Faith's husband and my mother's husband were both the second child of four children and none of these eight siblings, once they were married, ever had a child. Jim and Faith's husband both had the same combination of brothers and sisters, in the same birth order. Faith and my mother went to the same high school. There was so many 'coincidences', they came one after the other. To this date it is hard to remember them all. But from talking to Faith, we knew that Jim would indeed die and that my mum would be fine and go on with her life, just as Faith had.

How was it possible to dial a long-distance number on Christmas morning and get someone locally, who needed us (and we needed them)? How was it possible that she had the same family name? It was a Christmas that I will never, ever forget. The biggest gift to all of us was the realization that miracles do indeed exist.[1]

In 1996 MaryEllen began an online newsletter service dedicated to 'angels and miracles' and in less than two years had 40,000 subscribers world-wide, many of them writing to her with inspiring details of how contact with the angels changed their lives. Typical is the following, taken at random from her web site, from Carlotta:

> I have been tested lately in every phase of my life. It has been tough, but I am going to make it. When things go bad for me…it happens in bunches. At this particular point in my life, I am not satisfied with anything: my job, my home, my surroundings…not even my teenage daughter. I am a hard-working person and do my best to help others. I am usually a happy-go-lucky and optimistic person.
>
> When so many things hit you at once, you can only take so much, and I have been very discouraged. I caught the flu, was in bed for three days, my bank account was exactly 18 cents. I cashed in $2.30 worth of pennies so my daughter could have lunch money. I have friends and family that have been encouraging me through this bad time. I called one of my special friends, Margaret, she let me talk…and I cried and cried. In her wisdom Margaret said, you need to talk to your angels and let them know that you cannot endure any more. I got off of the phone and sat quietly…and told my angels exactly that. Today, with barely a voice to answer the phone, I went back to work.
>
> The first miracle was I was the ninth caller to a radio station and I won $1,000!!! I was in shock and of course I could not scream loud from being hoarse. Then about an hour later my boss called me and requested my presence in his office. I sat down and he handed me an envelope. The envelope held a Christmas bonus…equivalent to two weeks' pay. When I won the first time, I thanked God and my angels, over and over again…and cried. The second time, I realized no matter how down you are…or how bad it gets in your life, I have learned to ask my angels for help. It is a humbling experience. This has been a good day! Thanks for letting me share.
> Love and Blessings
> Carlotta

Can miracles be related to coincidences? If you pray for a miracle and it occurs, isn't that cause and effect? This could be so in a simplistic sense, but against this there is often such a high degree of improbability involved, a satisfactory outcome must have coincidence elements.

At a deeper level, when we talk of miracles, we are talking in many cases of parallel occurrences with coincidences. The two phenomena travel along the same path of apparent non-validity, of suspension of our normal prejudices and expectations. And there are times when they collide, enmesh, so that they become indistinguishable from one another. Coincidence equals miracle and vice versa.

I put the 'deeper' argument to author, freelance writer and creator of several synchronicity-based games Jeriann Sharf, who teaches that one way miracles come about is through 'creative visualization', a process she explains in her booklet *Miracle Making from the Ground Up* (self-published, New Jersey, 1997). Here is not the place to expand on her ideas, but they involve coming into harmony with 12 universal principles. And when she talks about miracles her words are meant also to apply to coincidences because she too believes in the duality of their experience. She reasons in her inimitable fashion that 'miracles' are really the science that scientists don't understand:

> There's not really anything supernatural about them…just super-unlikely. I think at one time (long, long ago) miracles were quite common (we simply went into the silence and made our demands knowing they would be met). But as Einstein said, 'How have we come to have so much knowledge, but understand so little?' I think the problem is, with our increased technological advances we have learned to analyse, pull apart, dissect, operate on, fragmentize, compartmentalize, but we lack the will to find MEANING. We can thank Descartes for that.

(Author's note: René Descartes [1596–1650] was a French philosopher, mathematician and writer. Unconvinced by scholastic tradition and theological dogma, he sought to get back to primary truth, to the very definition of knowledge or the reason why anything can be said to be true. The basis of Cartesian philosophy is summed up in his own words, *cogito, ergo sum* [I am thinking so I exist.])

> Coincidences and miracles cannot be understood via our ordinary cause and effect principles (physical energy), they must be understood by an acausal (non-physical) mode or meaning. When you are dealing in the unseen realm (where miracles live) then you must invent new rules…lean way out on sheer intuition, see with new eyes. In other words forget everything that you were ever taught about How the Universe Works…

Medical Miracles

Apart from the above discussion on the status of miracle-coincidences, the following story of medical miracles leaves us with the question: what can one call a spontaneous recovery from an illness that, given its normal run, is nearly always fatal?

Distinguished medical man Professor John Dwyer has been a doctor for 35 years. For much of that time he has been involved in research and teaching as well as patient care. He has come to know and trust scientific methods of healing. But he has also come to learn that there is something 'mystical in all of us'. He has seen proof of it in patients he has personally cared for whose recovery defied medical or scientific explanation – and chance:

> Their stories, even to a scientist, are nothing less than miraculous. A few days ago by chance I saw for the first time in 28 years a nun I cared for when I was a young resident. She is now 69 years old and in excellent health. She was visiting a friend in our hospital when she came across the ward to re-introduce herself to me after all those years. I did not recognize her, but I certainly remembered her easily. Sister Mary Joseph was dying in a cancer ward when I first met her. She had a most malignant tumour in her genital tract.
>
> One Friday morning I was doing my ward round and found her to be acutely breathless. A chest X-ray revealed her lungs were full of metastases – cancer cells – that had spread from the original site. She was ready to die and both of us expected that she would do just that on the coming weekend. By Sunday night she was feeling much better and extraordinarily, six weeks later, she was perfectly well. No sign of her cancer remained.
>
> I had previously seen a similar 'miracle' involving a patient with melanoma, the most malignant form of skin cancer, but in that case we did have evidence that the patient's immune system had suddenly and unexpectedly produced very large amounts of antibody against her tumour, explaining how she rejected her cancer, if not why she made this unusual and beneficial response. In Sister Mary Joseph's case, we had and still have no medical explanation for her sudden recovery. Did these radioactive rods that we placed inside her change the cancer cells so that her immune system was turned on and destroyed the cancer? Possibly, but I have never seen the same thing in other patients who were given exactly the same amount.

Sceptics may well put the sister's recovery down to chance – after all with so many people suffering from cancer, there are bound to be cases of recovery against the odds. But this is to ignore the 'mystical' that Dwyer talks about, and who would be more likely to call upon a spiritual force for a cure than a nun and her colleagues, and prayer plus cure equals a spiritual coincidence. Dwyer continues:

> One morning, the nurse in charge of my outpatient clinic asked if she could see me at the end of the morning session. She looked tired and obviously had lost some weight in recent weeks. When we were alone she told me she was becoming increasingly breathless on minimal exertion and had developed a troublesome cough, especially in the morning. She was a heavy

smoker and had been so for 30 of her 47 years. Fortunately, I refrained from any half-serious joking admonitions about her smoking that particular day, for the chest X-ray I ordered for her showed a mass in the right lung. It could only be cancer. A biopsy was performed and a pathologist saw through the lens of his microscope the very worst type of lung cancer.

Jane was the mother of four children, two of whom were young teenagers. She was naturally distressed at the news. I can remember her saying to me that she was not afraid of death but was scared of the dying process. 'I have nursed too many people in this situation not to fully realize what I am in for,' she told me.

About a month later, Jane developed pneumonia in her cancerous lung and was admitted to hospital delirious with a hectic fever, sweating profusely and acutely breathless. Following the instructions that she had previously given us about such an emergency, we only administered oxygen and a little morphine. Her family gathered by her bedside. Three days later her fever vanished and she started to cough from her lungs copious amounts of purulent material. Her pneumonia resolved and as the infection in her lung disappeared from her chest X-ray so too did her cancer. Jane made a complete recovery. Later, she did tell me that she had pleaded with God to be allowed to live long enough to see her teenagers through school. She believes what happened to her was miraculous.

In Jane's case there was a possible scientific explanation. It is conceivable that the bacteria in her lungs attracted the white blood cells of her immune system into the area where they attacked these organisms with such fury that in the ensuing mêlée they destroyed her cancer cells as well as the germs causing her pneumonia. Far-fetched, I agree, but then any potential explanation of what happened to save Jane's life would be certain to be described as incredible.

But miracles do not need prayer to occur. Dwyer again:

A few years later, I sat beside the bed of a 16-year-old boy dying because of a virus infection in his heart muscle. Well described but rare, this particular infection developed 'out of the blue' in a particularly healthy young man, strong, athletic and a stranger to the experience of being unwell. In desperation I had given the young man drugs to suppress his immune system in case, by attacking the virus vigorously, his immune system was actually contributing to the damage being done to his heart muscle cells. A biopsy from the right pumping chamber of the heart suggested that this indeed could be the case. However, the young man showed no improvement following the introduction of this therapeutic strategy. Breathless, exhausted and suffering from grossly swollen legs because of his heart failure, he was certainly in a critical condition. Neither the lad nor his family were the slightest bit religious. A heart surgeon who came to see him agreed his only hope of survival involved a heart transplant operation. The consensus was that his own heart was damaged beyond repair.

Could we find a donor heart in time? The chances were slim. One morning, soon after the decision had been made to attempt to find a donor heart, our patient, after a particularly uncomfortable night, suddenly started to pass a lot of urine. His breathlessness eased, the swelling in his legs started to decline and three weeks later he left our hospital perfectly well. We could not claim any credit for his recovery and no explanation could be forwarded from our collective experience or indeed from a search of the medical literature.

A coincidence of unknown origins? Perhaps we can find an explanation in José Silva's version of coincidence: when a higher intelligence – your higher intelligence – lends a hand to the picture but chooses not to sign it.[2]

Dwyer concludes that these stories illustrate that remarkable and unexpected cures happen, although extremely rarely. He says:

If you believe in miracles and that miracles are an example of divine intervention, then such cases support the possibility. If you believe it is only a matter of time before we understand more about the natural resilience of the human body under certain circumstances and that such understanding will explain these cases, then that's perfectly reasonable also. We all know that much that was in the recent past 'miraculous' or mystical can now be explained in molecular biological terms.

It would be short-sighted not to consider the possibility that cures have been wrought through some as yet unknown facets of human biology. But the influence of the human spirit, our intelligence – and other forces of which we at present know so little – cannot be ruled out either. As the following 'miracle' story with its strong overtones of the paranormal shows.

Invisible Guidance

An English woman went to her local doctor and told him she was hearing voices that were telling her she was seriously ill and needed help. Her doctor put it down to hallucination. She agreed to accept counselling and the medication the doctor prescribed. As a result the voices ceased and she went on holiday with her husband. While she was away, however, the voices returned. Some reports say they came back because she stopped taking the medication, others that she continued with it and they returned anyway.

The voices told here once again she was seriously ill and must return to England. They also gave her an address to go to. Her husband, who had sided with her doctor, thought if he took her to the address given it would show her that she was indeed suffering from delusions, that her problem was all in her mind. But the address turned out to be a hospital that dealt with brain tumours. She returned to her doctor and demanded a brain scan. He reluctantly agreed, although he was criticized by his colleagues for doing so – after all there were no indications the woman had any problem that would be picked up by such a procedure. That was until the results of the scan came through. They showed she *was* suffering from a brain tumour. In the *British Medical Journal*, the doctor, Ikechukwu Azuonye, describes how the operation was a success and the woman made a full recovery. On regaining consciousness she heard the voices for the last time saying, 'We are pleased to have helped you, goodbye.' Dr Azuonye said in a radio interview that had it not been for the voices she would have died. At one point, he was told by his colleagues that he had somehow caught his patient's hallucinations. Now he believes all doctors must keep an open mind as he has no doubt she 'received help from the paranormal'.

Just as Dr Azuonye has confronted the possibility of the paranormal, so Dr Dwyer admits that he had to be prepared to be 'brave' to talk about miracle stories. Miracles, like coincidences, are so easily dismissed as improbable, and the result of mere chance. One wonders, however, how many doctors around the world have run into similar paranormal and miracle incidences but are not 'brave' enough to talk or write about them? However, miracles do not always involve illness, as the following anecdote forcefully reminds us.

Protected by Angels

Carole Lawrence believes she lives under the protection of angels. It is the way she has been brought up, she says. 'I have no trouble at all in believing that I am surrounded by guardian angels. How else can I account for the many coincidences that keep happening to me?' She is a happy, joyful lady full of enthusiasm for life despite the setbacks in which it appears her 'angels' may have deserted her. She has many tales to tell that confirm her claim of heavenly protection.

When she was aged 11 and living in the Australian country town of Ouyen in Victoria's Mallee district, Carole was standing minding her own business in the town's unfiltered swimming pool. The water was usually a muddy, murky colour and quite opaque as it was on this day.

Suddenly she found herself deep in the dark waters, struggling for air and trying helplessly to regain the surface. Then the water turned into the most beautiful kaleidoscope and the usual chill went from it. She could hear beautiful voices singing around her and another voice telling her to go to sleep. Jut as she was about to close her eyes, the scene again changed. She was struggling for air, surrounded by harsh light, her lungs were bursting, her ribs felt like they were being crushed. Someone was attempting to resuscitate her.

As it turned out, her lifesaver was the school's fifth-grade teacher, a Mr Palmer. She found out later what had happened to her. A teenage boy had jumped backward into the pool, landing on top of her. Stunned she had sunk to the bottom of the murky pool. Mr Palmer happened to see the incident and dived in fully clothed when she failed to surface. Unable to see, he felt her long hair and used that to drag her to the surface. About a week later, the teacher came to see her. There were tears in his eyes as he said, 'Carole, when I was in Changi prison camp during the war, I used to wonder why I stayed alive when other, fitter, men died. You're my reason for surviving, I was meant to save your life.'

On 12 May 1996, Andrea H. Lashley's sister called at about 11.30 p.m. and said their father was having a heart attack. Andrea, who lives in Woodland, Washington State, needed to get to her father's side as soon as possible. His home, in Greenbelt, Maryland, was 3,000 miles (4,800 kilometres) away. Andrea called an airline and got a flight out for the next morning at 7 a.m. In the meantime her mother-in-law had called around some other airlines and found a less expensive flight with Northwest that was leaving and arriving at the same time, so Andrea decided to go with Northwest.

She had to change in Minneapolis, Minnesota. It was a long walk between gates and she was carrying her suitcase:

> I decided to rest as soon as I got to my gate and get my bearings. The gate area was very large with few people. I randomly sat down. Two ladies were sitting across the aisle from me. My first thought was that one of them looked like my cousin, Karen, whom I'd not seen in 11 years.

The three women exchanged uncertain glances for some minutes before one of them approached Andrea, who stood to greet her. Andrea goes on:

> It was Karen. She was travelling with her mother-in-law and husband. They had attended a wedding in Calgary, Canada, over the weekend and were flying back home to Greenbelt. They were also changing planes in

Minneapolis and flying into Baltimore on the same flight I was taking. We were really amazed. Karen's mother-in-law (the other woman) changed seats with me on the flight so I got to talk with my cousin the whole way home.

I could have chosen a different area to sit in, or I could have stayed with the airline I picked first. I was under a lot of stress and had to pack in a hurry. I really didn't have time to worry about which airline to travel on. On a Monday morning in the middle of the United States in the middle of an airport, I met up with my cousin I hadn't seen in 11 years. I consider that very amazing.

(Author's note: The 'small world' coincidence had come at a time when Andrea's spirits were low, when she needed an inspirational gesture to lift her spirits and offer her some hope and comfort, enabling her to finish her fraught journey with a sympathetic relative.)

chapter eight

Names

Coincidence at its friskiest has given many of us personal details in common with others. The most common example of this is a namesake. From inquiries and from my own experience, I have concluded that few of us who do have this problem are in a hurry to change any part of our own name, in spite of the confusion it sometimes causes. The practical Americans have dealt in part with the problem by using the initial letter of their middle names to differentiate between say a John A. Smith and a John B. Smith, but the rest of us just muddle through – anything but change what we regard, either consciously or subconsciously, as an important part of our own identity.

The problem of namesakes grows more acute the more other details between the pairs match.

In *Coincidences: Chance or Fate?* (pp. 210–11) I told the story of two American women who were both named Wanda Marie Johnson. They were both born on the same day, 5 June 1953, and were former District of Columbia residents who had moved to Prince Georges County, Maryland. Both were mothers of two children and owners of the same make of car. The digits in their social security cards and car serial numbers were similar. Their dual identities caused them no end of trouble with driving licences, credit cards and medical records.[1]

Interestingly in their interview with the *Washington Post* neither woman expressed a desire to solve the problem by giving up her name or part of it to overcome the difficulties. A betting agency put the odds at such a biological collision at five million to one. Given these odds, one would need to be a supreme optimist to outlay money on such a wager. Two women, both with the same name, born on the same day!

But coincidences have a habit of defying even the longest of the odds, as the following story shows. Two women, both called Belinda Lee Perry, were born on the same date, 7 January 1969. One is a distinctive, blue-eyed blonde, let's call her B1; the other an Aboriginal with curly brown hair and dark eyes (B2). So it's easy enough to tell them apart in the physical sense.

B1 told me, in a tone of voice that suggested she has now reached the stage where she is more bemused than annoyed by the coincidence, that she remembers her first hint of the problem came just after she had left high school. She went to register with the Commonwealth Employment Service/ Department of Social Security.

> It took me hours sitting in the office, as they went through files. I wasn't told what the problem was, but gathered this was to do with B2. They kept asking questions about my parents, etc.

This incident had her recalling that the health service Medicare had previously made some comments about claims she clearly had not made. Medicare later asked B1 whether she wanted her child on her own card (she does not have a child). 'Obviously our files were mixed and I would say still are,' she said, adding that B2 does have a child.

> We first truly became aware of each other when we both joined the same library, the City of Sydney Library. My library card had been cancelled because she had joined. I peered over the shoulder of the librarian and memorized the phone number on B2's card and later rang her, pretending to be the librarian, asking for further details for her library card records. Sneaky, huh? I asked her parents' name, etc. and was quite relieved that they were not also my parents!

> The next run-in was when we were formally investigated-interrogated by Austudy over our applications for student grants. An unpleasant experience.

> B2 was told she should pick up my degree when she enrolled for teaching at Sydney University. I get the impression that it was said in jest, but I'm not sure as they still gave her the same student number.

When B2 moved home, it was B1 who was struck off the electoral roll. As B1 explained:

> This happened each time we changed addresses, until the last election when I spent an hour or two – as usual – separating our files at the enrolment office.

> Our lives have been amazing similar. When we both finished school we both went to work for the New South Wales public service as clerks for about 18 months. Then we both worked at Sydney University for about the same length of time! THEN we both enrolled as 'mature' students at the University, me a lot earlier than B2 though.

B1 started out as an accountancy apprentice before switching to the Bachelor of Science course, gaining an honours degree in geology. Today, to avoid confusion, clipped to documents relating to the two women are photos of their namesakes.

Despite the problems caused to the two by portentous chance, when they met they found they got on well together. 'She's quite a nice person,' said B1, who encouraged her namesake in her studies. 'It would be nice to have another degree with my name on it,' she quipped.

I asked B1 the question that had intrigued me most in both cases: why did not one of them change her name? After a moment's thought she responded, 'You get used to it. Once I realized there was definitely another one and that she was legitimate it was a matter of pointing it out to every organization I dealt with.' She admitted she had given the name change some thought at one stage, then added with another bright laugh, 'but I couldn't think of anything worth changing it to.' B2 had moved and I was unable to contact her at the time of writing.

Our own name is our first point of formal identification between ourselves and others. We tend to believe it helps establish our uniqueness. Economist Rodney Small decided to put to the test the question, What are the odds of the average person having a namesake or namesakes? He used the Internet Search America service to find out how many people with his name are listed in all United States telephone books. Small, of Herndon, Virginia, found 23, including himself. What initially struck him as interesting was that one lives in Manchester, Connecticut, where he had once lived, and another in Virginia Beach, Virginia, another location where he has spent some time.

However, what caught his attention most was that there was a Rodney Small directly above his own current listing, at 1500 Massachusetts Avenue, Washington DC – another of his former addresses. Rodney notes that the address is a large high-rise apartment building, housing perhaps 500 people.

All his other 11 former residences were either private homes or garden apartments, so that his address was shared by only a handful of other people. He estimates that the total number of people currently living at all of his past addresses combined would be perhaps 1,100 at most. With an estimated one-third of the 260 million people in the USA listed in a phone book, he finds there would be one Rodney Small for every 3.7 million people (85 million divided by 23). Accordingly, the odds of finding another Rodney Small at a former address of his would be at best one in 3.7 million, divided by 1,100, equals one in about 3,400. However, this estimate does not account for the fact that some of the approximately 1,100 people who live at his former addresses would not be listed either. If the number listed is only 500, rather than 1,100, the odds increase to one in about 7,000.

Here is a man with mathematical skills breaking down by deduction what at first seem improbable odds of there being someone of the same name, living at a former address of his, and coming up with the figures that are nowhere near as high as one might imagine at first glance. Most of the population buy Lottery tickets with far greater odds.

Rodney's search for another name involved what he could not, with his scientific training, explain by logic. 'I experienced what appeared to be my most stunning coincidence ever,' he says. Mindful of the scorn of sceptics he carefully documented his many hours of research involved in this coincidence. His story is somewhat complex, but involves a search through the land records office at his local courthouse which began on 10 February 1993 for an estate transaction involving a Rachel Masterson (not her real name).

Unfamiliar with the operations of the microfilm machine on which he began his search, he put in the film cassette and used the operating knob to advance the film to what he thought was page three where the details of the transaction were supposed to be. On the screen appeared a few lines of writing carried over from the previous page with the signature of a notary who had witnessed the transaction; the signature was Rachel Masterson's. Until that chance sighting he had no idea Masterson was a notary. He checked the page number, and found it to be 127. He had scrolled way past the page he wanted but still found her name. He worked his way back to page three on which were the details he had set out to find. After checking them he left the office. But he was intrigued at the way he had come across the first sighting seemingly by coincidence, so much so that on 1 April 1993 he returned to the building to check the roll page by page for Masterson notarizations. Now familiar with the machine's operation, he went through the roll, which consisted of no less than 2,003 pages, and discovered no other Masterson notarizations. Her name had appeared on only two of those 2,003 pages. Dauntlessly he pressed on, examining 88 recent additional rolls of microfilm, a total of 180,000 pages, and found no other transactions involving Masterson. Her name had appeared twice and he had come across one by chance. 'I solicit explanations...that are in accord with the current scientific understanding of the laws of probability,' Rodney challenges.

Givens Names

Edward R. Givens and Edgar G. Givens of the small town of Sutton, West Virginia, are not related but their names and other similarities have plagued them for years. Edward lives at 410 Franklin Ave, while Edgar lives at 410 North Hill Rd. Edgar is 46 and Edgar 64. Edward has been receiving Edgar's phone calls all his life.

Peter Put His Foot in It

Peter J. Eyre, a 19-year-old Royal Air Force national serviceman, was home on leave when he trod on a tack which caused an infection in his foot. After a few days, he was hardly able to walk and in no condition to return to his unit. He went to see his civilian doctor, who passed him on to the local hospital where surgery under a general anaesthetic was carried out in which a very nasty abscess on his foot was lanced. Given a sick note for his unit commander by the hospital, his leg 'bandaged up like a Boris Karloff mummy', he was told to return in a few days for an examination and a change of dressing.

He duly reported as instructed and gave his name to the receptionist, who told him to sit and wait. Eventually a nurse arrived carrying a file, called his name and took him into a cubicle. 'Take off your tunic,' she ordered. He did so, thinking she was going to give him an antitetanus shot, or something similar. 'Which arm is it?' she asked, looking for a bandage. Then, seeing no sign of one, asked accusingly, 'You haven't taken it off?'

'It's my foot,' he said.

She referred to files. 'Not according to these it isn't,' she insisted. Peter protested that she had the wrong file. She looked at him and pursed her lips. 'Peter Eyre?' she asked. He nodded. 'Peter John Eyre?' she went on. He nodded again. 'Age 19?' she queried.

'Yes,' he said.

'Member of the Royal Air Force?' she persisted, looking up and down at his blue uniform.

Again he nodded and repeated insistently, 'But it's my foot.'

'Marital status?'

'Married.'

'Oh dear, this guy's single,' she exclaimed, finally relenting. She shook her head and quoted an address a few miles or so from Peter's home.

'No, I don't live there,' he said.

Peter, now retired, asked me:

What are the chances of a young fellow with the same full name as myself attending the outpatients department of a large city hospital on the same day? Even further, he was also in the RAF and of the same age. In fact, our birthdays were only a couple of months apart.

He says it has been one of the few times in his life he has been involved with the long arm of coincidence:

> …apart from things like coming across a new word and having to look it up in the dictionary and then falling over the same word in practically everything I read during the course of the next few weeks. But everyone has that kind of experience, don't they? I put it down to heightened awareness.

Apt Names

If I wanted a solicitor to carry out some confidential business for me I think I would feel comfortable with Mr Lipshutt, an Australian lawyer. In England, Mr P. K. Court, and his Scottish counterpart, McCourt, would also seem by their names capable of carrying on their profession as solicitors. I might think twice before deciding on Shropshire estate agents Doolittle and Dalley if I wanted a quick sale on a property!

Names apposite to a person's job have been around since, well, the village blacksmith was known as either Black or Smith. In other words, in the past people tended to be named according to the job they did. But that does not explain why today, when there are so many more occupations and one chooses one's occupation for a variety of reasons, people still find themselves pursuing a career whose description can be summed up by their name. Or conversely as a wry comment on the job they do. For example, Mr Neil Gamble was appointed head of the Sydney Casino in October 1966. He had been odds-on favourite for the job, while the yachting secretary of the Royal Prince Alfred Yacht Club is Jan Rowed.

I would feel I was being cued in watching a snooker championship broadcast by Steve Robilliard and that a sex researcher at the University of California knows what he was talking about – Marc Breedlove.

Mr Robert Citron is a former treasurer of Orange Country, California. He once offered a bottle of rare wine to anyone supplying a word in English to rhyme with 'Orange'. Other people who have made a career that suits their names are an Australian Food Foundation director, Mr John Cook, and an organizer with the Electrical Trades Union, Mr Kevin Power. Among the reporters on the *Sydney Morning Herald* are James Woodford, environment writer; Kathryn House, property writer; and Valerie Lawson, legal correspondent. Dr Kevin Borer is a British forensic firearms expert.

Woomb Doctor

At the time he was born, Bruce Mayes's father had just become mayor of the city of Toowoomba, Queensland. The father gave his son the town's name as his middle name. Mayes later changed this to Toomba, leading fellow medical students to joke he had taken the womb out of Toowoomba. Dr Mayes became a distinguished gynaecologist.

Girle Meets Gents

In Inverell, New South Wales, at the turn of the century there was a family named Boys, two families named Girle, families named Maiden and Mann and two families named Gents. Two of the Girle boys married two of the Gents girls.

Creative Fiction

Author Audrey Austin is often amazed at how often her fictitious characters 'come to life'. She meets couples identical to the ones she has portrayed. Also names she has 'invented' appear with the exact spelling in a newspaper. Her most fascinating coincidence concerning names occurred much closer to home. Her youngest daughter was named by vote. While she was pregnant Audrey asked her family and friends to gather one afternoon and for each of them to list the ten boys' and girls' names that they most liked. The names were then put into a hat and, as they were drawn, a poll was taken. The results, if a boy Jon, if a girl Joanne. On the day her daughter was born, in the same hospital and from the same suburb, was a baby girl whose mother had also decided to call her baby Joanne. The other mother was set on using the name so Audrey could foresee a problem when they both started at the local school. Further she did not feel like a complete change of name for her daughter after going to so much trouble to get it.

In the end she compromised by changing the spelling slightly, Johanne. Over the following weeks, it appeared she could not pick up a newspaper without coming across a Johanne. Johanna was common enough, but Johanne!

Some time later, when Audrey was discussing family trees, she suddenly remembered that the name of her father, whom she had never met, was Joe (Joseph) and his wife was Hanne. Thereafter, Audrey loved to relate that her daughter's name had been chosen not just by ballot but also by coincidence.

However, there is a punchline to the story. When Johanne was old enough, Audrey was mortified to learn her daughter had changed her name by deed poll to Joy. At the time she learned of the name change Audrey was writing a novel and she had named its central character Joy. Another fictitious character she had created had come to life in possibly the most unexpected of such events.

chapter nine

Fancy Meeting You Here

Very few of us have not had the experience of chance encounters in a strange place. This is known as the Small World Effect (SWE). Sceptics more often than not respond to such tales with the comment, 'How about all those times you travel somewhere and don't meet someone you know?' What about them? If we were going to meet the same old people every time we travelled it would hardly be worth going away. But the bottom line of such meetings should be an examination to see if there is some underlying meaning to the encounter.

Manly Meeting

Miami woman Mona Smith was sightseeing on Sydney's Manly Beach when she bumped into a man. Turning to apologize she found herself facing her old high school crush from more than a decade ago. There they were, thousands of miles from home, overcome with the dramatic Small World Effect, and romance followed.[1]

Double Act

Albert Rivers and *Betty* Cheetham of Swindon shared a table with another couple for dinner at the Tourkhalf Hotel in Tunisia in early 1998. The other couple introduced themselves, *Albert* Cheetham and *Betty* Rivers of Derby. All were in their 70s. Having overcome the surprise at their similar names, they kept talking and soon more similarities emerged. The two couples were both married on the same day and at the same time. Both couples have two sons, born in 1943 and 1945. Both couples have five grandchildren and four great grandchildren. The Bettys had worked in post offices in their home towns while their husbands had been carriage bodybuilders in railway workshops. Neither women could show her engagement ring as both had lost them, but they did have identical watch bracelets which had had the same links repaired.

Some undefined input or power appears to be involved in many such SWE stories. It is as though we are willing the meeting to take place. The following anecdote would appear to indicate this.[2]

Homesickness Cure

On a tour of Ireland, Adeline Wurst and her husband of Panorama, South Australia, were staying the night in a small guest house. A sudden bout of homesickness had overcome Adeline and she found herself at the window of their first-floor room gazing vacantly out into the street. She had been there only a few moments when a young bearded man walked slowly by. It took her a moment longer to realize she recognized him. 'There's Des,' she yelled to her husband and quickly opened the window. 'Des! Des! Stop! Stop!' she yelled into the street below to her nephew. Young Des, turned and slowly looked up, his jaw dropping as he recognized who was calling him by name. Adeline and her husband knew only that Des, who lived just 50 kilometres from them in Australia, had planned an overseas trip, but they had no idea where and when he was going. She has still not got over the circumstances that began with her bout of homesickness that forced her to gaze from the window at the very moment a relative from home happened to walk by.

Dream Comes True

The Rev. John W. Sloat teaches a course on paranormal experiences. He collects stories on the subject and tells of a 'marvellous' personal experience:

> In 1988 I drove to New York City to bring our son home after his sophomore year in college. I took along our grown daughter, Laurie, for company on the long trip, which takes eight hours.
>
> The night before the trip I dreamed about Evelyn; she is an 80-year-old former neighbour in New Jersey who still lives next door to the house in which I grew up. I have known her since I was four. She is like a second mother to me, but I don't remember having dreamed about her before.
>
> Travelling through New Jersey, Laurie noticed that we were going to pass close to my old hometown. She suggested that we stop and see some of the spots she remembered from her childhood, 20 years earlier, before my parents moved away. So we did.
>
> While we were in town, Laurie asked, 'Can we stop to see Evelyn?' I said, 'I'd like to, but we could only stay five minutes. It wouldn't be fair to drop in unannounced for such a short visit.' So, reluctantly, we decided not to stop.

We were already late, but Laurie wanted to see one more place, a spot by the river where she had fed the ducks as a child. So we crossed the bridge over the river, and I planned to turn left at the next street to go alongside the river, but I discovered that the road had been turned into a one-way street coming out. I said to Laurie, 'We'll go down the next street and go around the block.'

As I started to turn left at the second street, I had to wait for two elderly women to cross the intersection. As we drove behind them, I asked Laurie, 'Who does that look like?' and she said, 'It looks like Evelyn.' And it was. We jumped out of the car and had a wonderful five-minute reunion right there on the pavement.

We had left western Pennsylvania eight hours earlier and driven 400 miles (650 kilometres) to come to that precise spot to see the particular individual I had dreamed about the night before, at that exact moment she was crossing the street directly in front of us. If we had been 30 seconds earlier or later, or if the first road had not been changed to one-way, or if we had gone to her house as Laurie had suggested, we would have missed that rendezvous.

Evelyn, who was a mile from her home when we met her, later told me that because of her busy schedule she was an hour and a half late that day taking her daily walk with her companion.

These stories can hardly be lightly dismissed as random or chance encounters. There is evidence of some preconceived conditions relating to them. Adeline was feeling acutely homesick and part of that malady is the lack of loved ones around you – you are in a world where every face apparently belongs to a stranger. Then, with a flash of joy, a familiar face emerges from the crowd and the homesickness eases or vanishes altogether. There is a need in every one of us for the companionship of the people we are comfortable with, be they relatives, friends or colleagues. In their company our homesickness fades, or becomes less hard to bear. In Rev. Sloat's case, although he dreamed for the first time about his former neighbour and 'second mother', he had no real expectations of seeing her in the flesh the next day. Yet events conspired to ensure he did. The dream, therefore, takes on a precognitive aura. Even though, in practical terms, Mr Sloat thought such a meeting was not going to happen.

There is a further element to these two SWE cases – the timing. Adeline was amazed that she happened to gaze from the window at the very moment her relative happened by. While Rev. Sloat was just as impressed that, after driving for eight hours over hundreds of miles, he should arrive at the exact spot the woman he dreamed about the previous night was at that very moment. In both cases, as Rev. Sloat emphasizes, a few seconds either way and neither meeting would have taken place. So what was it that drove Adeline to the window? What made Rev. Sloat detour from his trip against his own best judgement? Was it a sixth sense? Or a need to see a familiar face? Or some synchronistic force?

Adeline Wurst has another traveller's tale to tell of an unexpected encounter that, while not strictly speaking in the SWE category, is worth repeating for its poignancy. On their first overseas visit to the USA in 1968 she and her husband were strolling near Fisherman's Wharf, San Francisco, just passing the time when they were approached by a Democrat Party campaign worker who gave them two 'Robert Kennedy for President' buttons. A few minutes later a car bearing the brother of the assassinated president appeared and stopped in front of them. The presidential candidate alighted all smiles, obviously pleased with the success of his campaign, and reached out for their hands. 'Greetings from Australia,' Adeline said as he took hers. A moment later he was surrounded by guards and ushered away. The next day, 5 June 1968, he was assassinated.

Face in the Crowd

Alyssa Sharf of Voorhees, New Jersey, on a weekend visit to Pittsburgh, a city of several million people, decided on an impulse to look up an old friend who had moved there. She found a public telephone and checked in the directory, but there was no listing under the name of the friend who had once lived across the street from her. A few hours later she heard a joyous yell 'Alyssssaaa!' It was the old friend who had spotted Alyssa from across the street.

I Know the Face

Grace Grigg heard the bell jangle as the door to her antique shop, Decorations, in Adelaide opened. Looking up from the tray of rings she was arranging, she was amazed to see a familiar face. 'It's John Cameron,' she thought. Grace's mind ran back 40 years to her childhood home in Aberdeenshire, Scotland, when she and her pal John would cycle to school together. After riding the five miles to the farm where Grace lived he would wait at her front gate, then the two of them would cycle another ten miles past farms and fields to go to school.

The man gazed at Grace without recognition. Grace presumed she must have aged too much for him to recognize her. Before she could say anything he asked, 'D'you have any medals?' He had an Australian accent, but then so did Grace after 35 years in Australia. 'Are you after British or Australian medals?' she asked.

102

'Australian,' the man said. 'I've never been to Britain.'

Grace gave a start. She'd been sure this was her childhood friend, but now as she looked closer she could see he wasn't, though he had the same thick black hair, dimpled chin and gentle way of speaking. She was disappointed. 'We don't have any right now,' she said, 'but if you leave your name I'll call you when we get some.'

'That's kind of you,' said the man. 'My name's John Cameron.'

Grace's hand was shaking so much she could hardly write – she just could not believe the coincidence. The man became a regular customer but Grace never worked up the courage to tell him about her friend.[3]

chapter ten

Diary Keeping

Joanne Stead of Leigh-on-Sea, Essex, must be one of the most assiduous coincidence diary keepers of modern times. Over a period of years her diary (or notebook as she calls it) built into six volumes. She stopped temporarily at the end of her sixth volume, not because the coincidences had stopped occurring, but because she realized there were too many in her life. Recording them had become time-consuming as they were, she had realized by then, an everyday event. Had there been one a week, she said, then she may have continued.

Joanne began using a mantra twice daily in 1963 and continues to do so. She says it has resulted in an 'effortless taming of a very unruly chameleon – *me*'. She philosophizes that the events in her life 'now just happen'. She expands on this:

> I have on a revolving potter's stand an ivory temple which contains a tiny
> Buddha. It has started moving to the left. Each time I move it back to face
> me, only to find it once again moves to the left until it is facing the wall. Very
> unsettling. Why?

Her notes show that the coincidences she records have at times served as an *aide-mémoire* to deeper meanings and greater understandings. Many of her coincidences had to do with reading or hearing some thought-provoking point in her search, then finding it reinforced by coming across the same point a short time later in a completely unrelated context.

Keeping her notebooks has brought her an awareness that she is developing in her work and study as a medium. Joanne has, as she says, lived a 'double life'. For many years she worked in positions of responsibility, while at the same time exploring more esoteric and artistic matters. Upon reflection, she realized one of her earliest remembered coincidences concerned this double life. She migrated to Canada in 1948 and 'saw' a sign on the window of a house where she was living:

'Citizens' Advice Bureau'. Shortly afterwards her attention was caught by a newspaper item on a Seafarers Centre.

It was not until several years later that she realized the significance of these apparently disparate phrases that had caught her attention but appeared to her somehow related. She returned to England and was made Lady Warden of a Seafarers Centre. After that she became full-time organizer of a busy Citizens' Advice Bureau in central London where she remained for many happy and exhausting years.

Her diary with its brief, even terse, notes is a perfect example for those who may be intimidated by the thought that recording their own coincidences requires lengthy writing. Those who find writing comes naturally may run on in their note-taking (I tend to do so, as my examples later in this chapter show), but it is not necessary. It is more important to put down the relevant details *at the time* even if only as a reference that one can return to. Doing so can largely obviate the problem that concerns many parapsychology researchers: false memory syndrome.

Dr Caroline Watt of the Department of Psychology at the University of Edinburgh says:

We often get people calling in who think they are having psychic experiences, such as precognitive dreams. People may be wanting to confirm their abilities or to get rid of them. As a first step we need to get a good description of what is going on, so we may ask people to keep a diary, noting every possible precognitive dream and whether or not it 'came true'. Doing this, people often find that they have been overestimating the frequency of their success rate, presumably because successes are so memorable. Recording actual performance can…make the non-coincidences less easy to ignore. (See Appendix, p. 229.)

Here are some recent extracts from Joanne Stead's diary:

5 December 1995 I bought from Samye Ling Tibetan Buddhist Centre, Scotland, a Tibetan Buddhist diary 1996–7 and to my astonishment found under First Tibetan month, March 1996, the name 'Jamyang Chentse Wangpo'. In my notebook, 15 April 1992, I had recorded: Awoke 4.30 a.m. with these words in mind; 'Why not? I will take – Wangpo as my guide.' I heard the full name of this unknown but as I awakened fully and reached for my bedside book, the forenames disappeared and only Wangpo remained. Upon seeing the diary I wrote immediately for more details to the Buddhist Centre. A few days later I got this reply: 'Jamyang Chentse Wangpo was a Tibetan saint and scholar of the nineteenth century. He was one of a group of lamas associated with the "ri-me" (non-sectarian movement).'

7 September 1996 I had just bought a metal spider's web with a crystal in the centre, and was hanging it on my window when, on the one o'clock news, while my hands poised to hang the web crystal, I heard Greville Janner, MP, talking about '…the spider's web of deceit…' The reason for buying this new crystal was because I was cleaning the inside of the window (which I rarely do) when I decided at the same time to clean my largest multifaceted crystal on the window. As I held it in my hand and dusted it, the catgut that had been holding it up for years suddenly gave way and came apart. How it remained on that window is a miracle as the crystal is very heavy.

12 October 1996 (See above.) Since I put the metal spider's web up I have been beset by reading or hearing about spider's webs. For example re-reading *Hidden Journey* by Andrew Harvey I found on page 28, 'The Mother – she is the spider and the world is the spider's web she has woven.'

19 October 1996 Yesterday posted airmail letter to Ken Anderson in Australia. This a.m. got his diary entry for 13 September [Author's note: see my entry under this date on p. 113]. He mentioned Jeri's *Fun Runes* game based on synchronicity. Now, when I was typing out the item for KA from my own coincidence notebook, I came across this entry: '11 September 1996: Went into local shop to enquire about pyramids. None. Bought rune charm instead. Chose "Loki", the ancient trickster from the pantheon of the Norse Gods, because it reminded me of the Cosmic Joker. I did not mention this note to KA reasoning thus: he is obviously a busy man; no time to plough through your meanderings about rune stones, etc. etc. So do not put it in your list of coincidences to KA.'

23 October 1996 Came home from a visit to the dentist to find mail awaiting. Among it was a newsletter which began, '"Relax, this won't hurt," said the dentist.'

24 October 1996 On BBC Radio 4 Professor Archie Royle told the story of an Icelandic medium circle session where a total stranger 'came through' demanding rum, snuff and tobacco. He said to one man who had recently joined the circle, 'You have my leg in your house.' The man denied this. The 'ghost' explained he had been at a party where he had become drunk. There was a severe storm and his companions had urged him to stay the night. However, fuelled by alcohol he had gone to the beach, fallen asleep under a rock and was swept out to sea. His body was later found with a leg missing. The newcomer to the circle had recently bought a fish factory in a tiny village. A carpenter who had built the house attached to the factory said that he had found a human thigh bone. It could not be given a church burial as they did not know whose it was. So the carpenter built it into the wall of the house. Dr Susan Blackmore, also on the programme, said if this story were true, then she was wrong to be a sceptic. Professor Royle said signed affidavits were taken from all those involved and the story of the ghost, investigated. [Author's note: after reading the above extract I wrote to Professor Royle at the BBC asking for verification and details, but received no reply.]

13 April 1997 Reading KA's book *Hitler and the Occult* and came across the line: 'Today is Friday 13 April. It is the turning point.' Well I have read the above today, 13 April 1997! So I shall now look for my turning point if there be one.

13 July 1997 The July–August 1997 *Theosophical Journal* arrived. On page 5 an item mentioned Dinosaur footprints found on National Trust land in Dorset. I glanced at today's *Observer Review* and saw, 'a dinosaur once walked through his kitchen...'

23 July 1997 Two days earlier I said aloud, 'I could do with some more money – how about £20,000?' Today in the post I got word from an unknown mail-order firm, *Health and Home Shopping*, that a sum totalling £20,000 had been allocated to me and others provided one of us won the Lottery on 31.12.97.

26 July 1997 Saturday. I have closed my coincidence notebook (No. 6) with the following items:

26 July 1997 On Thursday I ordered a book by telephone from a local store. *Being-in-Dreaming: An Initiation into the Sorcerers' World*, author Florinda Donner. Was told if it was in the warehouse it *might* arrive today (Saturday) and if so they would phone me. I had no intention of going out today, but the postman brought me this a.m. a mail-order blouse – wrong colour. Cross, I bundled it up and flew out of the house to the post office. Then I remembered the above book and decided to go to the book shop on the off-chance it had come. Inside the store three assistants were behind the counter. One with her back to me dropped the receiver and turned to face me holding aloft a book – *Being-in-Dreaming*. She looked somehow taken aback or scared. I said to her, 'Were you by any chance phoning me about the book?' She said, 'Yes, I was.' She must have put it down to sorcery I later realized. I tried to reassure her by saying, 'Those sort of things are always happening to me.'

28 July 1997 Mixed group of men and women in Eve's garden, Leigh-on-Sea. Joy, who does flower psychometry, came to our group. We had each bought a flower and placed it in the garden on a table. At that time she was absent. When she appeared she picked up each flower and with amazing accuracy told about the person who had placed it there. She said about me, 'This is a person who lives in two worlds at once. In one of which they are in touch with higher powers. It is a person who worked very hard for their knowledge which they impart to others without making them feel inferior.'

1 August 1997 *Transcendental Meditation* newsletter dropped through my letter box (I am not a member). On page two it mentioned that on 20 July, Maharishi's worldwide organization celebrated Guru Purnima Day…dedicated to the Vedic masters who have maintained the supreme wisdom of life. I decided to look in my personal diary to see what, if anything, I had written down on or near that auspicious day (bearing in mind the different time zones) and was rather taken aback to read the following: 19 July: Feel HAPPY and creative. Cleaned my little Shiva altar with the finest steel wool after years of leaving it darkened. Why, after years of leaving the little wall-altar untouched, I should decide out of the blue to restore it to its original brass I don't know (it is over 200 years old).

27 September 1997 Some months ago I had the odd experience of being overshadowed whenever I looked in a mirror late at night by the deeply lined face of a very, very old woman. My cousin Charles, I discovered, had for 30 years been keeping in an attic suitcases of family papers and photos. [Author's note: Joanne then asked if she could see the material and Charles and his wife brought it to her home.] They produced things I have never seen including a small framed pencil portrait of the overshadowing lady. She and I share many of the same features. She is our great-great-grandmama, Marie Madeleine Schachenmann of Innsbruck, Austria. I now keep her portrait on a shelf where I see it daily. Since then the overshadowing has ceased.

2 November 1997 Clear dream of my mother, Denise (in the dream she had been on vacation and had returned home). She was standing in my bathroom and on the floor I saw a bundle of laundry. Thought it an odd dream. Wondered if this meant I would be hearing of death of Uncle Henri in Malta, aged 96 and in poor health. Haven't dreamed of my mother for years.

12 November 1997 (See above.) One of Henri's daughters, Denise, telephoned to say he had died yesterday, 11 November, in Malta.

16 November 1997 (See above.) Jose, Henri's elder daughter, telephoned after she had returned from uncle's funeral in Malta. She told me that when Henri's first wife (her mother) had died in her sleep years ago, a washing machine had flooded and Henri had said to her, 'That's your mother, letting me know she's still around.' Jose also told me that when her daughter Julia, who lives in York, got back from Henri's funeral one of her tenants reported a leaking pipe and Julia said, 'It's my grandpa Henri letting us know he's still around.'

17 November 1997 This noon-time met one of the residents here in the hall. Hadn't seen her for ages. She had been in hospital for an operation. She said, 'I must thank you for those magazines you put through my letter box. I found them when I returned home from seeing the consultant before the operation and I was in pain and feeling low.' I had forgotten this incident of the mags (I think they were full of healing thoughts). She went on, 'How did you know I needed them?' I said, 'I didn't, but something did. I am a medium and this has happened before.' Years ago I was in London studying with a well-known Icon painter. I was at a Christmas fair and saw on the book stall a second-hand copy of *Self-abandonment: A Spiritual Classic* by Jean-Pierre de Caussade (Fontana, 1971). For some quite unknown reason I bought it for my tutor! Later, after reading it, he said, 'How on earth did you know I needed this book so much?' I replied, 'I did not know. But *something* obviously did.' Isn't it most strange! I have read this morning that 'channelling' is the modern form for the 'medium'. So this is what I feel I am, or am becoming, bearing in mind that I am very suspicious of what I call some 'unbalanced people' giving out to all and sundry pronouncements which there is no way of checking.

1 December 1997 About 20 minutes ago I came out of the post office with a rather preoccupied air. Someone rushed up to me and said, 'Hello, how are you? I haven't seen you for ages.' It was one of our residents. She then said, 'I'm off to San Francisco in the morning and will not be back until March.' I took a large illustrated book out of the shopping basket on my arm that I had intended to give to OXFAM and held it up before her eyes. The title? *San Francisco*. She was dumb-struck and so was yours truly. So I gave it to her as a memento of her coming trip. She said to me after she recovered from the shock, 'You must be psychic or a medium.' I replied, 'I'm beginning to think I am.'

2 January 1998 Letter from a friend, Diana, whom I had reproached for not writing down any suitable coincidences in 1997. She wrote to me [letter dated 31 December 1997] thus: 'Rang the Conran shop in Fulham [London] before Christmas to ask them to keep two of their string bags for me to collect. The assistant said, 'How strange, I'm just unpacking some more of them now.'

What my friend does not know as yet is that before Christmas I became obsessed with the idea that two string bags I had purchased earlier from Natural Edge in Leigh-on-Sea might be used as gifts for Diana and the other for friend Stephanie. I had already ordered and received two mail-order catalogue gifts for the above friends, so this obsession with the use of two string bags I had was odd, and lasted on and off for a few days till I got so fed up with it that I decided to keep these oh-so-useful string bags for myself and send them gifts from the mail-order catalogue. Apart from the oddness of the above incident, doesn't it show how much we are affected by thought waves (vibrations) from long distance? I have not seen my friend for some years due to the distance.

11 January 1998 (Sunday) Awoke between 5–6 a.m. and immediately these words came into my head: 'There *is* a magical other-land.' [Author's note: these words led Joanne to compose a poem in that early hour that concluded:
No, I didn't see fairies
I didn't see God
I just felt lighter
And I heard the grass grow.]

That finished I switched on Radio 4 to hear a countryman's voice say, '… where I was you could hear the grass grow…' [Author's note: the programme was called *On Your Farm* and Quentin Seldon was interviewing sheep farmer Harry Ridley and his wife Sylvia.] This coincidence has left me speechless.

Notes from the Author's Coincidence Diary

2 March 1994 Walking the dogs when the word 'outrage' popped whimsically into mind. Always a good word for a headline, I mused as we kept walking, 'outraged residents…', 'Leader says, "This is an outrage"', etc. Some few minute later, after the word had come and gone, my eyes fell on a magazine lying face up on the footpath. Across the top of its cover in large letters was its title: *Outrage*. I would like to be able to credit my fading eyesight with the ability to have seen more than about 100 metres along the street, across an intersection to the magazine lying on the footpath, but I am afraid I cannot make that boast. The appearance of the word without apparent cause in my mind and my coming across the magazine amounted to a synchronistic happening.

8 March 1994 At the library, looking for material in *The Times* index on Trevor Ravenscroft. Each time I came across an entry I made a personal note of it along these lines: 'Rav. 3 March 1973, p. 12'. Each time I collected two or three references I filled out a form to get microfilm copies of the paper, marking the form *The Times* and the month and year. The librarian at the desk then added a location code and number for the material before sending it to the stack storage area. About the third time I handed a form in I glanced down as the librarian was adding *The Times* location details. She wrote: 'RAV 297'.

9 March 1996 Having lunch with Martin yesterday when he suddenly handed me his osteopath's card. Jackie had asked me last week to get the address from Martin but I had forgotten to mention it to him. I assumed Jackie had spoken to Martin on the phone and asked him to give it to me. When I arrived home I handed Jackie the card without comment. The way she appeared to have been expecting it only confirmed for me that the two had spoken. Yet some doubt about the episode remained. While talking to Martin on the phone today I decided to clarify this. No, he had not spoken to Jackie. He was not sure what made him look up the card and bring it to our lunch, except that just before leaving home he had remembered I had been treated by an osteopath in the past and should I need the services of another...

21 March 1996 Yesterday I was searching for some information about a property and rang the Real Estate Institute. Unfortunately its staff were unable to help and I sat by the phone for some time thinking about my next move. Suddenly the name of a former colleague popped into mind: Gwen Edwards, one of Australia's leading real estate writers. But then I thought, 'No, she's a busy woman, it would not be fair to ask her to give time to a personal problem.' Besides I had not spoken to her for over a year which was remiss of me. The following morning the phone rang early. Of all people, it was Gwen. After we exchanged greetings and caught up with one another's news she explained she had called because she was planning an article on my suburb and wanted *my* help. I gladly gave it to her, then just as gladly and with no feeling of guilt raised my problem and she was most helpful. Of all the suburbs in Sydney – the city has more than 200 of them: I know, I wrote a book about them – she should choose mine!

21 March 1996 Fellow writer Glenn Cooper has mentioned several times in sporadic letters over the past year I should read *The Fortean Times* as it often had material of interest. Last Monday I determined to do something about it. Upon reflection it was not so much a rational decision as a positive impulse. When I called at the local newsagents, the owner did not have a copy in stock and said she had not heard of the magazine. However, she found it in a catalogue and said she would order a copy. Yesterday on the off-chance it had arrived I went back to the shop and she promptly handed me a copy. She was as surprised as I that it had arrived so quickly. 'Normally an order takes weeks,' she commented. 'They asked me whether I wanted the next edition or the current one. You didn't say which one you wanted so I asked them to send the current copy.' Last night I read it through and was suitably impressed by its even-handed approach to stories. I thought I had read it all, but tonight picked it up for a final check starting from the back, and that's when I came across a very favourable review of my book *Coincidences: Chance or Fate?*. Needless to say I had no idea the review was to be run. The whole episode has reinforced my view that giving in to positive, compelling impulses results more often than not in a satisfying synchronistic outcome.

6 April 1996 Esther Deans, the author of *Growing Without Digging* (Harper & Row, Sydney, 1977), rang very much out of the blue. She had, she explained, been going through some old papers and come across a letter I had written her. About to sit down and write to me, she had consulted her pendulum and it had advised her to ring instead – immediately. Esther holds the pendulum – usually no more than a peg dangling from a piece of string – in one hand and allows it to 'check' on the condition of seed, soil and plants in her garden. When the pendulum rotates clockwise they are positive, when it oscillates from side to side, they are negative. When the pendulum is stationary the plant, soil or seed sample is neutral. Her success rate has inspired many others to do the same. She began reading my letter to her and came to a reference to American magician and pursuer of fake psychics, James Randi (who is particularly sceptical of dowsers). I interrupted her to say that there was a television programme about Randi being broadcast tonight. Esther, who is in her eighties, took a little time to register and then she realized her pendulum had struck again. Carefully she took down the details. It was obvious she was not an avid watcher of television. She asked me exactly how she could find the station on the dial, but before I could explain added not to bother as her husband would find it as he was a television viewer; she preferred the radio in the evenings. Before she hung up we had to go over the whole episode again: she had come across my letter unexpectedly and the pendulum had told her to ring me, not delay by writing, and in doing so she had found the person I mentioned in that old letter who is of great interest to her was appearing on television that very night.

After the show was over Esther, a founding member of the Australian Dowsing Society, rang to thank me. 'If it had not been for this coincidence – coming across the old letter and being told to phone you – I would not have known about the show.' I did not tell her I had, by that stage, written two books on coincidences and was working on another and had in fact set aside her book to re-read as part of my research.

30 May 1996 In the mail this afternoon a letter from a colleague containing an article about UFOs, sent unexpectedly. Also in the mail, a copy of quarterly *UFO Magazine*.

31 May 1996 Had lunch with a friend who brought an essay that he wanted me to read. On my way home stopped off at the local newsagents. In a casual conversation with the shop assistant he mentioned he lived in the outer Sydney suburb of Busby, so faced a long journey to and from his inner suburban shop each day. That evening, I read the essay, which was about he early days of Sydney's water supply: the name *Busby's Bore* leapt off the page.

30 August 1996 Last week was shown the sledge Captain Scott took on his unsuccessful expedition to be the first to reach the South Pole. It is stored away in a local school, few people know of its existence and it is to me a mystery why no museum, especially a British museum, has not put in a claim for it. I have decided to write an article about it. Today having a drink with a journalist colleague, I mentioned the sledge and the possibility of an article. She gulped and said that last week she had written an article about the Antarctic explorer that was to appear in two days. There was no particular reason for having done so, just as there had been no particular reason why I should have chosen to go to the school last week having known of the sledge's existence for some months.

13 September 1996 Letter from Jeriann, who mentions in passing that my postal address, Newtown, is the same as her husband's home town and my PO Box number 429 is the same number as her last apartment. This reminded me that two days ago I received a letter from Joanne Stead of Essex, England, who had mentioned in passing a book distributor whose address is also Newtown, New South Wales. Joanne went on to say the company distributed a 'marvellous illustrated book and game in a box' which has much to do with synchronicity. This gave me a further link to this growing coincidence because Jeriann is the creator of her own game based on the 'principles of synchronicity'. The final link (I thought) took a while to emerge. Jeriann lives in a Stead Court, in New Jersey, which I do not think was named after Ms Stead or any of her ancestors, but one cannot be too sure. (Footnote: some weeks later, Jeriann wrote to point out that she and Joanne have the same initials, JS, and both have addresses that are a court, rather than street, avenue, etc.)

6 November 1996 Needing to track down a woman about an article I was working on, I rang a solicitor's office hoping for a lead as I knew she had had some dealings with him although some time before. The call was answered by a familiar voice, a woman friend of my wife's. I had not spoken to her for some time and was surprised to hear her voice under what I assumed were unusual circumstances. After identifying myself I went on, 'What are you doing answering the phone in a solicitor's office?' After a puzzled pause she responded, 'But I'm not in a solicitor's office – I'm at home.' She ran her own catering business from her home. Unthinkingly I went on to insist that she must be in the office. She broke in, her voice taking on a peeved edge, 'What's this all about?' After some further confusion, we worked out that I had misdialled two digits and instead of the solicitor I had reached her number which was unknown to me. But that was not the end of the coincidence. When I explained my mission she further surprised me by saying that her husband knew the woman well, so if I would care to call back in an hour or so…I did, and as a result found the elusive woman I had been chasing all morning.

1 December 1996 On an impulse I walked into Gould's book shop. There must be few places like it anywhere in the world. At any one time there are more than a million second-hand books crowded between its walls. One gets the feeling that any book you ever wanted is there – somewhere. The books overflow from the shelves onto floors, are stacked in high piles in the aisle and some just lie about on the floor and tables looking as lost and forlorn as a dog in a pound. Browsing, not quite knowing for what, I came across a hardback copy of *The Spear of Destiny* by Trevor Ravenscroft. I had tried everywhere else for a copy, including the State library (theirs had mysteriously vanished a week or so before I made my inquiry) as I needed it for research into my book *Hitler and the Occult*. I had been working with a paperback version, but needed to check that some material was also in the hardback edition.

With a whoop of joy I prised it from the tight-packed row on the shelf. Then I did a silly – and stingy – thing: ignoring the 'out of print' stamp inside its cover, I took out my notebook and pad, made a note of some brief but vital information that I had suspected was not in the paperback and replaced the book. A few days later I realized I should have bought the book on the spot. But when I returned to Gould's it was gone and no amount of searching or inquiries to the staff turned it up. I felt they may have burned it after it had been rejected once too often.

Perhaps I had been influenced by a similar incident at the store some months before. Looking for another rare book, Ellic Howe's *Urania's Children*, which had been published in the 1960s, I went once again to Gould's and asked the attendant if she had heard of the title. She had not so I asked directions to books on astrology and the like. As I neared the section my heart sank. This was obviously a popular section. Hundreds of books were stacked in their usual haphazard fashion, many jammed in sideways on the ledges; others comprised teetering stacks on the floor, and several of these had collapsed and had to be negotiated by pushing volumes aside with my foot. A path cleared, I noticed several books lying for some reason in glorious isolation on top of the shelf itself just below eye level. In that moment of focusing I saw *Urania's Children*. I stared open-mouthed, my mind racing. I glanced back at the counter where the assistant was busying herself with some chore or other. She could not possibly have raced ahead of me and placed it there. I glanced around for other customers; there were few. Had one of them over-heard?…No…ridiculous. This rare book was sitting apart, not on the shelf or buried in the piles, but on top, away from the apparent confusion surrounding it. Like *The Spear of Destiny* it also carried an 'out of print' stamp. I returned to the counter and bought it, having been in the shop less than five minutes

25 January 1997 In the State library I noticed an old colleague of mine, Walter Sullivan, sitting in a lounge chair. He glanced up as I approached and put down his book. We stood there chatting (quietly, of course) and as we did I happened to glance at another of the lounge chairs where, sprawled in it, fast asleep, with an open book resting on his chest, was a thin man in a dark blue suit with black hair and large black-rimmed glasses. Not unusual for someone taking advantage of those comfortable chairs to catch up on some sleep, but in this case, as I explained to Walter, the same man had been in the same chair in the same suit and glasses in the same position with the book (the same one for all I knew) on his chest exactly one week before at this time when I had last been in the library. We did note that he was breathing.

26 January 1997 Earlier today I had been going through some boxes of files looking for an item regarding a story Reader's Digest had asked for. Tonight I found a small yellowing cutting on the floor. It must have fallen from one of the boxes, one of hundreds of cuttings I have collected over the years. The undated item was from Column 8 (*Sydney Morning Herald*). It wished a 'happy birthday' to a woman born Leonore Australia Mullampy 78 years ago. About 35 years ago, the item went on, she married Lyndon Day and that's why she is known as Australia Day. The columnist added a happy birthday also to our country. Today (26 January) was once again Australia Day.

9 February 1997 A friend gave me a copy of *UFO Review 1969*, found in the house of a relative who had recently died. After glancing quickly through its yellowing pages I placed it on top of a book on my bedside table with the intention of reading it at leisure some evening. A few minutes later something I had casually noticed on the first page of the magazine made me pick it up and confirm what I had seen. The *UFO Review* editor was a Neville Drury. I picked up the book on which I had placed my copy: *Healers, Quacks or Mystics* by Nevill (no E) Drury, published in 1983. Was it the same man or a coincidence to the extent that both editor and author had similar names? A conundrum that I did not think I could solve without going to a great deal of effort, and for what purpose?

By this time I had returned to my desk. On it I found a note from my wife: 'ring Bill Chalker'. Bill is a scientist who has had a long-term interest in the UFO phenomenon. He represents the rational side of the UFO debate. We had not spoken for some months. It occurred to me as I reached for the handset that Bill would solve the problem of the two Drurys. Apart from the UFO link, why this thought had struck me I was not sure, but was full of confidence as I punched out his number. After we had dealt with his reason for contacting me, I told him about the coincidence. Bill responded as I had anticipated. He knew Drury, and they were the same person. As Neville he had been involved in the UFO debate back then, and had then moved on to other matters, the occult, alternative lifestyles, etc. He did not know why Drury had dropped the final E from his given name. I could not help thinking as we hung up that the coincidence that had occurred when I dropped the *UFO Review* on top of the book had been topped by the fact that I should find a message to call a man who had the answer to a question that, while not of world-shattering importance, was distracting.

2 March 1997 Returning last night from a philosophy lecture I settled in bed and read some pages from *Sophie's World* by Jostein Gaardner, a 1995 novel about the history of philosophy. One passage in particular caught my eye because it seemed close to what had been the topic of the lecture. The passage began: 'A former president of India, Sarverpalli Radhakrishnan, said once, "Love they neighbour as thyself because you are your neighbour. It is an illusion that makes you think your neighbour is someone other than yourself."' Shortly after this I put the book aside and went to sleep. Several hours later I awoke and, realizing I was not getting back to sleep, decided to read some more. Instead of picking up *Sophie's World* again, I decided I had had enough of philosophy for one night and reached for the novel *Fair Bride*, whose setting is the Spanish Civil War, written by Bruce Marshall and published in 1953. I opened it at the point I had reached about a week ago. Almost immediately I came across this passage '…the world has been lost to God through men loving their neighbours in the Lord. It is not your neighbour as we would have him that we must love; it is your neighbour as he really is.' The speaker is a church canon who has been condemned to death and is due to go before a firing squad at dawn. Two thought-provoking homilies on the same theme written many years apart and spoken by the followers of two different religions, Hindu and Christian. Still half awake I wondered whether I had heard the first passage at the lecture, or read it in *Sophie's World*. When I confirmed it had been from the first book I had picked up, I found a final coincidence. Each passage appeared on page 107 of their respective books, a right-hand page, each in the bottom quarter of the page.

28 March 1997 Shopping in King St today I ran into a neighbour who told me she had lost her wallet and had spent the past week 'running around organizing new credit cards, etc.' She said she was having difficulty remembering exactly what cards she had and never thought losing them could cause so much trouble. She was in quite a state. Arrived home to find in the mail a renewal notice from Credit Cards Sentinel which holds details of its clients' cards and other documents so that if they are lost it takes only one phone call…I promptly renewed my subscription.

20 April 1997 A few days ago I finished reading Gore Vidal's memoir which he had titled *Palimpsest*. It is, the American writer admits, an obscure word, which he had for years used incorrectly and even mispronounced. Having looked it up he found it apt as a title: 'Paper, parchment, etc. prepared for writing on and wiping out again like a slate.' It is also a parchment which has been written on twice; the original writing having been rubbed out. Vidal comments (page 6) this was 'pretty much what my kind of writer does: starts with life; makes a text, then a re-vision – literally a second seeing, an afterthought, erasing some but not all of the original while writing something new over the first layer of text.' The word *was* obscure and I could not imagine seeing it again in another context for some considerable time. Yet today I was reading this sentence, 'So far then, we have a sort of palimpsest on which a "manufacturers' democracy" has been overwritten on the monarchist constitution.'[1] Pritt's book, unlike Vidal's, is an obscure work. I had found it while undertaking some research for another book.

c. July 1997 Writing an article I used a quote that mentioned the 'Pacific island of Kwajalein'. I had never heard of the island and made a mental note to check the name before sending the article off. But it slipped my mind and, with the story gone and too late to change, I began to worry. Some days later I was skimming through Herman Wouk's *The Caine Mutiny* when I came across, on page 403, this line: 'His dropping of the yellow dye marker off Kwajalein…' I was looking through the book because I thought I had thrown it out years before, then a few days ago was cleaning out the attic and came across it. More than that, it was actually lying on the floor as though saying, 'I believe you are looking for me…'

24 July 1997 Item in the *Daily Telegraph*, page 7. A pedestrian was killed yesterday when he was hit by the side mirror of a truck when he had stepped off a median strip. It reminded me of yesterday, when I was waiting at a pedestrian crossing with my niece in King St, when we heard a loud slapping sound followed by the tinkle of breaking glass. Looking to our left we saw a man standing out from the footpath, holding his hand in pain. A bit further down the road a panel van had pulled up – its side mirror was bent and broken. Somehow the man's hand and mirror had come into contact. The injured man began yelling and advancing on the van whose driver promptly took off.

30 September 1997 Last week a relative took into her care an abandoned dog. Those who had been minding the dog temporarily had given her the name Billy. The relative decided that was no name for a female, thought a bit and came up with Bella, similar-sounding so as not to confuse the dog. In the early hours of Sunday morning, the relative's house caught fire. She was lucky to escape with her life, but Bella was not so lucky and perished. Jackie [my wife] had flown to visit her brother and his three sons on the Saturday. The following day, only hours after Bella had died, their dog was rushed to a veterinary clinic. He was found to have plastic bags in the stomach, the result of someone throwing scraps over the fence without first removing the bag. For a time it looked as though their dog was not going to make it, but she did. Her name: Bella. None of those involved in this anecdote knew of the other dog's existence. They live more than 600 kilometres (375 miles) apart and are seldom, if ever, in contact.

22 October 1997 Reading a story in the newspaper about the lack of literacy skills among students, the news comes on the television – its lead story: lack of literacy skills, etc. The number of times that this happens puts this segment into the 'mere coincidence' category. However, at first glance it would seem not a coincidence to be reading a news story that is the main item of the day only to have it come on the radio or television at the same time. (Another thought on this – the reports I receive from people this happens to often are a fair indicator of the hectic lives we are living: reading and listening at the same time!) It does not happen only with a major story; often it's a minor one, a few paragraphs that are also a footnote to the news bulletin, reached at the same time. When it does happen it has a wonderfully reinforcing quality, prodding one to return to the item and read it more carefully.

23 October 1997 After saying (see previous item) I have not experienced the effect of reading a news item only to have it come on air for some time I noticed it again tonight.

30 October 1997 Checking a quotation from *Julius Caesar* I looked up the Shakespeare entry in *A Dictionary of Famous Quotations* (Pan Books edition, London, 1974). The plays are listed here in alphabetical order, and I looked under 'C'. The play was not there, but my eye was caught by the title of another play, *Cymbeline*. I could not recall this play, certainly not in any detail, and was starting to have the feeling that my classical education was somehow lacking. I went in search of Caesar under 'J'. Later that night I glanced at the arts page of that day's newspaper and read: 'What is old is new again, A new production of *Cymbeline*, one of Shakespeare's more obscure plays, is opening downtown this week…'

31 October 1997 On my way to see a colleague I found myself thinking of my forthcoming wedding anniversary and my thoughts drifted from there back to the early days of our marriage, finally settling on the last place we had lived in England – a flat in Putney. A few minutes later in my colleague's office, she picked up a book from her desk and handed it to me. She had just bought it at a second-hand library sale. 'It's Jilly Cooper's,' she explained, 'about the time she lived in Putney. It's even got a map of Putney Common. You may be able to recognize some things in it.' She knew my wife and I had lived in the London suburb for some time. I did not ask her whether she had put the book aside to show me the previous day when I had arranged my rare visit to her office, or it had been lying on her desk for some time and she had spontaneously chosen to give it to me – I was too confused to ask, I guess. I do know that only a few minutes before, the same London suburb in which we had lived more than 20 years before was on my mind for the first time in ages as I approached the office.

14 November 1997 In the post arrived a cute photo of Judith Oliver's granddaughter, Alison, wearing the full-size Australian rugby union jersey I had sent her when she was born – a joke between Eleanor, Alison's mother, and me. I had been in England when they beat Australia and Eleanor, then heavily pregnant, had taken great delight in ribbing me about the win. I put the photo down next to the newspapers on the table. Then I realized that the front page of the top newspaper on the pile, the *Daily Telegraph,* was carrying a large photo of the Victorian Premier, Jeff Kennet, pulling on an Australian rugby jersey – an exact copy of the one I had given Alison.

19 November 1997 A relative rang to say he was now a father. The inevitable question arose about what they were going to call their new son. They said they had been discussing the name Cowan, but were having problems with the possible unfortunate nickname, Cow, and didn't know whether it should be spelled Cohen, in which case it might be thought the child was Jewish, or Coen, which he said they had found to be the Irish spelling. My suggestion was to say, tongue-in-check, that Cowan was Irish for the Scottish Ken so why not name it in honour of their uncle! The suggestion was not greeted with much enthusiasm. I suspect it may have something to do with Barbie's partner, Ken. Since they came on to the market there's been a distinct lack of new Kens. I did not expect to hear any more of the matter. But last night, I found in a newspaper a reference to 'post-modern filmmakers Joel and Ethan Coen...'

20 November 1997 A further newspaper reference (see previous item), this time to an Eleanor Cairns-Cowan.

2 December 1997 *That* name has appeared again: 1. an article by a Nik Cohn; 2. a young artist in the news, Margaret Coen.

9 December 1997 Sitting enjoying the Sydney Harbour ferry crossing I noticed the woman next to me on the ferry was reading a folder. On its cover: 'Deborah Farr Personnel'. I glanced away from the title and my eye was caught by the name of a moored yacht we were at that moment passing: Farr.

21 December 1997 For days now whenever I have opened a book, magazine or newspaper I have come across the word 'anomalous'. In the early hours this morning, unable to sleep, I picked up *The Australian Review of Books* and my eyes fell on it almost immediately in an article. Before going to bed I had been reading Theodore Roscoe's *The Web of Conspiracy* and came across it on the third line I read. (*Macquarie Dictionary* definition of anomalous: adj., deviating from the common rule, type or form; abnormal, irregular.)

3 January 1998 Watching a skateboard at the beach a few days ago Jackie recalled that the first story she had written as a journalist was about the 'new rage' of skateboarding. The newspaper had used her then teenage brother John (now a mature airline pilot) on his skateboard to illustrate the article. I reminded Jackie that she had mentioned this several times recently. Today she received in the post from a relative a copy of that very article. The relative had been going through some old papers and came across it, deciding on an impulse to send it to Jackie rather than destroy it as he was doing with the other papers. A premonition, a psychic message? The article had certainly been on Jackie's mind. Did her thinking prompt the relative to a clean out his papers and find the article, or was it the other way around? And why should we have noticed a skateboard rider at the beach. Coincidence? I think so.

28 January 1998 I gave a copy of an early coincidence book of mine as a birthday present to Tiffany, a cheerful young waitress in the coffee lounge where Martin and I usually meet once a week. As we talked she mentioned she was moving from her flat at the beachside suburb of Maroubra at the end of the week. Matthew, Martin's nephew visiting from South Australia, offered, 'I'll be at Maroubra on Sunday for the beach handball championships.' Matthew, it turned out, was playing for his state in the event. As the subject was coincidence, we found it amusing, given the number of beaches in Sydney, that two people who had not met before, one a stranger to Sydney, were suddenly linked. Half an hour later, sitting on the train, I opened the *Sydney Morning Herald* and my eyes were drawn straight to the front page, Column 8: an item recalling a ship wreck in 1931 caused when confusion over steering orders had it turning towards the shore 'straight for the Maroubra post office...'

29 January 1998 Jackie's birthday; arranged to meet her in the City to buy her lunch. We decided, for no particular reason except it seemed to be half-way between the places were going to be, to meet outside Angus and Robertson's book shop in the Imperial Arcade. Having met we began discussing where we were going to eat. Glancing round I saw a menu board on the footpath for a coffee lounge in the arcade – its name: Tiffany's (see previous entry). We ate there.

30 January 1998 Watching a film on television, the hero asked the heroine what her favourite film was. *Breakfast at Tiffany's*, she responded (see previous entries).

4 March 1998 For some reason I had a compulsion to spend a few hours this afternoon trying to design a new national flag. Taking a break I turned on the radio to find Parliament had been debating the proposal for a new flag that afternoon and had decided it can only be changed by a national plebiscite. I have never before tried to design a flag.

10 March 1998 A tree maintenance company kept an appointment to give our magnificent Sydney blue gum a check. By coincidence (how else to describe it?) it was a windy day so that it gave the company rep ample opportunity to observe the state of the branches as they flailed about. After some time he pronounced the tree to be in generally good condition, but, pointing to some dying branches, suggested it could do with a bit of pruning. Inspection over, we fell into a discussion which got around to the well-known legend of gum trees shedding their branches without warning. I pointed out I had been living in our house for 17 years and had not seen the tree lose one major branch in that time. He agreed it was unlikely to happen, even with old trees in Sydney with its damp climate, but in drier conditions in the Outback it did happen.

Reassured there was no immediate problem, I arranged for the pruning to take place in a fortnight. After he had left I went out to do some shopping. When I returned half an hour later I happened to glance out of the window and was shocked to see a large, healthy branch had sheared away from the tree, destroying the clothesline and almost covering our small backyard. Had anybody been under the enormous branch they would most certainly have been seriously injured or even killed – gum tree wood is very heavy. The limb that had come away was not one of those marked for pruning. It was replete with fresh green leaves. Surveying the damage I had an eerie feeling that the tree had been listening to our conversation and, in an act of perversity, had decided to prove us wrong.

Coincidence File I

Balance of Nature

In September 1992, Tony Mills of Bishopston, Bristol, enrolled on an advanced course at the Transcendental Meditation (TM) Academy at Roydon Hall, Kent. He was there for one year, paying for the course by working on the staff at the hall. His stipend was £40 sterling a month and his bank account became largely redundant for the year. It fell to £6.94 which he simply left there. In March the following year, he was in touch with his mother, who said that she had received a letter for him from the Inland Revenue. On opening it she found a cheque for £33, which she said she would pay into his account.

Over the following few weeks, he checked the balance of the account, when he had an opportunity to pass a cash machine. It stubbornly remained at £6.94. He decided to ask the bank for a summary of recent transactions to see what had become of the cheque. He was handed a slip at the counter, which showed a credit for 10 March of £33. The next transaction was 16 March, a direct debit from his account to the World Wildlife Fund which he had joined the previous year and totally forgotten the fact that the next year's membership was to be automatically debited. The amount of the debit was exactly £33. Tony says:

> This was the only activity that my account saw within the six months surrounding it. It called into question the very way that I viewed the exchange of money, the role of the Inland Revenue and the deserving quality of the WWF. I and my account seemed to be merely the path that this worthwhile money took to its destination. Some of the other staff at Roydon said that this was a side benefit of TM, and the phrase they have for it is 'nature support'. I will leave you to draw your own conclusions!

Personal Greetings

In 1946, members of the Australian Waratah Rugby Union team that had toured England in 1927–8 held a reunion in a Sydney hotel. They decided to send greetings to Mrs Gordon Shaw, widow of their manager, who had been a generous hostess to many members of their team. After composing a telegram they sent it off to Mrs Shaw, who lived at Bombala in the Snowy River country, hundreds of kilometres south of Sydney. At the end of their reunion they piled into a couple of cars and headed for the seaside suburb of Collaroy to visit Huck Finlay, an old Waratah laid up with illness contracted in a Japanese prisoner-of-war camp. The drivers got lost and pulled up at a street corner while Wally Meagher got out to ask directions. The male occupant of the house they had randomly selected was giving instructions, when a woman's voice called out from inside the house, 'Is that you, Wally?' A moment later out came Mrs Shaw, who was holidaying in Sydney.

Crossing Over

A man whose daughter was killed by a train at a level crossing four years before died at the same spot and the same time. The train was also driven by the same driver, Domenico Serafino.

Vittorio Veroni, 57, used to drive back and forth to work several times a day over the Via Cartoccio crossing near Reggio Emilia, northern Italy, where his daughter Cristina, 19, was killed in 1991. The crossing, unmanned and without a protective bar – the legal norm for Italy's local railways – was equipped with two flashing lights and a bell to warn motorists of approaching trains. The crossing itself was situated near a bend. His daughter had been hit on the crossing on a bright winter morning, and Vittorio drove over the crossing for the last time in his Renault on a sunny morning in November 1995. When the train driver, Domenico Serafino, spotted the car on the line and braked, it was already too late. His engine ploughed into the car and dragged it for several dozen metres.

Suggestions that Vittorio had decided to take his life at the place where his daughter had died were repudiated by his family and the train driver. Investigators said his death was accidental. Vittorio's son, Andrea, 22, described it as an incredible, absurd, fatal coincidence.

Month of Fall

The world's most famous stock market crash was in October 1929. In October 1987 the markets crashed again, as they did in October 1997. In practical terms, however, this gives us very little to go on if we want to predict some future crash.

Identipic (1)

Colin Eves was standing outside his local shopping centre when a man approached and introduced himself as Derek from the local post office. Derek went on: 'I've seen a photo of you. You were looking out over Sydney Harbour.' Derek persuaded Colin to return to the post office where he produced some prints that had been found loose in some incoming mail. They were indeed pictures of Colin. His mother had taken them on a visit to see her son, and had sent them from Harrogate in Yorkshire. (Source: *Sydney Morning Herald*, Column 8, 24 January 1994)

Identipic (2)

Andy Sothern lost his new camera in the mud at the Glastonbury Festival in England. It was returned to him after Kirsty Kelly-Lewin found it, developed the film and recognized him from one of the photographs taken on the dance floor of a club in Nottingham. She had picked up the camera after losing hers in the same way. (Source: Paul Sieveking, Editor, *The Fortean Times*)

Met his Master

Swami Rama tells the story of a German psychiatrist who in 1955 had recurring visions of the Swami's Master and felt this unknown man was calling him to come to India. After seven days, the doctor went to Frankfurt airport and bought a ticket to India. He fell asleep in the airport lounge and missed his flight. When he awoke he saw Swami Rama – who had been sent to Germany to learn aspects of Western psychology – and approached him. The doctor showed the Swami several drawings of the man he had seen in his recurring vision. The Swami immediately recognized them as his Master. The coincidence meeting was fortuitous for both men. The Swami arranged for the doctor to meet the Master and stay with him in India. In turn, the doctor arranged for the Swami to visit different institutes and universities throughout Europe. (Source: *Living with the Himalayan Master*, edited by Swama Ajay, Himalayan International Institute of Yoga Science, 1978, p. 467)

Hail Kolumbus

A Colomb family researcher in England wrote to a former colleague of hers who worked in the University of Western Ontario, Canada, asking for her help in tracking down relatives of Charles Colomb, her Swiss grandfather. The colleague wrote back to say she had received the letter on 12 June 1995 and had looked in the *Ontario Free Press* that day. Her eye was caught by the following small advertisement:

Happy 7th Birthday, MICHELLE LAUREN KOLUMBUS, Love Mum and Dad.

The colleague sent a copy of the notice to the researcher saying it may not be what the researcher wanted...but it was! The researcher had combed telephone directories without success for the name Columbus – a variation of the name Colomb – and did not know there was yet another variation spelt with K. It gave her a whole new field in which to research her ancestors.

Coming Clean

On BBC Radio 4 on 15 February 1996 the 9.00–9.30 a.m. programme was *Face the Facts* in which Audrey Edwards, on hearing of the murder in a prison cell of her mentally ill son, said, 'I immediately started hoovering [vacuum-cleaning] the house from top to bottom.' The programme was followed by *Cause Célèbre* in which 'Monica', after kissing a priest the night before, said, 'I think I got the Hoover out.'

Linked through Pencil

Joseph A. Reif, an American living in Israel, recalls that about 20 years ago a colleague was in London and picked up some teaching materials for him. However, he was going first to the United States before returning to Israel, so he said he would mail the material as soon as he got to New York. While waiting for his turn at the check-in at Heathrow airport, he fell into a conversation with someone in the adjoining queue. The other person turned out to be a neighbour of Reif, who lived in the same apartment building and was on his way back to Israel. The result was that Reif got the materials the next day.

Reif, a teacher at Bar-Ilan University, Israel, has another story of a fortunate encounter. He once had a neighbour from Australia, but about 15 years ago the Australian had moved, and two years later Reif himself moved to a new address. They had not seen one another since. While in Sydney for a conference, he met a cousin of the former neighbour who asked him to pass on his regards when Reif got back to Israel. Naturally Reif agreed, but once back home he could not find the new address or phone number of his former neighbour, nor did he know where he worked.

One day he was driving through the small town of Nes Ziona and saw a billboard depicting a pencil. The billboard had been erected by the local municipality to wish children a good school year. The Hebrew text was: 'Have a successful year of studies'. In the bottom right-hand corner it added, 'First priority for education' and in the bottom left-hand corner, 'With best wishes, Yosi Shevo Mayor'. The reason it caught Reif's eye was his interest in pencils. He corresponds with Professor Henry Petroski, of the Civil Engineering Department at Duke University in North Carolina, who is the author of *The Pencil*, a 400-page book about its history. Reif decided to return the next morning and photograph the billboard to send to the professor. Afterwards, sitting at a nearby bus stop, a car passed by, stopped and the driver got out and offered him a lift to Yehud, a town about 11 kilometres (7 miles) further along the road. As Reif declined the offer the man looked at him more closely and, apologizing, said he looked like someone he knew who lived in Yehud.

As the man was getting back into his car, he asked Reif where he was going; just a few stops down the road, he replied. The man offered to take him. On they way they talked and Reif explained why he had taken the picture of the pencil. The driver said he was an engineer but knew nothing about the history of the pencil. Reif went on to say he had just returned from Australia. The driver responded that he worked in a laboratory with someone from Australia – and it turned out he was the cousin to whom Reif was to pass on the regards. When they stopped the engineer wrote down the details and promised to be Reif's messenger. Reif said that the people he told the story to in the following week all denied it was just coincidence, but rather that it was a deliberate act of divine will to help him finish the good deed that he had set out to do. But he had doubts. He felt some of them had made the comment simply because that was the 'thing' to say. From his knowledge of these people they did not run their lives with a constant reference to the Almighty and they probably would admit that pure coincidence was a more likely answer.

Keeping in Touch

Mrs Pat Adcock of Breaston, Derby, is an only child and has more relatives in Germany than in England. She does have a first cousin, however, who lives with his wife in Grassington, Yorkshire. Pat's husband chose Norfolk as a venue for a short holiday. On their way to Cromer, Pat suggested they pull off the road to eat at a pub before going into the town. As they were walking back towards the pub a car drew up and her only relative in England, Len, was inside. He asked, 'What are you doing here?'

Len and his wife had been visiting some friends in the region and had been on their way to Cromer for lunch when they so unexpectedly came across his cousin. They spent a few pleasant and unexpected hours together. Pat was left wondering at the odds of them being on the coast road at exactly the same moment.

Some time later Pat was composing the above anecdote in a letter to me when a letter arrived from Len's wife telling her they were on holiday. The two generally communicate by phone and Pat found it strange, not only that she received a letter with the information in it, but that it should arrive on the very day after she had spent the previous evening mentally re-living the earlier strange experience. Pat is obviously an aware person and says she has experienced many coincidences in her own life, many of them involving her friends, similar to those related in *Coincidences: Chance or Fate?*.

Self-Admission

Steve Ford searched frantically for his beloved dog, Jo Jo, a Labrador retriever, after being told he had been hit by a car outside his home. Unable to find him, he called the Audubon Animal Hospital to tell them that Jo Jo had been injured and that he would be bringing him in, if he could find him. But Jo Jo had already admitted himself. Following the accident Jo Jo had apparently run about a mile from Ford's home to the animal hospital. He suffered bruises but no broken bones. Jo Jo stays at the Audubon when his family is away. (Source: news item in the *Herald-Leader,* Lexington, Kentucky)

Like Father, Like Son?

When a young service station attendant in Pueblo, Colorado, accepted a cheque payment for petrol, his life changed dramatically. Noticing the signature John Garcia on the cheque he asked the man who presented it, 'Were you ever in the Air Force?'

'Yes.'

'Were you ever in Thailand?' John nodded.

'Did you ever have a son?'

At that moment realization came over John: the attendant was Nueng Garcia, his son, whom he had not seen for 27 years. In 1969, John, then a US serviceman, had left Thailand when Nueng was three months old. John lost touch with him when Nueng's mother started seeing another man. Nueng later settled in the USA, but the strange part about the reunion was John's comment that he had never used the petrol station where his son worked before, he was not even low on fuel and he hardly ever paid for anything with a cheque. (Source: this report appeared in various publications in early May 1996)

Sticks up for Job

Onkar Singh works the midnight to dawn shift in the Circle K convenience store in Seattle. He likes the job and has no plans to give it up, despite the fact that within a year he was the victim of six of the seven hold-ups at the store. In two of the robberies he was roughed up and in the others he was threatened with guns, but never seriously hurt.

Speech is Golden
A woman who started out in life with a reading problem overcame it to graduate with honours in arts from Queensland University then began further studies to become an academic lecturer. Her name: Vicki-Ann Speechley-Golden.

Double Life
In 1997 two biographies of a famous film director were published at the same time, both titled *Stanley Kubrick: A Biography*. HarperCollins published John Baxter's book and Donald I. Fine/Penguin Vincent LoBrutto's version.

The Kryptonite Curse
The comic book story of *Superman* has brought anything but light relief to those who have been involved in it since its inception in 1938. The two creators of *Superman*, Jerry Siegel and Joe Shuster, never saw any of the millions of dollars that were made from the comic books, films and television programmes of their superhero. Both aged 17, they sold their rights for a pittance and in 1978 were discovered living in penury.

The actor Kirk Alyn, who played Superman in the 1940s Saturday matinee serial, claimed that it had ruined his career. He never got another job in Hollywood. The grim coincidences continued. George Reeves, who fought for Truth, Justice and the American Way on television's *Adventures of Superman* in the 1950s, was finished when the hit series finished after six years. He too was unable to find work. He took up professional wrestling. In 1959 he committed suicide.

Christopher Reeve, who donned the costume in the 1970s and 1980s, was thrown from his horse in 1995, broke his neck and ended up on a respirator and in a wheelchair. His accident followed years in which his career had been crippled by typecasting as the 'man of steel'. Margot Kidder, who co-starred as Lois Lane in all four of Reeve's *Superman* films, damaged her spinal cord in 1990 in a car accident while filming a television series. Confined to a wheelchair for two years, she was unable to work and her life declined into painful poverty.

John Haynes Newton and Gerard Christopher played the caped crusader and his son for the 1980s series *Superboy* and have both since disappeared from the limelight. Marlon Brando, who was enticed out of retirement to play Superman's father in Reeve's original 1978 film, was also hit by the Kryptonite Curse. In 1995 his daughter Cheyenne hanged herself, while five years earlier his son, Christian, had been convicted of murder for shooting Cheyenne's boyfriend. Richard Pryor, the villain in Superman III, was struck down soon after filming was completed with multiple sclerosis and, like Reeve and Kidder, confined to a wheelchair. Pierre Spengler, the producer of the four *Superman* films, was made a bankrupt.

Fax Faux Pas

Tory government members were delighted when an article attacking the Labour leader Tony Blair appeared in a London newspaper in the pre-election days of 1995, under the by-line of Bryan Gould, a former member of the Labour shadow cabinet. The *Evening Standard* headlined the article 'Tony Blair's fatal lack of vision'. Among its criticism was the claim Blair's only thought was a 'desire to please the public'. It appears that, with the deadline approaching, an executive was waiting by the fax machine for Gould's article to appear – but at that very moment an unsolicited article, also by coincidence about Blair, appeared on the machine and was rushed into print. A further coincidence, the writer of the piece that went out under Gould's name was Nick Howard, the son of Britain's then Conservative Home Secretary Michael Howard. The newspaper ran a front-page apology and Tony Blair's critics who had leapt on the article with such glee were forced into silence. Nick Howard explained that his father had nothing to do with the piece; it was all his own work. Blair won the ensuing election by a big majority.

Case of the Three Doctors

The names of three of the doctors who attended mystery writer Agatha Christie towards the end of her life were Stabb, Carver and Quick.

Quentin Que?

Standing in the corridor of the ABC television studios, a sound recordist was telling a colleague he had just bought a house in Quentin Street in a seaside suburb of Sydney. The friend did not hear the street name and asked him to repeat it. 'Quentin!' he stressed raising his voice. At the moment one of the ABC's best-known reporters was walking past – Quentin Dempster. Hearing his name being uttered with such emphasis he swung around somewhat startled, waved his hand uncertainly to acknowledge what he took to be a greeting, then walked briskly on. The embarrassed sound man had never met Dempster. (Author's note: I was still chuckling over the story when I picked up a book that night that I had put on my bedside table some days before but had not until then had a chance to read. The title of the book was *London Diary: The Story of an American Reporter's Experience in London during the Blitz*. Its author: Quentin Reynolds.)

Washed Out

A performance of the musical *Singing in the Rain* was cancelled at Edinburgh's Playhouse Theatre after it was flooded with hundreds of litres of water from a leaking sprinkler system.

Going Together

Salvatore Silvio and his wife, Maria, met in Sicily when he was eight and she was five. They married in 1933. In their 62 years of marriage they were inseparable and went into a nursing home together, although they stayed on different floors. Maria, who had been suffering from dementia, lapsed into a coma, but their sons decided not to tell Salvatore to avoid upsetting him. Still without knowing of his wife's condition, he too went into a coma, although he had shown no signs of ill-health. Neither recovered. Salvatore died 15 minutes after his wife. A relative commented that they had always said they would go together.

Joint Celebrations

A Mr and Mrs Cummins were celebrating their wedding anniversary in a restaurant when they realized the pair behind them, a Mr and Mrs Beasley, were also celebrating theirs. They got talking and, as the conversation progressed, discovered they were all married on the same date, spent their honeymoons at the same resort at the same time and had celebrated anniversaries at another resort at the same time. The couples went halves on a Lottery ticket. (Source: © *Daily Telegraph*, 26 April 1995)

Greens Against Pork Barrelling

A Green Party candidate for the Australian Parliament was a Mark Berriman, who is also a vegetarian. The Green Scientist for the year in 1992 was Professor Martin Green.

Hoisted by their Own Petard

Six delegates representing members of the Lift Operators Union entered a lift on their way to negotiations on the 35th floor of a Melbourne office building. After rising a few floors the lift jammed. In London at a conference given by the Electricity Association a few months after the above 1995 incident, there was a power failure.

First, First Aid

In October 1995, Michael Springer saved the life of a baby by catching her when she fell from a third-floor window in Philadelphia. Seconds before he had turned a street corner to see the 17-month-old toddler dangling from the window and whimpering. Michael, aged 45, told reporters that this was not the first time he had come to somebody's aid. In 1980 he had comforted a man who had been shot inside a pool hall until paramedics arrived. In 1989 he had done a similar thing after coming across the victim of a shooting. In 1995 he had stemmed a stabbing victim's wounds until police came.

Ghost at the Helm

In *Coincidences: Chance or Fate?* I told strange tales of ghostly presences that appeared to bring comfort and hope to men whose lives were in peril. The first concerned three British officers trekking across Turkey after escaping from a prisoner-of-war camp in World War I. All swore they were joined by a mysterious stranger whose very presence encouraged them to push on against the odds. In the second incident Antarctic explorer Sir Ernest Shackleton and two companions crossed South Georgia Island in a desperate attempt to find help for their marooned party. All felt they had been joined by a fourth person whose presence was reassuring.

Writing in the *Daily Telegraph* (13 April 1997), columnist Dr James Le Fanu claims that there are dozens of other similar cases of shipwrecked sailors, polar explorers and mountain climbers in which a guardian angel seems to have joined them when their lives were in danger. He concluded that their appearance is more ghostly than hallucinatory.

Joshua Slocum (born in Novia Scotia, 20 February 1844) was the first man in recorded history to circumnavigate the world single-handedly in a small boat.

Conditions for solo sailors were very different in 1895, when Slocum set out on his voyage, from those enjoyed by present-day sailors. There was no radio or aircraft to come to his rescue. Any sailor who undertook offshore voyages was literally on his own. Slocum set out from Boston harbour in an old boat (built *c.* 1800) he had re-built himself. The *Spray* was 36 feet (11 metres) in length with a beam of 14 feet (4 metres) and a gross tonnage of about 13 tons. At the start of his voyage the weather was fine and he reached the Azores after an 18-day crossing of the Atlantic. Slocum relates in his book of the voyage, *Sailing Alone Around the World*, that shortly after leaving the Azores bound for Gibraltar he found himself doubled up with cramps. He blamed his condition on the plentiful supply of plums supplied by the locals together with a white cheese given him by the Americana Consul-General. He was sailing into heavy seas and between bouts of pain managed to double-reef the mainsail and set the *Spray* on course before going below where he collapsed on the cabin floor in great pain. Slocum did not know how long he lay on the floor, but when he came to, looking out onto the companionway, he saw to his amazement a tall man at the helm, his rigid hands holding the spokes of the wheel in a vice-like grip. With his large red cap and shaggy black whiskers, Slocum took him to be a pirate.

The apparition had Slocum forgetting both the storm and his illness. As though he had read Slocum's thoughts, the stranger said, 'I have come to do you no harm. I am one of Columbus's crew. I am the pilot of the *Pinta* [one of the three ships under the command of Columbus when he found the New World] come to aid you. Lie quiet, *señor* captain, and I will guide your ship tonight...You will be all right tomorrow.'

That night Slocum lay on a mattress in the cabin listening as heavy seas crashed over the sloop washing away everything movable. Next morning he found the *Spray* had kept on a steady course and made 90 miles (150 kilometres). By noon the gale was moderating, the sun appeared and the worst of his illness had worn off. He was dozing on deck when his friend from the night before re-appeared. 'You did well last night to take my advice,' he said, 'and if you would I should like to be with you often on the voyage for the love of adventure alone.' Finishing what he had to say, he again doffed his cap and disappeared as mysteriously as he came. 'I awoke much refreshed and with the feeling that I had been in the presence of a friend and a seaman of vast experience.' Was this a case of hallucination brought on by Slocum's illness, together with the stress of the perilous situation in which he found himself? A clue perhaps lies in the fact that he says some pages later he was reading Columbus's book of voyages at the time of the incident. Can we suppose his delirious mind, under considerable strain, fixed on the book to conjure up an imaginary rescuer? Possibly, except for the fact the somebody or something guided his ship safely through that wild night, giving Slocum, who should have been at the helm, time to recover in the comparative comfort of his cabin. Not only to recover, but to make good progress. Few fevered hallucinations are that helpful. A clue appears to lie in his final words describing the experience, a 'feeling that I had been in the presence of a friend and a seaman of vast experience', for it mirrors the feelings of the other men in peril who had been comforted by a ghostly presence.

Slocum does not report any further visitation from the Columbus helmsman, but notes that he made the run across the Indian Ocean of 2,700 nautical miles in 23 days, of which he spent only three hours at the wheel, a remarkable achievement in the days before self-steering gear. Was he again helped by the ghostly helmsman who 'liked' to be with him? (Sources: Joseph Slocum, *Sailing Alone Around the World*; based on 1985 version, Ashford Press, Hampshire, pp. 241–5. Further material from the *Daily Telegraph*: articles by Walter Sullivan, 8 September 1995, and Margot Pitkin, 9 September 1996)

Opportune Omen

An Australian man in his forties was strolling along Bay Street in the Melbourne suburb of Brighton when he bumped into a Lottery sign. He took it as an omen and bought a ticket, although not a regular player. He won $A5 million.

Personal Calls

Columnist Scott Ellis ran an item about Victoria Evans, who had decided to phone her sister Sally, but had misdialled the number. She ended up on the phone to a total stranger who lives about six streets from the intended house. By some astronomical odds, Sally was visiting the house Victoria had accidentally dialled. The following day in his column Scott followed the story up with a second item. A similar thing had happened to another reader, Bill Orr, who, while working at a city cinema, was taking a break in a nearby milk bar. He had been rung by a friend who had misdialled and found himself connected to the milk bar where Bill was at that very moment. On the third day Scott had to call a halt. 'It seems there are dozens of people who have had amazing phone coincidences to report,' he observed The *most* amazing of the last batch of reports came from Jeff Etcell. A few years back his boss at work was trying to phone a branch office when he somehow got a crossed line. He found himself listening to a conversation between his wife and his daughter. (Source: © *Daily Telegraph*: 28, 29 and 30 August 1996) chapter twelve

Coincidence File II

Death of a Princess

A number of coincidences of varying degrees of significance surrounded the tragic death in August 1997 of Diana, Princess of Wales.

The film *Diana and Me* was on the point of release when Diana was killed. The film concerns an obsessive fan who teams up with a paparazzo to pursue Diana. In reality Diana died in Paris fleeing the paparazzi.

Also held back from release was the book *Royal Blood*, which tells of an extremist right-wing plan to murder Diana in order to prevent her from marrying a Muslim. At the time of her death Diana was said to be on the point of announcing her engagement to Dodi Al-Fayed, the son of Egyptian billionaire Mohammed Al-Fayed, and a Muslim.

Kylie Minogue held back from release her new album *Impossible Princess*.

Diana died violently in the car crash in Paris, a few days after the violent death of fashion designer Versace. On the day of her funeral, 6 September 1997, Mother Teresa died in Calcutta, the two stories competing for space in news bulletins and newspapers. All three were known throughout much of the world, and it is often the case when one famous person dies for a cluster to follow. Of course, it does not need to be a series of VIP deaths, engagements, falls from grace, plane crashes etc. Clustering effects occur at all levels of society. However, in this case each of their deaths was a front-page story. Furthermore Diana linked the three as a person known to the other two.

Half-mast

There was some surprise, even indignation, that Buckingham Palace, the Queen's residence in London, was one of the few buildings not flying a flag at half-mast. Eventually the Queen bowed to public pressure – to some extent – by ordering that a flag be hoisted as a sign of

134

mourning, but to the top of the pole as flags are not, by tradition, flown at half-mast over Buckingham Palace. However, as it was being raised, it stuck half-way up the pole and efforts to move it further proved fruitless.

Comforting Hand

Almost seven years to the day before Diana's death, Dean Woodward, a computer operator from Nottingham, was involved in a horrific car crash. At the time Diana was visiting Prince Charles at Nottingham's Queen's Medical Centre where he was recovering from a broken elbow sustained while playing polo. She emerged from one visit to find Dean's mother crying in a corridor. Moved by her distress, over the following four weeks Diana spent time at Dean's bedside in the intensive care unit, stroking his brow, squeezing his hand and offering words of comfort to his family. Dean came out of his coma, but Diana kept in touch and sent him a get-well card. What had led Diana to show so much compassion for a stranger? Dean said that Diana had told the family that, after seeing his mum crying in the hospital, bells started ringing in her head and she knew she had to come and see him. (Source: *Daily Mail*, 2 September 1997)

Some may see all of the above incidents as products of mere 'chance'. However, this negates the exploration of the very real depth of this subject. We can accept as 'chance' the release of films, books and albums about Diana – such was her fame that creative imaginations were bound to be stirred by her life. However, some might say that these productions were predicated on neither her life, nor her death and that the creators drew their inspiration from the universal mind where all knowledge dwells.

The habit of analysing events that impact on society in general, such as the death of Diana, can help us reveal the role of coincidences in general.

Luck Links Newman and Redford

Australian veteran television personality Peter Luck was travelling to England in 1972 to take up a Churchill Fellowship. He stopped off by chance in Cannes where that year's film festival was in full swing. Through a set of circumstances he found himself having lunch at a table where one of the other guests was actor Robert Redford. At that time Redford was receiving widespread international acclaim for his role in the film *Butch Cassidy and the Sundance Kid* in which he co-starred with Paul Newman. As the afternoon progressed, the other guests drifted away from the table until Luck and Redford found themselves alone. They were getting on well and talked on over several cups of coffee.

Shortly after they had parted, Luck was waiting at the reception desk of his hotel to collect his key. A woman standing next to him spoke with an Australian accent. At that time few Australians attended the festival so Peter greeted her. She turned out to be a journalist, also passing through Cannes for no particular reason. She had been working for *The Australian* newspaper back home and was hoping to land a job in London. She asked him what he had been doing. The young Luck enjoyed casually dropping the line: 'Oh, I've just spent the afternoon having a long lunch with Robert Redford.' She responded with a look that was a mixture of envy and doubt.

Luck's story moves on to New York some months later, where he stopped on his way back to Australia having completed his scholarship. He was taken to a party by some acquaintances and found himself in the company of Paul Newman and his wife, Joanne Woodward. He naturally mentioned his meeting with Redford in Cannes.

The next day he boarded a bus and found himself sitting next to the reporter he had last seen in Cannes. Unable to find work in London, she had moved to New York. She recalled their last meeting, in a manner that suggested she still thought he had been kidding her about Redford, then asked what he had been up to in New York. Luck took a deep breath and began, 'You're not going to believe this...' She didn't.

Taken at the Flood
The appearance of John Barry on 12 April 1997 at Joseph-Beth Booksellers in Cincinnati to promote his new book, *Rising Tide: The Great Mississippi Flood of 1927 and How it Changed America*, was preceded by the flooding of the Ohio river. The store took advantage of the coincidence to help publicize both the book and the Red Cross's efforts to aid flood victims in Cincinnati. (Source: *Publisher's Weekly*, 7 April 1997)

Two Stars Fade
Two of Hollywood's most famous actors, James Stewart and Robert Mitchum, died within hours of one another.

Alliterative Poll
The first three names and addresses on an electoral roll appeared as follows:

Adams, Arthur, Arundel Ave, Allandale
Burns, Bernard, Brighton Boulevard, Bondi
Campbell, Charles, Carlton Crescent, Carrington.

Like Fails to Meet Like

When Japanese television programme researcher Fujiko Oksuka made a new acquaintance, she soon realized there were many things about him that reminded her of a close female friend of hers. She resolved they should meet. Some time later she was having dinner with the man and broached the subject. Just as she was saying, 'I really think you should meet my friend,' she glanced towards the door of the restaurant to see her friend entering, unfortunately with another man. (At the time of writing she was planning to organize another meeting with just the three of them present.)

Birthday Surprise

When she was in Canada, Dorothy Herron rang her friend Martin Cochrane in Australia on a whim. They had not exchanged a word for nearly a year. Martin assumed Dorothy was ringing him because it was his birthday. But Dorothy admitted she had not known this. She had rung on an impulse. Dorothy said, 'That's funny, because I did the same thing to Kathy just a month ago – rang her because I had not spoken to her for ages – and it was her birthday.'

A Few Records

A caller to Stan Thompson's show on ABC radio station, Mount Gambier, related that the previous day he had been driving back from Adelaide at high speed towing a caravan he had just bought, when a wheel came off the van. Apparently the wheel nuts had not been properly tightened. This had all the makings of a very dangerous situation. At the very least the axle should have sheared as it hit the road surface, but in this million to one case, at the precise moment that the wheel parted company with the axle, the U-bolt holding the axle dropped neatly into the top of a soft drink can that had been on the road. It prevented the axle from coming into contact with the road surface and kept the car on an even keel. The driver was able to replace the wheel, screw the nuts on properly and proceed.

The story does not end there. After appearing as a guest myself on the show, I was making idle conversation with Stan, who told me of a coincidence that had happened at precisely that moment the previous day. He had been interviewing a leading Adelaide anaesthetist who had made the point that the days of using gas and drips onto a face mask were virtually gone. These days most anaesthetics were given by needle. 'As we finished talking I reached for a piece of music to play,' Stan went on, 'and you'll never guess what I put my hand on: *Classical Gas*.' We laughed, and as he had done the previous day with his guest about to leave, Stan reached out for some music. He glanced at the disc, then he lapsed into silence. 'Now you'll never guess what's happened – what do you think I've just selected – *Axle Eight*! This is incredible.'

Lunch Lurch

Some years ago when Kimberley Kijanowski was a freshman at the University of Illinois she was having lunch with some other students in the cafeteria. One of them, Sam, began telling an amusing story, waving his hand about for emphasis. Suddenly Kimberley sensed he should stop doing it and told him so. Sam ignored her and the others scowled at her interruption. Kimberley could not give an explanation as to why she was so insistent and Sam proceeded with the story and the gestures. A few moments later another student, James, came into view carrying a tray loaded with food. She knew with a certainly she could not explain what was about to happen and called out to warn James, who also ignored her. Turning to Sam she begged him to just stop for a moment, but it was too late. James was passing Sam's back just as his arm shot out once again, only this time it hit the tray spilling its contents over the floor. In the confusion her roommate turned to her: 'How did you know that was going to happen?' she asked, amazed and impressed as she at last realized why Kimberley had been so insistent.

Handy Bookmark

At a dinner party in London, Judith Oliver found herself sitting next to a man who, in the course of their conversation, said he had once been a Member of Parliament. Judith had worked in the Houses of Parliament at Westminster for some time during the 1980s, but she could not recall him. A few days later, she got out her 1987 edition of *Dod's Parliamentary Companion*, which has more than 2,000 pages containing the biographical details of all 650 MPs and the more than 1,100 peers in the House of Lords. It had been at least ten years since Judith had last used the book, which had become dated as a result of the 1987 elections. It fell open at the page where she had long ago inserted a bookmark and the first name and picture she saw, on the top of the right-hand page, was that of the former MP.

Self-Protection

As he was leaving his house for the railway station, James Martin picked a book at random from his bookshelf to read on the train journey. Passing through the local shopping centre he was held up by two Bible-wielding young men who told him they wanted to talk to him about God. Martin soon had them retreating when he produced his book and held it up to them. Its title: *Why I'm Not a Christian,* by George Bernard Shaw.

Sympathy Pains

In the outer Sydney suburb of Camden, Wendy Souter was awoken in the early hours by a sharp stinging sensation in her leg. She thought she had been bitten by a spider. But when she examined her leg she found no sign of a bite and no spider in the bedclothes. The pain soon disappeared. Before falling back to sleep she noted the time on her bedside clock: 2.35 a.m. She had been awake some five minutes. The next day she received a call from her daughter who lived many kilometres away. She told Wendy that she too had been awoken in the early hours by some instinctual need to check on her baby. Torch in hand she opened the nursery door and the beam immediately fell on a deadly funnel-web spider on the floor advancing towards the baby's cot. The time her daughter noted was 2.30 a.m.

Double Tragedy

On 24 October 1996 a news report told of how a girl, aged 15, found the body of her father, who had committed suicide. The girl phoned her mother at work to tell her. The mother's colleagues offered to drive her home to her hysterical daughter. En route the car crashed, killing the mother.

Gold Strike

A coal miner in the Burragorang Valley of New South Wales was driving his tractor into the shaft when he caught sight of an object glinting in the black waste on the sides of the shaft. He stopped the tractor and recovered the object – a golden wedding ring. Although there were no markings on it to identify its owner, the miner (who did not want to be named) knew the moment he picked it up that it belonged to his father, who was also a miner. Some days later he saw his father and asked him if he had lost anything recently. The father replied that he had indeed lost his wedding ring, whereupon the son was able to produce it.

Fluke finds of lost articles are not uncommon, as coincidence-minded readers know. But what gives this story an added dimension is the son's certainty of the ownership of the ring. He was at a loss to explain his feelings. Naturally, from his tractor he had been unable to see the ring in any detail. We can speculate that maybe, after examining it, there were certain flaws or subtle peculiarities about the ring which the son, without being consciously aware he was doing so, had noted over the years. There are obvious differences in even plain golden rings such as width, quality and colouring etc. Others may propose another explanation, that the ring itself had absorbed enough of the father's aura, so that when the son first glimpsed it he was driven by the emanations coming from the ring to rescue it.

Born to Brew

The licensee of the Edinboro Castle Hotel, Bathurst, is a John L. Brew.

Snow Children

In January 1967 Christine Guillemet was born in a snowbound car in France. Her mother had been unable to make it to hospital because of the weather. Thirty years later in January 1997, with France in the grip of some of its worst winter weather for a century, Christine gave birth in her own snowbound home, near the very spot where she had been born. The weather conditions had also made it impossible for her to reach hospital.

Coincidence Coincidence

Billy Bryson notes in his best-selling book *Notes from a Small Island* that in the early 1980s he was working as a freelance journalist in his spare time and had decided to write an article on remarkable coincidences. In his research he gathered a large amount of information about scientific studies, probability and the like, but he had not come up with enough examples to fill out the 1,500-word piece. So he wrote to the magazine to whom he had proposed the idea saying he would not be able to do it. Leaving the letter on top of his typewriter with the intention of posting it the following day, he went to work at *The Times*. In the lift he saw an announcement of a sale of books sent to the newspaper for review. Pushing through the milling crowd of fellow journalists, the first book that caught his eye was: *Remarkable True Coincidences*. He had found his source. When he opened it the first story that caught his eye concerned a man named Bryson. (Source: Bill Bryson, *Notes from a Small Island*, Black Swan paperback edition, London, 1996, page 205)

War Tag

A group of Australians who had fought in Vietnam were back in the country, after 30 years, inspecting the old battle zone. A teenage Vietnamese boy approached them at one village and singled out one of the veterans. He had a serviceman's dog tag around his neck and explained his father had given it to him to sell to the Australians. The veteran looked at one side of the tag and said, 'Oh, that's my blood group.' He turned it over and saw his own name and number printed on it.

Sticky Wicket
Arthur Snow, aged 91, was driving his Metro car when it careered down an embankment at an isolated bridge over the River Avil, near Minehead, Somerset. The car ended up on its side and Arthur was pinned to his seat by the steering wheel. He lay there for more than 30 hours, his cries for help going unheard. In a last desperate attempt to attract attention he began waving his walking stick from the window and it was this latter effort that saved him. Tim Heley, a contract gardener, had decided on the spur of the moment to mow the grass at an empty house near the spot where Arthur lay trapped. As he worked, Tim noticed the car but dismissed it as abandoned – until he saw the walking stick sticking up like a periscope. Tim said he had only gone to that particular house by chance. He could have chosen any day of the week to go there. Had he left it until the end of the week, Arthur would almost certainly not have survived. (Source: *Daily Mail*, 28 August 1996)

Forget-me-not
The name of the woman in charge of PR for the Alzheimer's Awareness Week in Victoria, Australia, was Tasha Forget.

All Legal
A Sligo law firm: Argue and Phibbs.

Wedding Cake
Engagement notice in the *Latrobe Valley Express*: Sultana–Cake. Shirley Sultana is happy to announce the engagement of her daughter Kerren to Paul, second son of Edith and Greg Cake.

Cleaned Up
New South Wales Lotto promoted a $9-million draw with advertisements featuring a group of happy prize-winning office cleaners. Among the three winners was a syndicate of cleaners from the Optus office in North Sydney.

Lucky for Some
Irish tourist Joe Paterson broke an arm and both legs when he fell over

a cliff near Italy's Lake Como. He had bent down to pick up a 'lucky' four-leaved clover when he lost his balance.

Bone of Contentment
When Nora Van den Camp of Simpson, Australia, married Andrew Bone in 1994 she became Nora Bone.

Never Volunteer
London police were looking for people to use in an identity parade and randomly selected several from the street. One of the volunteers, who was not told the purpose of the line-up, was quite happy to take part for the £7.50 fee. Unfortunately for him witnesses identified him as one of a group of men involved in an assault and robbery. The unlucky volunteer later pleaded guilty to the charge.

Last Rites
The Rev. James Alexander, 83, came out of retirement to conduct the funeral service of his old friend Gertrude Watson, who had died aged 86. As he was going through the ritual he suddenly clutched at his heart, collapsed on the lectern and died.

Work Hazards
In *Coincidences: Chance or Fate?* (p. 145) I told the story of four sales-women who, after sitting in an office chair at the Cardiff Arts market-ing office, became pregnant. The female staff finally insisted that the seat be given to a man. A similar phenomenon has occurred at a super-market in Kent, where nine women who worked at cash till number 13 over a period of ten months became pregnant. Perhaps they should follow the example of the Cardiff women and insist a man work that cash till.

Happier Holiday
Alec and Vivienne, a couple from Fremantle, Western Australia, were on holiday in London, thanks to a $A700,000 win in the State Lottery, when news came through that they had won again – this time $A1,200,000. The couple said they planned to continue their foreign holiday. Lottery officials said they had beaten odds of 64 million-to-one to win twice within six months. (See the Appendix, p. 229, for an 'expert' opinion on the chances of someone winning the Lottery twice.)

Much in Common

When he was aged 25, Rae Cummings met Estelle and later discovered they not only had similar surnames but shared the same birthday, 20 November 1917. The two decided that would be the perfect day of the month on which to marry. The omens were a pointer to a happy marriage of more than 50 years.

Dutch Shout

Strong ties are often developed in adversity and none was stronger than that forged between two youngsters, Bill Harsveld and John van der Rest, in World War II. As the Japanese rolled southward the two boys were imprisoned in the city of Semarang Java in the Dutch East Indies (now Indonesia). Bill was just 11 years of age when he was separated from his family – his much younger brother, sister, and mother were placed in a separate prison camp, while his father was sent to the infamous Burma Railway as a slave labourer. Bill and John became inseparable and managed to escape just before the end of the war. Both were eventually repatriated to Holland where they parted company for the first time in four years of hardship.

Bill was reunited with his family, all of whom had managed to survive their years of privation. He was conscripted for national service while John joined the Dutch Navy. Bill became engaged and migrated with his fiancée Maria to New Zealand. There they settled and 38 years passed without a word from John.

In 1994, John's sister Zusje Tavenier and her husband decided to visit New Zealand and John asked her to try to establish contact with Bill. Zusje said she thought that would be a hard task as the country was some nine times the size of Holland, with a population of 3.5 million. By the time they began their caravan holiday, Zusje and husband had put thoughts of locating Bill at the back of their minds. Camping at a remote North Island resort, Waikeremoana, on the shore of a large lake, they wanted to make a booking for another motor/caravan ground in Taupo, also in the central North Island. Zusje found the only public telephone in the area and picked up the telephone directory. As she did so it slipped from her hand and fell open on the floor. She bent to retrieve it, and the name 'Harsveld' seemed to leap off the page. It took her some time to overcome her feeling of incredulity that the book should have fallen open on the one page that contained the name of her brother's war-time friend, which was also a rare name in New Zealand. She had still not recovered fully by the time she dialled the number. Maria Harsveld answered and asked Zusje to speak in Dutch so she could understand her. Zusje asked whether her husband was Bill Harsveld, previously of Holland and a friend of John van der Rest? Once this was confirmed, their holiday schedule was quickly re-arranged and the two couples met in the Harsvelds' home town, Hamilton, also on the North Island. During the meeting, Bill rang his old prison partner and they spoke for the first time in nearly 50 years. They have kept in touch ever since.

Scales of Justice

Looking for a project with which to occupy himself, David P. Nugent decided to restore his rusty old set of bathroom scales. He sanded them back to the bare metal and then painted them bright yellow. He was pleased with the result; they looked brand new and the problem of the rust rubbing off all over the bathroom floor had been solved. But there was another problem he knew he just could not overcome, no matter how much effort he might put into it: the scales measured in imperial rather than metric. The following day he was removing some card-board from the communal rubbish bin to make room for other rubbish when to his surprise he found a practically new set of bathroom scales – with a metric measure. Putting it down to an act of God he gave his old scales to the St Vincent de Paul Society.

Luck of the Draw

Colin Rowley was about to move to a new town and decided to seek the advice of a clairvoyant. The clairvoyant foretold of a new car for Colin, smaller than the XB station waggon he was presently driving, and its colour would be blue. Colin's response was cynical: 'Oh yeah. With what money? I'm broke.' The clairvoyant could not offer him any advice on that problem. Some years later Colin was at an Australian Rules Football game in Perth, Western Australia. Just before three-quarter time he was in a queue for a kiosk when a teenage girl began working her way along the line selling raffle tickets – the prize was a car. Colin's financial situation had not improved as much as he would have liked in the intervening years, nevertheless he bought one $A2 ticket. Ten minutes later the winning ticket number was announced: 3585. Colin looked down at his ticket: 3584. He had missed by one winning a new Ford Laser, whose colour was blue and smaller than the car he was still driving. To add insult to injury, the first prize was not claimed. Colin was glum for weeks afterwards.

Death Notice

In 1992 an old friend of Jackie Deigan of Chelmsford, Essex, died. The friend was in her eighties and had been one of Jackie's teachers. Two days later a handbag her late friend had bought her 15 years earlier fell to bits.

Life Song

Veteran performer Jade Hurley was on stage singing *Life Begins at 40* from his album *Life, You Wouldn't Be Dead for Quids*, when he collapsed with a heart attack. Jade survived.

You Wouldn't Read About it

Book editor Carl Harrison-Ford had been feeling bad for some weeks about the fact that work pressure had prevented him assessing a novel which had been sent to him some months before by a would-be novelist. He was about to start a six-month residency in a college, and resolved to pack the manuscript and work on it while he was away. He picked up the hefty bundle from where it had stood for so long on his study floor and placed it on his desk. He was just looking at the first page as the phone rang. The caller was the hopeful novelist, who explained he had just finished a project that had kept him so occupied for months he had not had a chance to even think about his manuscript. It had popped into his mind that morning. 'The good news is that I have it in front of me at this very moment...' Carl began.

chapter thirteen

Coincidence File III

Cover Story

In *TIME Magazine* on 7 June 1963, the cover story was the death of Pope John XXIII whose short reign will be mainly remembered for calling the historic Ecumenical Council in 1962. The following week the magazine's lead letter was from a Judith Weber of Milwaukee: 'I just received my copy of *TIME Magazine* (7 June) and I couldn't believe my eyes. Is it just a quirk of fate or coincidence that Vol. 81, No. 23 has on its cover Pope John the 23rd, who died at the age of 81?'

Safety Signs

The day after Thanksgiving, Jill Thomas of Jacksonville, Florida, and her son Jimmy, aged 6, were on their way back from West Palm Beach where they had gone to visit Jill's best friend, Angie. The traffic on the road during this four-day holiday period was very heavy and Jill decided to take a break. She had seen several signs along the way indicating an exit was coming up for fast-food restaurants, including both a McDonald's and Burger King. As they passed further signs, they began discussing which of the two they would have a snack at. Jill pulled the car off the six-lane highway when she saw the sign indicating the restaurants were off the next exit.

All they were able to find was a small store, where they bought soft drinks. Jill asked its owner where she could find the McDonald's or Burger King which had been signposted every mile or so along the road. He said the nearest of either was 50 miles (80 kilometres) away. Back on the road again they had travelled only a mile or so when the traffic began to back up, and soon they came to a pile-up again: a van had collided with a car. As they passed the accident, Jill recognized the van as the one she had been travelling directly behind before she pulled off the road in search of the phantom fast-food restaurants.

As the Crow Flies – and Flies

Frank Landstrom was playing golf in Spring Hill, Florida, on 19 October 1997 when a crow grabbed his 14-carat-gold bracelet from a golf cart and flew off.

A few hours later, and 35 miles (55 kilometres) away, Tom Johnson found the bracelet by his car wheel when he pulled into a supermarket parking lot in Clearwater. Two weeks later Tom's wife read the story of the crow's daring robbery in the local paper. Tom phoned Frank and asked him to describe the bracelet. It was clearly the same one. Tom refused a reward when Frank came to pick it up. 'I didn't want the money,' he said. 'I already had a great story to tell.'

Ornithologists say crows are capable of flying 35 miles, but not normally while carrying something as heavy as a bracelet. One expert suggested that the original bird might have dropped the bracelet and another picked it up and carried it to Clearwater. Perhaps there was a crow relay team. (Source: Paul Sieveking, Editor, *The Fortean Times*)

Early Warning

Mrs Sykes of Huddersfield wrote to the *Daily Mail* telling how she was reading an article over breakfast one morning titled 'Early warning signs that may save your heart', when her husband began suffering from severe chest pains, tingling in his fingers, sweating and nausea. As instructed in the article she waited 15 minutes to see if the pain subsided. When it failed to do so she rang for an ambulance and her husband was taken to the coronary care unit in Huddersfield Royal Infirmary where the staff confirmed he had suffered a heart attack. 'They were delighted I had got him to hospital so quickly and after treatment he's now recovering,' Mrs Sykes told the newspaper. (Source: *Daily Mail*, 14 February 1997)

Juliet's Fortune

Juliet Mercieca of Malta says that when her mother's kitchen caught fire everything it in appeared to have been totally destroyed. On top of the burnt heap that was about to be loaded in a truck she found, still intact, a toy car belonging to her young son that she had been vainly looking for for ages. Its number plate was still clearly legible. Juliet took it as a sign of good fortune and played the numbers in the Lotto – they were the winning numbers.

Juliet was born on 7 September 1957. When she bought a flat in Malta, it was number 7. The flat block is in Sapphire St, Sapphire being her birthstone. Juliet's next-door neighbour in a block of 18 flats is Romy, short for Romeo – Romeo and Juliet!

Dead Man Walking

Playwright Frank Gauntlett was pretty sure he had come up with a unique fictitious name for his latest play, a murder mystery entitled *Who Slew Reg Smedley?*. On the day after the play's opening night, he received a phone call from a real Reg Smedley. Once Mr Smedley had convinced Frank he was who he said he was, the playwright invited him to see the show. What else could he do? (Source: Scott Ellis, © *Daily Telegraph*, 29 November 1997)

Writers search their imagination for suitable names for their fictitious characters. One problem about the naming process is that unless they are writing an extremely comical piece, the name has to be plausible – while not offending, or, worse, libelling a real person. Creating a character for a novel I was working on I finally came up with what I believed to be an original surname for a woman, Dupree. The name seemed to me to reinforce the character of the woman: young, sophisticated, with the suggestion of the exotic, and best of all it came from my imagination and so was hardly likely to offend. Months later while doing some research, I came across a 1981 article written by an Anne Dupree.

Poems Presage Murders

A poem written by murder victim Caroline Dickinson, 13, eerily foreshadowed her death. Six months before she died in July 1996, she wrote the following lines:

Small child crying, weeping, dying
Alone on the concrete floor...

No one worries, life full of hurries
Rushing past the concrete door

Someone hops, halts, stops
Standing by the concrete door

While on a school excursion, Caroline, of Cornwall, was raped and suffocated on a mattress on the floor in a French youth hostel. One of the other students heard her feet drumming on the floor as she struggled, but thought she was having a nightmare. (Source: *Daily Mail*, 23 July 1996, p. 7)

Her story is eerily reminiscent of another teenager whose story I told in *Coincidence: Chance or Fate?* (pp. 278–9). Two weeks before she was shot dead by a berserk gunman, she wrote the well-known lines :

Do not stand by my grave and weep
I am not here I do not sleep

I am the star in the dark night sky
Do not stand by my grave and cry
I am not here, I did not die.

At the time relatives thought it a strange thing for the normally effer-
vescent young girl to do…

Several readers wrote to me regarding this poem pointing out that it
has been used many times as an epitaph. For example, by an airman
who had written it in a letter to his father shortly before he had died.
Virginia Hanson (co-author of the *Reader's Guide to the Mahatma Letters*)
also left instructions that it be read at her memorial service in 1991.
She had written it out under the title 'Immortality' as a message to all
who knew and loved her.

It was also read by Frank Hick at the end of an interview he gave on
an Easter Sunday, 16 April 1995, on the BBC Radio 4 *On Your Farm* programme. Hick, aged 90, is a ploughman's son, born in the Vale of York,
a beekeeper, retired railway employee and author. The BBC says that of
all the poems Radio 4 broadcasts it is the most popular.

What Goes Round

Tony Mills's mother enters many competitions, but seldom wins.
However, in a local draw her luck changed – in a manner of speaking.
She found herself the possessor of a mountain bike, a gentleman's
model. She was due to collect her prize on 17 January, a Saturday, and
asked her son whether he wanted it. He declined the offer as he had a
good mountain bike of his own that he used every day to get to the station on his way to work. On 14 January, a Wednesday, his bike was
stolen. The circumstances meant no insurance money. Then he remembered his mother's offer. He phoned her and asked if the offer still
stood. It did and he had a new bike that Saturday night.

Cathy's Day

Catherine Cline of Jacksonville, Florida, finds coincidences manifest
themselves in her clairvoyancy. She discovered her gifts at an early age:
'As a child people would tell me what was planned or intended and I'd
reply "that won't happen", and invariably it didn't,' she explains. 'I
was thought of as sassy.'

She relates one series of events that happened to her in the 1970s
when she was a single mother of two and also a foster mother. It was
on a Sunday in May when the Feast of Pentecost coincided with
Mother's Day. She awoke, not with any expected anticipation about
this special day for mothers but with the words 'flat tyre' crossing her

mind. A flat tyre was the last thing she wanted, she told herself as she put the thought out of her mind and began organizing her day. She was going to load her brood into her large AMC Pacer station wagon, take them to church and afterwards make the long drive to visit her father. Just as she was about to set out, the phone rang. It was Sharon, a friend, asking if Catherine could give her and a friend, Bob, a lift to the church. Somehow she managed to make room.

Following the service, she retraced her route to drop Sharon and Bob off, before setting out to visit her father. About halfway home they came upon another friend, Frank, from the church. He was an elderly Englishman 'with the mechanical ability of a goldfish' and was standing by his car on the side of the road looking helplessly at a flat tyre! Catherine realized how fortunate she had been in giving Bob a lift as he set about changing the tyre. Frank had been on his way to the post office on a road he had not used before. He did not know what made him decide to take that route, but he was congratulating himself he had, otherwise how else would he have been able to deal with the problem? Catherine did not bother telling him they had not planned to be there either. But she did tell him about the words that had woken her that morning – relieved that they had not applied to her car.

After saying farewell to Frank, Catherine opened her large door to get behind the wheel only to have the wind slam it so hard on her thumb that her daughter had to unlatch the door for her to remove the injured finger. By the time she had dropped off Sharon and Bob, the injury was causing her some discomfort. In addition to the throbbing, her ears were ringing and she was feeling too nauseous to attempt the journey to her father's.

As she pulled into the driveway the phone was ringing. On the line was another friend, deeply distressed. Like Catherine she too was a foster mother and one of her young charges had just died, a crib death. Forgetting her own troubles, she called Sharon to her house to look after her children then drove to her friend's home to comfort and help her through the ordeal. Hours later as she was recalling the day's events she realized she had not noticed any pain in her thumb for some time. She held it up and found the swelling had disappeared completely. 'There wasn't a mark, no bruise, nor a white line on the nail, nothing,' says Catherine. 'I took on someone else's burden and mine was lifted. I can find no other explanation.'

Knew He was Ill

A photographer arranged to take pictures of Dr Macfarlane Burnett, joint winner of the Nobel Prize for medicine and one of the world's foremost authorities on influenza. Dr Burnett failed to keep the appointment – he had influenza.

When their Time Came

Three of four speakers at a forum on euthanasia ended their speeches, 'Unfortunately, my time is up.'

Unhappy Birthdays

Wayne Holland's grandfather died on his wife's birthday and some years later his (grandfather's) daughter died on her husband's birthday. Now members of Wayne's family dread birthdays.

Lingering Song

Teresa Holland, then aged 15, was watching some music clips she had taped on video. Halfway through a Howard Jones song, she realized she had to go out and she stopped the video. She thought the tape had not stopped so she pressed the stop button again. Then she realized that the video had stopped – at exactly the same place that Howard Jones's song was on the television.

Intriguing Indian Story

Hari Haran Iyer of Pimpri, Pune, India, writes:

> By chance I borrowed your book *Coincidences: Chance or Fate?* on 10 January 1996. At that time my sister-in-law was seven and a half months pregnant. Next day (11 January) she was admitted to a nursing home for high blood pressure. On 12 January, morning, the doctors diagnosed that the child was not getting enough oxygen due to her high blood pressure.
>
> The doctors decided to take the child by normal delivery and sister-in-law was given medicines for that. Then she developed pain in the afternoon of the 14th and delivered a male child at 4.45 p.m. Immediately the child died. The coincidence is that my father also expired on the same day, 14 January, at the same time (4.45 p.m.) in 1992, due to cardiac arrest. When my sister-in-law delivered the child I was keeping your *Coincidence* book in my hand. Really it was unbelievable. My twin brother, an engineer by profession, could not make himself available for my father's funeral because of distance and the unavailability of a flight. So I had to do all the rituals. He arrived the next day. So there are two possibilities: one it was pure coincidence, the other may be, since my brother (elder) couldn't make himself available for the funeral to do the final rites, our father was born and died again for him. My brother looks like my father and I look like my mother. So, he was giving him more affection. Whether the soul is there in the universe or not, that is a

difficult question. But if you accept this, it is my father's soul that must have gone to the child who was suffering.

Made a Boar a Friend

Kim Colville of Carpinteria, California, says she and her immediate family experience any number of events and wonders if God has his fingers in every pie or if 'my angels' (as she calls them) are contributing to all her coincidences. The Carpinteria resident says, 'I know nothing about physics, a little about metaphysics. I am not a religious person, but I have become extremely spiritual.'

She cites as an example a coincidence that affected her family. It began when they sent their adopted son to a YMCA camp for the summer. When he returned they were naturally interested to know how it had gone, and what activities he had been involved with. They did not expect the reply he gave them. He told them he had encountered an animal with tusks and bristles and had reached down and patted it where it lay apparently asleep under a bush. Kim asked her Honduran-born stepson what happened next and he said it had awoken and run off in a cloud of dust.

Kim joked to her husband that their son had had a vision because of his Mayan ancestry – that is, if Indians from Central America had the same experiences as Native American Indians. Later that day, she rang an old friend who had a Druid Oracle set of cards. Kim had vaguely recalled seeing a card on which was a wild boar – for that was what they had assumed her son had come across. Her friend confirmed the existence of the card and said the message that went with it advised that if you make friends with such a creature, you will have leadership abilities.

That night they went out to dinner at a nearby restaurant in Summerland. Glancing around, Kim spotted a wild boar's head above the door. When she pointed this out to her son, he became frightened and said that it was exactly the animal he had been talking about. It finally brought home to them the reality of what the ten-year-old had done and the risk he had taken. That same evening, Kim and her husband retired to their room and turned on the Discovery Channel, to find a programme about wild boars.

Relative Strangers

Over a period of several years Ruth Maguire and her schoolteacher husband had built up a firm friendship with another teacher and his wife. As it turned out the two women had something in common: both were researching their family history. Both came from Oldham,

Lancashire, and they joked many times that they might be related to one another, although they had no grounds on which to base the comment.

While researching her father's ancestors Ruth Maguire found that her great-grandmother had a brother called Ashton Whittaker, who was born in the Oldham area in 1847. One morning in the course of a conversation with her friend on the phone the friend mentioned that her great-grandfather had the unusual name of Ashton Whittaker! On comparing notes they found that Maguire's great-grandmother and her friend's great-grandfather were brother and sister and therefore they shared the same great-grandparents. They are now faced with a problem: are they great-great-cousins, first cousins twice removed, or just plain amazed at the coincidence of actually being related after having joked about it so many times? (Source: letter to *Family Tree Magazine*, June 1996)

Mrs Maguire later told me a further intriguing story of family genealogical coincidence. Her daughter, now in her late twenties, graduated from the University of Birmingham and found work with a large car manufacturing firm in Essex, where she lived at various addresses, before moving to a tiny village called Broomfield near Chelmsford. The village has one main street, a church and a hospital, and borders on some beautiful countryside.

When her daughter telephoned with the news of her new address, Mrs Maguire said, 'I could not believe what I was hearing.' After the conversation had ended, Mrs Maguire searched through her family history papers for a branch of the family called Childs and there found a copy of a page of the parish register for the church at Broomfield with an entry for 29 June 1815 showing the marriage of an ancestor, William Childs, to a Sarah Rayner! 'While my family is obviously aware of my obsession with family history,' Mrs Maguire went on, 'they have never taken a serious interest in the side of the family just mentioned and the village of Broomfield has never been mentioned by me. It was as if the family had just come full circle over the last 180 years and had now returned to one of our villages of origin.'

Street Meets

In Guildford, Sydney, one of the city's oldest suburbs, three streets near to one another are named Ruby, Oswald and Kennedy. Real estate agents say most houses in Guildford range from 110 to 60 years of age, so the three streets were named long before the names themselves were linked when President Kennedy was assassinated in 1963 by Lee Harvey Oswald, who was in turn murdered by Jack Ruby.

Supernatural

Some coincidence-prone people report that they also experience vary-ing degrees of premonitions in the form of dreams and intuitive flashes, while others undergo experiences that can only be described as supernatural. No studies, as far as I am aware, have been undertaken of people who undergo such experiences regularly to see if they too are coincidence-prone. It would be a fair bet that this latter group has a high degree of synchronistic awareness. The following are a few anec-dotes from people who have shown that coincidences play a signifi-cant role in their lives.

Carole Lawrence and her friend Penny were on their way home from visiting a friend in the small Australian country town of Ouyen in Victoria's Mallee. They had been told not to use the old wooden rail-way bridge because some girls had been 'accosted' on it recently, and instead they were to go via the railway crossing. In 1910 a young rail-way ganger, jilted by his girlfriend, had committed suicide by hanging himself from the light stanchion overhanging the middle of the bridge. Since then it was reputed locally to be the coolest spot in Ouyen, apart from the iceworks. Those who chose to stand beneath the yellow light cast by its single shaded bulb on a hot night were soon enfolded by a chill.

In the early evening the two girls set off for home and, disobeying their parents' instructions, decided to go over the bridge. It appeared to be deserted as far as they could see, but at one point the bridge swings sharply to the left and they could not see beyond that point. As they rounded the bend, they spotted a man swaying from side to side coming towards them. They did not recognize him but could see he was drunk and, with the bravado of youth, decided they could out-smart a drunk any day. But just as the three of them arrived at the 'haunted' stanchion the man lunged at them, grabbing Carole by the arm. She screamed and tried to pull free, while Penny took her other arm and attempted to pull her clear. But his grip was too strong. Suddenly, to the astonishment of all three, a woman was standing there. The woman poked at the inebriated man with a rolled parasol and he released his grip. Carole could not take her eyes off the appari-tion. The woman, whom she had never seen before, was dressed in old-fashioned clothes – a long lemon-yellow dress with a very tight-fitting bodice. She held the man at bay with her parasol as she addressed the two girls: 'Is this gentleman bothering you young gels?' They both yelled, 'Yes,' in unison. 'Well, then run along home now and don't look back.' As they departed they realized the man was quivering in fear. They ran swiftly off the bridge and down to the embankment where they ignored the woman's caution and did look back to where the two figures continued to stand under the light. They were too far away to hear what the woman was saying to the man. But judging by his cowed appearance he must have been very frightened. Then the woman vanished as suddenly as she had appeared. After looking around wildly the man also fled the bridge. They never saw the woman again. Penny told her parish priest about the incident. He was over-joyed and told her she was a blessed because she had seen her guardian angel. Spurred by the response, Carole sought out their family's Presbyterian minister and told him the story. His response was, 'Little girls who go around telling such wicked tales should have their mouths washed out with soap and water.'

Carole's eerie coincidence is similar to another ghost story of more recent times in Barnsley, Yorkshire. In 1997, Daniel Geraghty, aged 12, was walking home after a fishing trip, when, in a remote lane, he saw a girl dressed in old-fashioned clothes. He was able to give his father, Ken, a detailed description of the apparition: the girl was wearing a black choker, white lace gloves and a knee-length red velvet dress; she was carrying a stick or a broom. Ken was so intrigued by Daniel's story that he drew a detailed sketch based on the description that appeared in a local newspaper. Jean Maloney spotted the story and recognized the ghost as her aunt, Emily Whiteley, who had died in 1908 at the age of 11 when a shotgun discharged as it was being cleaned at Champney Hill Farm, near the lane. Mrs Maloney produced an old photograph of Emily showing her wearing similar clothes, including the black choker. After seeing it Daniel confirmed that it had indeed been Emily whom he had seen. Mrs. Maloney said Emily had loved to play in the lane.

Clair Hawkshaw of Norwich had a disturbing dream in early hours of 26 April 1991 in which she found herself sheltering under a bridge watching some shacks being torn apart by a tornado. It was something she had never experienced in real life and she was disturbed by the experience. The following day she saw on television footage of a wild tornado that had torn through the American Midwest killing more than 30 people at about the same time she had 'seen' the storm. One of the scenes showed a cameraman sheltering under a bridge as a shack was being ripped apart in the background, just as in her dream. Claire says she has been receiving clairvoyant messages since she was a child and finds them something of a strain. 'It's hard to say under what circumstances the experiences happen,' she wrote. 'It acts on its own accord. It just depends if you are awake enough to notice its calling card...'

Kere Fleming of the Gold Coast, Queensland, writes of a few of the many 'extraordinary coincidences' that have happened to her that manifest themselves in premonitions and precognition. Her daughter and family of three sons visited her from England, where they were living at the time After they had left, Kere had a vivid dream that the youngest grandson had become lost in a park and people were running around looking for him. The dream was so real (as precognitive dreams most often are) she awoke feeling upset. Unable to rid her mind of the dream she rang her daughter, but everything was fine, so she did not mention the dream, as her daughter was very sensitive to her mother's forebodings. About four months later the dream recurred, waking Kere from her sleep. The following day her daughter phoned her from Paris where they family had been living for the past six weeks. 'You'll never guess what happened to Andy yesterday,' she began. Kere replied, 'He got lost in a park,' and went on to tell her about her dreams. The equally incredible part of the story was that Andy, who was just four years old, was guided by some sixth sense of direction to find his own way back from the park, crossing busy streets to arrive safely back at their new home, while police and volunteers were running around the park looking for him.

Deana Sampson of Stradbroke, Sheffield, claims her dead brother came to her in a dream and told her she was going to win the Lottery. She said that in the dream he handed her a toffee tin she had once used to pick out numbers for the British National Lottery draw. Brother Glynn was most emphatic about his mystical forecast. Mrs Sampson searched out the tin and used it to choose an extra line of numbers. The line did not come up but one of her regular numbers scooped the pool winning her £5.4 million in October 1996. (Source: *Daily Mail*, 8 October 1996)

House Call

Stephen Iacono, of Picnic Point, Sydney, had just picked up his cousin, who had flown from Melbourne to spend a few days with his family. Earlier that year the cousin had been on a cruise of the Pacific where he had made friends with a girl from Sydney. He had been in touch with her and was going to meet her the next morning. They were driving away from the airport along Forest Road, Arncliffe, when Stephen asked his cousin where the girl lived in Sydney. He said Arncliffe, to which Stephen asked what street she lived in. He replied that he had her address in his suitcase which was in the boot of the car. Stephen mentioned they were on the suburb's main street, Forest Road. At which he exclaimed, 'That's it – that's the name of her street.' Stephen immediately pulled over and offered to drop him at her house if he wanted to get the address from his suitcase. He declined, saying he would catch up with her in the morning as arranged. The next day Stephen drove him to his friend's place. When they found the house, Stephen was amazed to find it was across the road from the very spot where he had spontaneously pulled over the previous night. 'I have had a few coincidences happen to me but that was probably the most "random" event of them all,' he commented.

Royal Decree

Margot Pitkin, editor of the 'Historical Features' sections of the *Daily Telegraph,* had just pulled a story up on her computer screen to edit it as her phone rang. A man with a strong European accent was on the line explaining he had been a reader of her section for many years and why, he demanded, had there never been a story on Queen Astrid of Sweden, who was a most impressive figure? Margot froze – the story now before her on the screen was about Queen Astrid. She was too surprised by the coincidence to ask him what reason he had for making the call and managed only to assure the caller that such an article would be appearing within the week. Obviously pleased at the prompt response to his inquiry, the loyal fan of the Swedish Queen hung up.

chapter fourteen

Coincidence File IV

Knowledge Beyond Time

Eve Wright's sister, Chrissie, died on 23 January 1983. Exactly nine months later, her daughter, Leanda, gave birth to a son, Joshua. Joshua was about 19 months old when his mother took him to visit his grandmother in Byron Bay, New South Wales. 'We were chatting away when I noticed Joshua had wandered off,' said Eve. 'Minutes later he wandered back holding a photo of my deceased sister. Very clearly he said, "Chrissie". My two other daughters were also present and we all heard it – the hairs on the back of our necks stood up. It was one of those chilling moments. You see, we'd never mentioned my sister in front of him and he'd never seen a picture of her. Our photos were usually kept in the top of the wardrobe but that morning I just happened to have brought them down.' How did he know the name of the woman in the photo?

Years after, Dublin-born Eve still has no explanation for the startling event. Joshua himself has no memory of it either. But the four adult witnesses attest to it to this day. There is a footnote to this tale. They all saw Joshua slide the photo of Chrissie into his pocket, and it has not been seen since.

Faithful Teddy

Mairi Hedderwick, from Inverness (Scotland), was given a teddy bear when she was a baby in the 1940s. He lay about her former home in the Isle of Coll, until he was finally thrown out with some old household rubbish. The rubbish was dumped at the other end of the island and was washed out to sea. Six months later, the teddy found its way around the island and was washed up near her home. Again she got rid of it before moving from the island. When she returned to the island two years later on a holiday, she found her teddy washed up again. Source: (Source: Paul Sieveking, Editor, *The Fortean Times*)

Money Worries

We all worry about money, or rather the lack of it, but David Ball of Frinton-on-Sea, Essex, has found that, sometimes, the worrying is misplaced. He writes:

> At the beginning of my second year in Nigeria I found what I should have known but didn't – that I had to pay income tax for one year in arrears and one in advance all in one go. I got them to agree to take so much down and, I think, £34 per month for four months. That was a lot of money to me then and, as I drove the 240 miles (385 kilometres) from Kano to Kaduna, my headquarters, one day I was wondering how I was going to find it. When I arrived in Kaduna, my boss, about to go on leave for four months, said, totally unexpectedly, 'I put in on your behalf for acting pay during my leave and I've just been told it's been approved.' It worked out at an extra 30-odd pounds a month.
>
> Once, during my leave from Nigeria, in about 1960, I went to bed somewhat concerned (again) about my financial situation which I had just worked out. '£150 in the red!' I said to myself, 'Whatever shall I do?' The next morning I received through the post a letter from Kaduna saying that they had changed the rules regarding contributions to widows' and orphans' pensions. As a bachelor I need not contribute in future and if I didn't I was due for a refund of £150.
>
> On 23 October 1996, I went to bed in a similar, but less frenetic state of mind. I had just spent £1,840 on a new lap-top computer, was totally confused about how to work it, decided I much preferred my old one (this one!) in many ways and had I wasted nearly £2,000? It wouldn't break me but the situation was uncomfortable, especially as I had spent weeks working out exactly what I wanted. 'At least,' I thought, 'I shan't miss £1,000 of the money which has been sitting in Premium Bonds which have paid me £50 in two years. I'll draw that out. But what about the rest?' This morning almost the first thing I heard when I woke up and switched on the radio news was that the Halifax Building Society's pay-out to account holders (I am one, but had forgotten about this conversion bonus thing) would take place early in the new year and would be about £1,000 each.

(Author's note: As I was writing this last item into my computer I found myself nodding my head in sympathy. It was only later that I realized why. I was in the same position as David Bell. I was using my new computer and had only last week declared that I preferred my old one *and* that I had wasted my money. Last night I had been worrying how I was going to pay the next instalment of $A500, when in the following morning's mail there was an unexpected cheque for $500 for an article I had written – I had expected to be paid only $200 and had not expected that to arrive so quickly after the article was published.)

Got the Time?

In 1996 a student from Salisbury, Wiltshire, lost his wristwatch while dancing in a nightclub in Jersey. Two months later he and a friend were waiting at Basingstoke railway station and struck up a conversation with two girls, He asked one of them the time and remarked that the watch was just like the one he had lost.

The girl replied: 'Is your name Nick Coombes?' It was indeed the missing watch engraved with his name which she had found in the nightclub. (Source: Paul Sieveking, Editor, *The Fortean Times*)

Weighty Tomes

On a day when the weight problems of Australian spin bowler Shane Warne were front-page news around the nation, a customer in a Sydney suburban post office noticed on the book rack Warne's biography, *My Own Story*, next to a book titled *The Adventures of Young Fatty*.

Old News

On 4 April 1995 Max Gillen, the manager of an Adelaide cellulose fibre company which recycles newspapers for insulation, noticed a yellowing copy of a newspaper in a three-tonne stack of newsprint and pulled it out as a matter of interest. It was dated 4 April 1938.

Thumbs Up

A student who thumbed a ride with a stranger got into a car driven by his long-lost brother. Tim Henderson, 29, hitched a ride with diving engineer Mark Knight from Newcastle to London. The brothers had never met because their father had divorced Mark's mother and remarried. (Source: Derby *Evening Telegraph*, 2 February 1996)

Coincidental Purchases

Graphic artist Jon Foster of Cambridge met his girlfriend, an accountant, in a café for an evening meal and, during their talk about the day's happenings, she said she had been to a book shop. Jon replied that, coincidentally, he had also been to a book shop.

'Talking of coincidence...' she responded as she produced the book she had bought and placed it on the table. It's title was *Cosmic Coincidences*. Jon caught his breath as he took in the title. What was going on here? He took out his book, and it was now his girlfriend's turn to gasp. They looked at one another, each wondering what had compelled them both to spontaneously choose that day to go to separate book shops and buy the same book. 'There had been no previous discussion on the subject at all,' Jon assures me. 'There could have been nothing further from our minds yet on this particular day we had each been to a book shop during our respective lunch hours...'

How I Loved Thee

June Benedict of Hove, East Sussex, is the widow of a former college principal who died suddenly of a massive heart attack. Some years after this tragedy, she was being driven by a male friend, Alec, through her neighbouring town of Brighton. While doing so they began discussing poetry, modern and traditional. June said that when she had first met her husband they discovered they shared a love of a particular poem by Elizabeth Barrett Browning from *Sonnets from the Portuguese*. She started to quote from it: 'How do I love thee? Let me count the ways...' At that very moment they passed an advertising screen, one of those that are constantly changing messages (usually for cars, soft drinks, cigarettes, etc.) and the top line flashed over: 'How do I love thee? Let me count the ways...' Stunned, she asked Alec whether he had seen the line appear as the words came from her mouth. He affirmed that he had indeed. June says, 'Neither of us can explain what drew our eyes at that particular moment to the advertising board. Nor can we comprehend what an Elizabeth Barrett Browning quote could possibly be advertising. I might add that this friend is a very down-to-earth materialist, with no beliefs whatsoever in ESP, life after death, etc. Alec sees it as pure coincidence, but I believe it was beyond mere chance or coincidence.'

The last line of the poem is '...and, if God chose, I shall but love thee better after death'.

Strange Links with Dead Pilot

Australian Air Force Sergeant Tom Hamilton had just stood down from duty for the week on a Friday in September 1976. He headed for the mess, about to get his weekend off to a good start with a few beers and passing the time with some of his fellow NCOs. But as soon as he had walked through the door, the mess manager advised him that Operations had called. The wreckage of an aircraft had been uncovered on a lonely beach north of Stockton on the lower north coast of New South Wales. A helicopter was about to leave for the scene and he, an expert in aircraft recognition, had to be on it.

It took them half an hour to fly from the Williamtown air base in clear spring weather to the site. Tom, along with two other servicemen, unloaded a selection of digging tools and a radio from the helicopter, which then headed back to the base.

Guided by a section of silver metal uncovered by the elements they

161

began digging furiously – inspired by thoughts of the cold beers waiting for them back at the base. Soon, enough of the wreckage was uncovered for Hamilton to be able to identify the type of plane: a Sabre jet, from 75 Squadron, and, judging by its wing markings, it had met its demise in the early 1960s or late 1950s. Further excavation revealed the identity of the aircraft from markings on its body: A94-924. This sent a chill through Hamilton, as earlier that year he had constructed a model of that very aircraft for his private collection. But that was not the end of the story.

The cockpit section was still hidden and when Tom radioed the details they had found so far back to the base he asked if the fate of the pilot was known. It was. In February 1960 Flight Lieutenant R's aircraft had suffered an engine malfunction and, rather than eject, he had attempted to land on the beach. At the last moment, however, he noticed a group of fishermen in front of him and manoeuvred to avoid them – a decision that had cost the young pilot his life. Because of the remoteness of the site, the Air Force, after removing R's body, had buried the bulk of the wreckage and it had lain there for more than a decade and a half until the winds and tide had begun to expose it.

Some time after the incident, Tom was transferred to the Fairbairn base in the Australian Capital Territory. When he was unpacking he found among the 'junk' that had somehow got into his goods the oil cover panel of the wreckage. He had recovered it in order to identify the aircraft and put it aside meaning to throw it out. Later he moved to Richmond air base, where he was once again unpacking when he came across the oil cover he had thought he had long since discarded. This time he decided to keep it and placed it in his garage, which he had converted into a crew room. Its presence made a good conversation piece during the many parties he held there. At one of them Tom was telling the story of A94-924's demise to an American couple (he was a US Air Force detachment commander). Next morning he was browsing through his bookcase when he noticed a book by Winston Churchill on the American Civil War. He could not remember seeing it before and thought one of his children must have obtained it from the school library and forgotten to return it. Thinking his American friends might be interested in it, he took the book from the shelf and was surprised to note it carried the stamp of the Williamtown officers' mess. Hamilton remembered then he had appropriated a number of books from that mess when it had closed its library – but they had, he thought, all been related to subjects that interested him, that is to do with aircraft. A book on the American Civil War was of no interest to him. However, when he opened the book, he froze in disbelief.

Inscribed on the title page were the words: 'Dedicated to my late brother Flight Lieutenant R. Accidentally killed 1960.' This was followed by his brother's name – an Air Force engineering officer. Later that day he showed the book to the two Americans when they called. Having heard the story of the crash the previous night, they were as stunned as Hamilton to hear the sequel. Naturally Tom decided to keep the book. A week later he was at Mass, the book and the young pilot still very much on his mind. When it was time he included R's name in the prayer for the dead. The next time he went to get the book, it was missing from the shelf, and despite many searches for it, it remains missing to this day.

Birthday Shock

In September 1997 the roof of the thirteenth-century St Francis of Assisi Basilica collapsed in an earthquake. Most damaged were masterpieces by Giotto, Cimabue, Cavallini, and other painters who laid the foundations of later Western art. Residents of the town of Assisi noted that the earthquake had happened on St Francis's birthday, 26 September, and recalled that Brother Leo, one of the first followers of St Francis, had pronounced an anathema on the 'sumptuous edifice' of the basilica when work began in 1228, arguing that it was contrary to the simple and Spartan principles of the saint: 'Sooner or later it will fall down,' the friar had prophesied. (Source: *The Times*, 28 September 1997, p. 18)

Unhappy Anniversary

A man and his wife were each charged in court with having committed bigamy. Each was remanded in custody until 9 April, the date of their 29th wedding anniversary.

Bad Year for Birds

The Peregrine Investment Bank was named by its Hong Kong-based chairman Philip Tose after the swiftest and deadliest member of the falcon family. Tose quickly turned it into one of Asia's biggest investment banks and by 1996 it ranked as the Asian-Pacific region's leading equity underwriter, outstripping rivals such as Morgan Stanley and Goldman Sachs. Its future seemed assured, except in the eyes of Hong Kong's *feng shui* masters, who predicted that 1998 would be a bad year for birds – and so it proved, as millions of them were slaughtered in Hong Kong in an attempt to stop an outbreak of a virulent flu virus that was spreading to humans. The Peregrine Investment Bank went bankrupt.

In yet another coincidence, a major part of the investment bank's problems were the result of a bad loan of $US365 million to an Indonesian transport company named 'Steady Safe'. Sadly it proved not to be.

Winning Voice

In 1994 in Perth, Western Australia, a newsagent punched out a Lottery ticket by mistake. He offered it to the next customer in the shop, a 26-year-old man. The man had only gone into the shop to pick up a newspaper, so shook his head and turned to leave. At that moment, however, he heard a disembodied voice telling him to try his luck. He turned, hand reaching for his wallet...A few days later he was the winner of $A7 million.

Face in the Wallet

Travelling home on a packed train Ian Heathcote suddenly realized he had lost his wallet. Resigned to the fact it was gone for ever he got off at his usual station, reported the loss to the police and went home. Two days later, a commuter on a city-bound train noticed a wallet under his seat and checked the contents. No cash but the driver's licence picture bore a striking resemblance to the man who sat next to him at work and the surname was the same. A few inquiries later and the man's colleague, who turned out to be Ian's brother, phoned to tell him he could fetch his wallet whenever he wanted. (Source: Scott Ellis, © *Daily Telegraph*, 14 January 1995)

XI Files

In a local league cricket match in Yorkshire, Hampsthwaite and Studely Royal played a tie, each finishing all out for 154. On the same day the two clubs' second XI sides met and they too played a tie – finishing all out for 154. In both games Hampsthwaite batted last and both innings ended with the last ball of the 44th over when the batsmen were run out.

Laws of the Series

The birth of Emily Beard of Gosport, Hampshire, completed a string of numerical coincidences for the family. She was born on 12 December (12/12) 1997 at 12.12 p.m. Her father, David, was born on 4 April (4/4) at 4.40 p.m. Her mother, Helen, entered the world on 10 October (10/10), her brother Harry on 6 June (6/6) and her maternal grandmother Sylvia on 11 November (11/11).

Cathy Comes to Life

When Cathy Fryer was aged 20 she came across a book titled *Kathy Fryer*. It centred around a young woman who had health problems (as had Cathy), who was always cold and liked to take very hot baths (as did Cathy).

A Toss Up

On 26 January 1996 (Australia Day) *Daily Telegraph* photographer Matt Munro was assigned to cover the Big Day Out rock concert. He positioned himself on stage before the audience of between 30,000 and 40,000 mostly young people. Suddenly a young man was thrown above the heads of the people in the crowd and an alert Matt pointed his camera and caught the man an instant before he fell back into the arms of his mates.

Back at the office, the technician processing his film pointed at the shot of the flying man and said, 'Hey, I know this bloke.' The two men marvelled at the coincidence.

The story did not, however, end there. Exactly 12 months later, Matt was assigned to the same annual outdoor concert. This year it was bigger – with an audience estimated at 40–50,000. Again Matt was fortunate enough to photograph a man as he was thrown into the air by his excited mates. Back at the office, the same technician who had processed the film a year before was dumbstruck when he came across Matt's latest effort. 'It's the same man as last year,' he said, looking at Matt in wonder. Until that moment Matt had not realized himself what he had done. He had certainly not set out to repeat his effort from the previous year – who would back themselves against such odds?

Lie Became Truth

June Benedict, who now lives in Hove, East Sussex, met Benny during the last months of World War II when she was just 15 years old and he a young US Aircorps lieutenant stationed in England. They met only three times before he was sent back to the USA, but obviously there was a deep attraction between the two. For three years they corresponded and in his letters he spoke of his wishes and plans for her to go to the States and eventually marry him. For several reasons, one being she was still so young, she eventually stopped writing. Eventually she met an English boy to whom she became engaged. Benny in the mean time had written to tell her he too had become engaged to a hometown girl.

That would appear to have been the end of the affair. Then one evening about a year after his last letter, June and her fiancé were returning home from a local dance and she said (apropos of nothing), 'I have received an invitation from Benny from America inviting my mother and I over to visit with his family.' She had received no such letter but some impulse had led her to blurt out what she believed to be a complete untruth. She says:

> To this day, I can't explain why I said such an untruthful thing and without reason. Besides we had had no contact for so long. The following week, imagine my amazement when I did receive a letter from Benny inviting my mother and myself to Detroit, Michigan, to stay with his family. Needless to say my mother returned to England alone and I stayed and married my young lieutenant. We were happily married for 39 years, until his death in 1987. We returned to live in England in 1963.

Bomb Aplomb

At the height of the controversy over French testing of nuclear weapons in the Pacific in 1996, the French consulate in Los Angeles was besieged with angry phone calls (as were French consulates and embassies everywhere). But those who rang France's man in Los Angeles were not sure what to make of him when he gave his name, Jean Marie Lebom.

News Tip

A plumber watching a television news segment sat up from his lounge chair when he saw in the background a white utility van. It looked just like his, which had been stolen two days earlier. He rang the newsroom, who told him the location, and a few hours later he was reunited with his vehicle.

Timely Training

On Sunday 28 April 1996, a Royal Hobart Hospital two-day trauma course for the Royal Australian College of Surgeons was winding up and the 16 leading local and interstate surgeons were beginning to relax or preparing to fly back to their homes around the country. Elsewhere in Hobart, the head of the Tasmanian ambulance service had just dismissed a class of volunteer paramedics who were undergoing training in disaster work.

Then came news of a shocking tragedy. Gunman Arthur Bryant had gone berserk at Port Arthur, south of the Tasmanian capital, killing 35 people and injuring 19 others. In the grim hours that followed, the freshly acquired skills of both surgeons and volunteers were put to vital and instant use.

166

For some surgeons and paramedics it was the first civil tragedy they had had to deal with and probably the worst they will ever have to face.

String of Robberies

When Judith Stone (not her real name) arrived home one evening in March 1995, she found her house had been burgled. The thief, or thieves, had taken the only thing she considered to be of real worth, her string of pearls. She rang her friend, Anne, who lives in another suburb, to report the sad news. Anne had bought the pearls for her on a recent visit to Hong Kong as a birthday present. In addition she had bought another string for herself. After listening to Judith, Anne commiserated, and then told her that her flat had also been broken into a few days earlier and the only thing of worth that had been stolen was her pearls.

Real Life Exercise

A platoon of Air Force cadets from the Edinburgh Base in South Australia taking part in an exercise were told their task was to find a fake marijuana crop. The exercise took on an unexpected turn when the young airmen came across a real crop of marijuana comprising 160 plants valued at $30,000. The police took over the 'exercise'.

It Never Rains, but it Pours

As a university student, John Peck of Brogo, New South Wales, was very cynical about superstitions, especially those his fellow students appeared to believe in. One day, a friend arrived at a lecture with what was then a new type of umbrella, opening with a push-button. Another student dared someone to open it in the lecture room and thereby bring bad luck upon themselves. John took up the dare, opening it wide and holding it over his shoulder, and scorning other students who told him he had done something foolish. 'Within one week,' Peck recalled years later with a wry smile, 'I had a car accident, my flat was broken into and I broke my ankle. Now that's just crazy, but until I had opened that umbrella indoors none of these things had happened to me.' John remains a sceptic.

Intuitive Win

An office worker who went to buy a Lotto ticket found an already processed entry on the counter. A mental flash told her the numbers were the ones she needed. They were. She won $A1.3 million. An attendant at the shop said the ticket had been processed in error for a customer who had wanted different numbers.

Millennium Profiled

Two television programmes went on air at the same time in the USA, and in other countries, that were eerily similar, leaving their producers baffled about how it came about. One was NBC's *Profiler*, in which Ally Walker plays Sam (short for Samantha) Waters, a retired FBI forensic psychologist renowned for tracking serial killers, and who helps police solve grisly cases with her psychic-like ability to visualize a murder through the killer's eyes. The other was Fox's *Millennium*, in which Lance Henriksen stars as Frank Black, a retired FBI agent who is renowned for tracking serial killers and who still helps police solve grisly murders through his psychic-like ability to visualize a murder through the killer's eyes. In *Millennium*, Frank Black relocates with his wife and young daughter after they are menaced by a stalker. In *Profiler*, Sam Waters relocates with her young daughter after being stalked. 'I had no idea that this other show was out there,' *Profiler* Executive Producer, Ian Sander, told *People* magazine. While *Millennium* Executive Producer, Chris Carter, said, 'I didn't know there was a show called *Profiler* until after our pilot was done.' Earlier in the year two shows about hospitals that are very similar, *ER* and *Chicago Hope*, came out at the same time. The producers of all these shows put the similarities down to coincidence. What else?

Miners Match

Kathleen Silver of Box Hill, Victoria, attended a reunion for overseas war brides. She found herself drawn to another woman whose name tag said 'Goldie' – hers naturally enough was 'Silver'. After chatting for only a short time, they found the coincidences of their lives were far more than having the names of precious metals. They had both come from England and had both lived in the very same street in Hove, Sussex, before embarking for Australia. They had both met their Air Force husbands at the Brighton Regent dance hall. Both had been married by the same minister at the same church! In addition, both had one daughter and two sons, with one son in each case living in Perth, Western Australia. It had taken them 50 years to meet, but, in the words of the World War II song, they parted with a firm resolution: 'We'll meet again...' (Source: *This England* magazine)

chapter fifteen

Coincidence File V

If the Key Fits...

Robert Beame was a sales representative travelling the state of Iowa. One morning in 1954 he was leaving the hotel where he had spent the night, and crossed the street to his new car to load his suitcase and other items that he had taken into his room the night before. He then climbed behind the wheel, noticing his briefcase was lying on the front seat where he had left it the previous night.

He proceeded to drive to his first business appointment for the day in another town. A few miles out of town he reached over to extract some material from the briefcase. But the papers he pulled out were not his! Bewildered, he pulled off the road to have a closer inspection. That simply confirmed his original finding. He sat there for some time wondering what was going on. Had somebody replaced his briefcase during the night? If so, for what reason? His eyes strayed around the car. Nothing else appeared to be out of place. There was no indication that it had been broken into or in any way interfered with. On a sudden impulse he reached out and opened the glove compartment. It took him only a moment to realize the items in there did not belong to him. In another moment her registered with a shock that somehow he had got into the wrong car!

Robert immediately turned round and drove back to the spot where he had parked the night before. Standing there was a man in front of an identical car that proved to be his. There was a further coincidence, one that more than made up for the trauma he had experienced. The owner of the car that he had taken in error was a man he had roomed with in college seven years earlier. During the time in between they had had no communication. Robert had not known where his old college roommate was living. When the two men examined their cars they found they were identical down to the hood ornament that had to be specially ordered.

'Needless to say we spent many hours renewing our acquaintance and marvelling at the coincidence that had occurred,' said Robert, who now lives in Milton-Freewater, Oregon. 'As I recall my key fitted his car but his key did not fit mine. This is true, so help me. I have related this story to many friends during the years,' he added. There is, of course, no reason to doubt Robert's story; good coincidences stories are always too incredible to have been the product of someone's contrived imagination.

All in the Family

On Sunday 23 April 1832, the *London Examiner* carried the following marriage announcement:

> At Saco, Maine, on Christmas Eve, 1831 by the Rev William Jenkins, Mr Theophilus Hutcheson to Miss Martha Wells; Mr Richard Hutcheson to Miss Eliza Wells; Mr Thomas Hutcheson to Miss Sarah Ann Wells; Mr Titus Hutcheson to Miss Mary Wells; Mr Jonathan Hutcheson to Miss Judith Wells; Mr Ebenezer Hutcheson to Miss Virginia Wells and Mr John Hutcheson to Miss Peggy Wells.

Intuition Guides Her to Family Tree

Catherine Cline of Jacksonville, Florida, allowed her intuition free rein in the two and a half years she spent working on her family genealogy. She writes:

> I have had such an easy time getting back to the 1700s that others in my genealogy group have passed being in awe of my success. I can quite literally walk into a strange library I have never been in before and go to the shelves and take out a book and turn to my family in it. This even happens when the book has no apparent relevance to the town it is in. In Lincoln, North Carolina, I found a book on Swiss immigrants and turned right to Chrischona Tschudi, a great-grandmother of mine, whose national origin I did not know – the rest of our ancestors are English and Scottish (and one Frenchman, Richard Beauford) and I was drawn to this index of Swiss emigrants. There are genealogists who have devoted 20–30 years to finding the third and fourth generation of their ancestors. In two and a half years I have found 16 generations on one side…there are 1,015 ancestors in nine generations and I am missing only four.

> I can read of a grave of an ancestor and, when I go to the cemetery, I find my way directly to the grave with only the cemetery name to go by. In fact, sometimes I don't need a map or directions to the cemetery. Rational research this is not – but I am able to prove and document every bit of it!

I went to the college at Hampden-Sydney, Virginia, to find and photograph the graves of my great grandparents, Samuel Blaine Wilson and Elizabeth Hanna Wilson. When I told the college campus guard, 'I am here to find Sam Wilson's grave,' he said, 'Sam Wilson ain't dead.' A General Samuel Wilson is the present college president. He lives in a house called Middlecourt, purchased c. 1890. My ancestor Samuel Blaine Wilson was professor emeritus of theology and languages [at the college] when the Union Theological Seminary was on the campus, 1841–69. He died in his home in Middlecourt. Yet 130 years later another, apparently unrelated, Sam Wilson lives there. The Union Theological Seminary moved to Richmond in 1890 and the college continued at Hampden-Sydney. Was I drawn to my family's roots and guided by their spirits?

In 1945, when Catherine was four, she was taken to a Taylor family reunion at Tabernacle, Tennessee. For various reasons her side of the family lost touch thereafter. It was not until 1994, spurred on by her genealogical research, that she tried to return. By then no one was alive that she knew to ask where Tabernacle, Tennessee, was. She bought maps and atlases and could not find it in any of them. But she decided to go to Tennessee anyway, to see houses and graves of family members:

Driving along the highway from Paris (my father's family home) towards Memphis where I was to meet other first cousins (none of whom had a clue where Tabernacle was either) I passed a roadside historic marker commemorating the family reunion camp meeting held annually for more than 120 years at Tabernacle. The marker said the site was 1.7 miles (2.7 kilometres) down a narrow road. I had found it. Furthermore, I did so in the week of the reunion. The one week a year anyone would have been there. My mother's cousin, Beth, embraced me as if I had not been away 50 years (she's 82) and introduced me to all the cousins of varying degrees – who all share my peculiar shade of green eyes. It was eerie but warm and wonderful to have stumbled onto my family again. Coincidence? God? Who knows?

Linked by Numbers

When Ken F. Bowden of Bacup, Lancashire, met his wife-to-be they found her parents had married on 24 April 1929, while his had married on 24 September 1927. Her father, Philip Bacon, died on 24 February 1974, his father, Jonas, on 24 February 1989. Ken also has a clutch of number 23s to add to his list: Fred, his favourite uncle (Wilfred Weaver), married his mother's elder sister and died on Ken's mother's 63rd birthday on 23 January 1960; Uncle Fred's father (Alfred Weaver) died on 23 January 1939 – exactly 21 years earlier. Uncle Fred himself was born on 15 December 1890 and his birth was registered on 23 January 1891 – just six month before Ken's mother was born on 23 January 1897.

Taken for a Ride

One day in 1923, an attorney in Illinois was defending a case, when an employee from his office arrived and whispered the news that his car had been stolen. Unable to leave the case, the attorney instructed the messenger to tell the police. Some time later the messenger returned to the court to tell him that the police had found his car and arrested the thief – who was the son the man the attorney was at that very moment defending.

Name Loan

Mrs Suzanne Venecek, of Downers Grove, Illinois, noted a one-off instance of a name-coincidence. Her adopted mother's name is Evelyn Shostrom, which she has never considered to be a common name. However, when she approached a large bank in Chicago for a loan to replace the home she and her husband had lost in a tornado, the women she dealt with was another Evelyn Shostrom.

Memory Cheque

Earlier this century, a barrister sat up one night to write letters. At about 12.30 a.m. he went out to put them in the post. On undressing he found he had mislaid a cheque for a large sum which he had received during the day. He hunted everywhere in vain, went to bed, slept and dreamed that he saw the cheque curled round a railing not far from his own door. He awoke, got up, dressed, walked down the street and found his cheque in the place he had seen in his dream. He concluded that he must have noticed it fall from his pocket as he walked to the letter box without consciously remarking it and his deeper memory awoke in slumber. (Source: Andrew Lang, *A Book of Dreams and Ghosts*, c. 1930)

Marilyn's Ghost

Sarah McIntyre, of Bilgola Plateau, New South Wales, and some other young teenage girls held a seance one evening in one of the girl's bedrooms. They decided to try to make contact with the late Marilyn Monroe. They stopped abruptly when they heard her girl's mother approaching. The mother put her head around the door and said, for no apparent reason, 'There's a Marilyn Monroe show on television if you want to watch it.' They never held another seance.

Balloon Went UP

David Nugent was working as a courier for a large pathology company. On a delivery run in Melbourne in 1987 he was listening to Radio 3 replaying the live broadcast of the crash of the *Hindenburg*, the German airship, at Lakehurst, New Jersey, exactly 50 years ago to the day. Thirty-five people were killed in the crash that brought an end to the airship era. Just as the radio commentator was saying , 'Oh, the humanity' as the flaming ship broke up in the air, David noticed an inflated silver balloon drift towards some overhead power lines, hit them and explode in a puff of smoke and a flash of light.

Ring on her Toes

A woman from Connecticut told me that a newly engaged friend of her mother's lost her engagement ring on Misquamicut Beach, Rhode Island, some years ago and, despite the assistance of a metal detector, was unable to locate it. About a year later she returned to the beach and was rubbing her toes through the sand when the ring she had lost popped to the surface. Misquamicut Beach is about a mile long and several hundred feet wide, and is usually crowded with people.

Till Death Us Do Part

In a fatal accident in Paris in 1996, two cars collided head on at high speed killing both drivers – who turned out to be man and wife. The couple had been separated for some months and neither knew the other was going to be driving that night. Although police did check the possibility of a bizarre murder-suicide, they soon ruled it out. It was so dark they could not have recognized one another, and it was concluded that it must have been an accident.

In Melbourne in 1979, a couple were driving cars that collided. However, neither husband nor wife was injured and when they emerged from their wrecked vehicles, to the delight of the crowd that had gathered, they embraced. (Source: *Coincidences: Chance or Fate?*, pp. 165–6)

Cool Move

Suni Cabrera was hot and uncomfortable in her Puerto Rico apartment, so much so that she did something she did not normally do in the evenings – she went to sit outside on the porch. She remained there for about an hour listening to recorded music. In the end she decided she was feeling no cooler and retreated to her living room where she found the book she had been reading and settled down. A few minutes later there was a 'dreadful crashing' sound on the porch. She turned on the porch light and found to her 'utter amazement' that the heavy wooden railing had come loose from one of the porches above her in the con-dominium and fallen across the sofa where she had been sitting. Suni was left to ponder what had driven her to seek relief from the heat on the porch in the first place – and what had led her to decide that it was no cooler there and return to the living room in time to save her life.

Well Named

Linda Eisenberg became pregnant with her second child soon after her father, Marvin, died in 1981. Linda and her husband decided to name the baby, when it came, after her father. It is Jewish religious tradition to name children after deceased relatives. Baby Marcy was born at 7.23 a.m. on 23 July (American style: month 7; day 23). This was also her father's birthday. The timing and date of the event profoundly affected their family, said Linda's sister Holly Bossert of Baldwinsville, New York.

Why They Remember 4 December

Bill and Maria Harsveld married on 4 December 1957 (4/12/57). Their first child, Joyce, was born on 4/12/58 and their first grandchild was born on 4/12/86.

Lost in the Desert Storm

On 18 January 1991, two days into the Desert Storm operation during the Gulf conflict, Marine Chief Warrant Officer Guy Hunter Jr., flying a reconnaissance mission with Lieutenant Colonel Clifford Acree, was shot down by an Iraqi missile and bailed out deep in Iraqi-held terri-tory. Before he was taken prisoner, Hunter buried his wallet in the sand. In January 1997, six years after the war, the mud-soaked wallet appeared in Hunter's mailbox in Jacksonville, North Carolina, still containing his credit cards, family photos and $47 in cash. It had been unearthed by a Sri Lankan labourer working in Kuwait who had passed it to the Marines. (Source: Paul Sieveking, Editor, *The Fortean Times*)

Great Escape Movie

Young Hilary Sumner of Unionville, Connecticut, found herself for some inexplicable reason watching television in the middle of the day. It was something the ten-year-old never normally did. As she flipped through the channels she came to an old black and white war film. She did not particularly care for war films, or black and white movies. But some intuitive instinct had her watching the whole movie with intense interest. It told the story of a woman spy who had escaped from Germany in World War II by taking medication that made her appear clinically dead. When the movie ended, she ran excitedly upstairs and told her mother about the great movie she had just seen. Her mother grew even more excited as she took in the details. Her daughter had watched the movie version of a book called *Escape* that her grandfather, Egon von Mauchenheim, had written 40 years earlier. Before that day, Hilary had never heard of either the book or the film.

Impatient Patient

One night in the 1970s, Carole Lawrence was a patient at the Woden Valley Hospital in Canberra. She was sharing a ward with three other women and a storm was raging outside. The elderly patient nearest to her was in an extremely excitable state and kept crying out that the window next to her bed was going to fall in. The nursing staff tried to calm her, but she persisted with her claim. A doctor suggested a sedative, but the woman refused. As the night wore on she kept up her wailing. Finally the night sister called a maintenance man to reassure the woman. By that stage the other women in the ward were unable to sleep and were being comforted by the nurses with cups of tea. The maintenance man went to great pains to explain to the distraught woman that her fears were groundless, the window could not possibly fall in. It was fastened solidly into the wall and there were no signs of any fault or cracking around it. His words appeared to offer the woman some comfort and in the early hours calm returned to the ward. The wind too died down. Just as they were all drifting off to sleep, the elderly woman decided to go to the toilet. She had no sooner left her bed than the 'safe' window fell across her empty bed with a resounding 'thwack'.

Night Thoughts

Sharon Martens, of Milwaukee, Wisconsin, vividly remembers two outstanding personal examples of intuitive coincidences. When she was 14 she met in church, then later at school, Michael, a boy she liked very much. They seemed to think alike and were looking forward to building a friendship. One night she had a disturbing dream: she and Michael were at a basketball game and he told her he was leaving town on Tuesday. In her dream Sharon cried at the news. At the same time part of her wondered why he had specified Tuesday. Later in the week, Michael approached her at school and told her he was leaving – for Colorado. His family had made a quick decision and that was that. The crestfallen Sharon asked when they were going. By now half-expecting the answer she was subsequently given: the following Tuesday.

The second case of intuitive coincidence happened to Sharon when her daughters were about seven and three. One quiet night, the girls were asleep in their bunks, her husband was out of town and she had just turned out her bedside lamp and settled in when she heard her eldest daughter, Anna, talking in her sleep. She mused, 'How strange she sounds when she does that. It sort of gives me the creeps. At least she doesn't walk in her sleep.' Her musing, driven by some compulsion, began to dwell on the last thought – how awful it would be if she got out of her bed and disappeared out the back door. The thought made her feel most uncomfortable. Wide awake by now, she heard Anna jump from her top bunk. Alarmed and also with a feeling something eerie was happening, she fumbled for the light and her glasses and was out of bed just as she heard Anna reach the back door. She caught up with her daughter as the little girl was trying to open the door. Still half asleep, Anna mumbled something about coming to find her mother, because she had heard her calling. With Anna safely back into her bunk, Linda lay awake the rest of the night wondering what it all meant. Did she have a premonition as she had had years before over Michael's departure? Or did Anna somehow 'hear' her thoughts and move to obey them? Sharon told me she was thinking of starting a journal of synchronistic events. While she thought they were few, she added, 'Maybe I will be surprised if I determine to be more aware of them.'

Fossickers Find Fortune – Twice

A fossicker read a newspaper report about a fellow fossicker's find of $A200,000 in notes buried under a railway station in Balaclava, Melbourne. Hoping lightning would strike twice he rushed to the site and within 15 minutes had found another $A200,000 in bundled notes only 10 metres (33 feet) from the first lucky strike. Police had no explanation as to why the money had been buried at the quiet suburban station.

Lucky Look

British Airways air stewardess Joanne Savage was serving drinks to passengers on a Jumbo flying between London and New York when something caused her to glance out of a window, just as a gap appeared in the dense cloud cover. In that split second she noticed smoke rising from the sea. Advised of the sighting, 747 captain Dave Cobley switched to the emergency channel and picked up an SOS signal. As a result an American rescue helicopter was called and three fishermen were plucked from a burning vessel, 160 kilometres (100 miles) off the coast of Cape Cod, Massachusetts.

PC's Number Came Up

After he had completed his education, Tony Eyre decided to join the Derbyshire police force. He was allotted the number PC 972. Four years later his younger brother, Steve, decided he too wanted to become a police officer, but not in the same force as his brother, who had been promoted and was doing well and he did not wish comparisons to be made. Steve joined the Lincolnshire force and was issued collar number PC 279. Although called a collar number, it is not worn on the collar but the shoulders – the name is a relic from earlier days when tunics buttoned to the throat. Tony, incidentally, is still a police officer and currently a uniformed inspector (which means he no longer wears a number). Steve served for 15 years before being invalided out after he was injured calming down a nightclub brawl with other officers.

Psychic Post

A letter posted in Scotland ended its journey in Margot Pitkin's office mail box in Sydney. As she was about to open it, she realized the letter, posted to both her and her husband, bore their private address. How it found its way through automatic sorting machines and the mailman to her business address (which is completely different to her home address) the postal service was unable to explain.

If the Cap Fits...

In the autumn of 1996 Roger Nussbaumer, president of a furniture manufacturing business in the USA, was leafing through a mail-order catalogue. While ordering a military field watch over the telephone, he had an inexplicable urge to buy an army coat, cap and rucksack. When the cap arrived he found that it had 'R. Nussbaumer, Co. 3, Troop 1' on the name tag in his own handwriting. It was the cap he had surrendered in 1970 when he left the Swiss army. The mail-order firm had made a large purchase from the Swiss army in the spring of 1995, including 3,000 Swiss alpine caps. These had been individually bagged, making it nearly impossible for anyone on the company to have matched Nussbaumer's name with the cap. (Source: Paul Sieveking, Editor, *The Fortean Times*)

Art Dogs Real Life

With President Clinton deeply involved in a sex scandal, war suddenly loomed with Iraq in early 1998. At the same time a film came out telling the story of a fictitious US president who orchestrated a war to divert attention from a sex scandal. Producer and actor in the film

Wag the Dog, Robert de Niro, said it was just a coincidence. More like just another case of the life imitating art.

Sang at their Wedding

Tony Mills of Bristol planned to ask his good friend, Harriet, to sing at his wedding in June 1996. He had casually mentioned it to her some months before the wedding day. As the time approached, for various reasons the reception was arranged in something of a hurry. The manager of the pub in which it was to be held said that he would take care of the entertainment; he knew of this great singing duo. Tony realized he must phone Harriet and explain so that she would not be offended about the change in plans. Before he could begin, Harriet greeted him saying she was glad he had called because she had mislaid the wedding invitation. Glad of a temporary diversion, Tony recounted the date, place and time, and the fact the reception had been arranged for the evening as he lead up to his apology. Harriet, however, was not surprised. She was booked for that evening, to sing at a wedding reception – and it was that of Tony and his bride.

Revolutionary Reunion

Russian-born Eugenie Fraser, who grew up in Scotland, was on board *The Mulberra*, en route to join her husband in India, when she heard a woman singing in Russian. She turned out to be a Norwegian whose father had been Norwegian Consul in Archangel for many years. Eugenie mentioned that she was also from the north Russian city. Amazed that two people who had lived there had found one another on a India-bound ship, the singer asked Eugenie where she had lived in Archangel. 'In Olonetstaya Ulitza, ' she replied. The singer said her doctor had lived there and described him, a big, dignified man. Eugenie knew him well – her mother had married one of his sons. The two women spent much of the rest of the voyage discussing the events of the Russian Revolution that had swept around them during the tumultuous years in which they had lived so near to one another (Source: Eugenie Fraser, *A Home by the Hooghly* [Mainstream, London, 1989], pp. 12–13)

Blackout Hits All Blacks

Auckland, New Zealand's largest city, was turned into a virtual ghost town in February 1998 by a crippling power failure when all four major cables that supply the city with electricity failed. A day later, thousands of miles away across the Tasman Sea, another major city, Brisbane, the Queensland capital, was also hit by a major blackout when all four power stations servicing the city and surrounding region broke down at the same time. Both cities have populations of more than a million and were thrown into chaos. Power industry sources said the chances of a major power failure happening in one major city were greater than those for winning a Lottery – but two separate cities thousands of miles apart in different countries? Days after the blackout in Auckland, the cause had still not been found, while a spokesman for the Brisbane electricity suppliers described the failure there as a freak and 'very, very unusual that all four generating units should break down at the same time'.

chapter sixteen

Coincidence File VI

Free Call

Jon Foster of Cambridge had arranged to meet a friend in a large city pub. He arrived early and decided to ring the friend to let him know he was there. As he picked up the coin-operated pub phone's handpiece he heard breathing on the line. He had not yet dialled the number or put any money into the machine. 'Hello?' he said. A voice that he recognized immediately replied, 'Hello?' It was his friend on the line who told him he had dialled the pub expecting to pass on a message via the landlord to say he was on his way down there. But before he heard a ringing tone, there was Jon on the line. 'This may be one of those "you-had-to-be-there" stories,' Jon told me, 'but to me, a participant, only one word sums them up...Spooky.'

Owls Grim Message

When Catherine Brunson was 21 years old she read the book *I Heard the Owl Call My Name* by Margaret Craven. It tells of the Native American legend of the owl as an omen of death. In early 1991, impressed by its contents, she gave it to her mother, Judith Brunson of Ruby, Louisiana. Some years before this, Catherine had given her another 'owl' present, a wind-chime shaped like the bird. In the autumn of 1991, Catherine and her husband moved into a house in Shreport, Louisiana, where they found an owl wind-sock belonging to her neighbour hanging listlessly over their side of the fence. By now Catherine had become convinced that these events amounted to an ill-omen. Days later she told her mother she had 'just run into' the book *I Heard the Owl Call My Name* three times in a few days. The expression on her face showed she was very concerned and Judith did not know what to say. Soon afterwards Catherine awoke at night calling out, 'What, Daddy?' This brought her husband out of his sleep and she told him she'd heard her father call her name. Despite her concerns, in the summer of 1991 Catherine gave her mother a picture of three owls in a frame. On the day before Thanksgiving that same year Catherine suffered severe chest pains and went to her doctor, who at first diagnosed pneumonia. But a month later the results of X-rays showed she had inoperable lung cancer.

Although her condition deteriorated Catherine was still alive a year later. On Christmas Day 1992, Judith visited her daughter in hospital. At home that night she had begun writing in her diary an entry on her daughter's condition when the owl wind-chime her daughter had given her many years before began to tinkle. Judith Brunson has five wind-chimes hanging in her window, but the owl chime was the only one moving. The window was not open and in any case conditions outside were calm, with no breath of wind. That Christmas a friend at work gave everyone a bird letter opener – Judith's was an owl. 'So,' Judith surmises, 'as the owl foretold, Catherine died on Easter Sunday, 11 April 1993.' It was Judith's birthday.

After a relapse of some years, owls returned again to Judith's life, causing her to wonder whether another death was imminent. In February 1995 a cousin gave her a kit containing a rock and three owls – the owls are meant to be glued to the rock. It made Judith so uncomfortable she hid the kit at the back of a drawer, unglued. That same night after she had gone to bed, some owls began 'carrying on' right over her house. She lives in wooded country and regularly hears owls, but this was the first time they had been so close to her house.

A week later she was driving to church when an owl flew in front of her car, looking down at her, then flying ahead of her to settle on a limb and watch her as she drove past. A few weeks after that came the most mystifying owl coincidence. She had gone to stay with her other daughter in North Little Rock, Arkansas. On her visits she always stays in the same bed in the room of her daughter's two twin girls, who were then aged seven. Above her bed there was a picture of an owl. Her surviving daughter knew of the owl coincidences involving her sister and next morning Judith rather pointedly raised the subject of the owl picture over her bed, saying it had rather shaken her. The daughter responded, 'Momma, there is no owl picture up there!' 'Well, maybe I have owls on the brain,' Judith responded, 'but it truly looked like an owl to me.'

The daughter went to investigate and when she returned said, 'I don't want to give this any more importance than I have to, but I've never seen that picture before.' The two woman could only speculate that the twins had hung it. This turned out to be the case. But they knew nothing of the owl symbolism surrounding their aunt's death, they had just somehow been drawn to the picture.

Things became even more disturbing for Judith a few days later when her good friend from high school days told her that she was in her backyard when she heard Judith call 'Hello', as she usually did when she arrived. Her friend responded by calling for her to come on through. When Judith did not appear, the friend went to investigate and found no one there.

In July of that year, Judith and her oldest granddaughter visited the Aquarium of the Americas in New Orleans and as they passed through the rain forest they came across an owl. Judith was by now fearful that all these sightings meant her own death was being foretold, despite the fact she was in good health:

> The power of the sightings is hard to convey in a description, but that owl flying out to get my attention as I drove to church, then sitting on a limb where he could watch me, had a feeling more than I can convey. I am beginning to believe that we all get these symbolic messages but we do not notice them, or if we do, we brush them aside as mere coincidence, just not significant, because we've been through so many generations of being 'rational'.

Judith promised to arrange for her family to let me know if she did die. I replied suggesting that the experience involving her daughter and the owls, both real and symbolic, may have heightened her awareness of the creatures and that in any case owls were also a symbol of books, of learning and of knowledge. I was relieved when Judith appeared to agree. She wrote back saying that it had been over a year since the spate of incidents and she was not aware of any real illness. She goes on:

> Therefore this might be a message of transition. Maybe I will live in an entirely different manner. I am due to retire shortly and plan to attend retreats, etc. Maybe I will move. I never did think of the owl as evil – just a messenger.

At the time of writing I am pleased to say that in the 12 months or so since our last correspondence I have had no word from Judith's family.

Down to a Tee

Rhonda Russell of Hastings, Victoria, wanted to phone her uncle, who had moved some months before. She rang directory inquiries and was given a number and address. When the phone was answered she asked, 'Is this Brian Maher of – St, Yarrawonga?' 'Yes,' responded a male voice she did not recognize. After a long awkward pause, the man went on,

'Perhaps you want the other Brian Maher of – St? I have his phone number.' Two Brian Mahers in the same street and they knew one another? 'Yes,' said Mr Maher, 'we play golf together. We're good friends. Now for that number...'

Mother and Daughter

On her daughter's first night away from home – she was visiting a friend – Barbara Spencer of Levelland, Texas, had a dream that a skunk was at their door. Next day when her daughter returned home she told her mother she had awoken frightened in the night, after hearing a noise under the bed. She looked and saw what she thought was a skunk – it turned out to be a sock. Barbara then told her of her dream. On another occasion Barbara drove to a local store to do some shopping. While there she had a sudden desire to buy some doughnuts, something she had not done in a long time. When her daughter arrived home that afternoon, she said she sure wished she had some doughnuts! Barbara says:

> Coincidences are pretty common to me. That may be because I'm interested in odd happenings and am always on the lookout for them and recognize them when they do happen. General coincidences that happen frequently are my daughter and myself will be thinking the same thing at the same time – this happens a lot. My daughter was supposed to be born 25 January, but was born 6 January. When looking in a diary I kept as a kid, I noticed I'd written that I had been learning to cook and had made my first cake on 6 January 1979. Now every 6 January I bake her a cake.

Swap Shop

Katie Pierce put her shopping bag down in the public toilets in a shopping centre in Canberra. When she arrived home she found she had picked up the wrong bag. She had been shopping at Grace Brothers and the bag she had was from another department store, David Jones. When she went through the contents, she felt in no great hurry to retrieve her purchases, for her fellow shopper had bought the same items: a Garry Larson desk calendar, an Anna Geddes baby calendar and one pair of boxer shorts – hers had the Phantom logo on them, the other shopper had bought a pair with a Yogi Bear emblem (Source: *The Canberra Times*, 7 December 1994)

Nine Life

When Neridah Mullington was pregnant, doctors told her the 'due date' would be 27 July (2+7=9). A few weeks later she was given a scan and told a new date of 18 July (1+8=9). When the 18 July arrived she was not in labour but was admitted to hospital with high blood pressure and was induced the next morning, 19 July at 9.19 a.m. The baby, Kris David, was weighed and measured and found to be 9 pounds (4 kilograms) and 19 inches (48 centimetres) long. Mrs Mullington had read an earlier book of mine and was intrigued by the mystery of numbers and the role they play in our lives. She took her son's 9 'number' one step further by counting the letters in his name: Kris David has 9 letters and Mullington has 10 letters, giving a total of 19 letters. Neridah has two other sons, but finds nothing significant in their pregnancies, birthdays or weight.

Lion's Share

A mother complains that her middle daughter, a Leo, kept getting Libran boyfriends one after the other. Eventually she married one of them, but they were divorced. So she resolved she would avoid Librans. After turning down a few more Librans she married a man with her own star sign. They had a son – he is a Libran.

Dead End Streets

A funeral director has his premises in Terminus Street, while another is in Mort Street.

Men for the Job

A stray herd of cows near Exeter, Devon, were rounded up by Police Constables Glen Bullock and Nick Bull.

In Expert Hands

The Penrith District Operations Centre near Sydney, which co-ordinates bushfire and flood emergency operations, has as its manager Stephen Frost. His deputy is Rosemary Hailstone.

The Last Anzacs

Ted Matthews, one of the last surviving members of the approximately 16,000 men of the Australian and New Zealand Army Corps (ANZAC) who in World War I landed at Gallipoli, Turkey, on 25 April 1915, died in December 1997, aged 101. He was given a state funeral. Nine days later, Doug Dibley, the last surviving New Zealand Gallipoli veteran, also aged 101, died.

The landing at Gallipoli (at what is now known as Anzac Cove) was a defining moment in the history of both countries – more than 11,000 soldiers perished on the Turkish battleground. Each year

25 April is commemorated in both countries with parades through cities, towns and villages.

A further coincidence: Matthews survived for another 82 years because a notebook he had slipped into his tunic pocket stopped a piece of shrapnel from piercing his chest.

Deadly Words

Colombian drug baron Pablo Escobar read of his own death. Tom Clancy, the author of *Clear and Present Danger* – which later became a Hollywood box office success – based his fictitious drug baron on Escobar. Clancy describes how his drug baron is shot dead by the Colombian national police as a result of an intercepted cellular phone call he makes to his family. In real life the police used a computer that identified Escobar's voice on the phone and within minutes located him and moved in for the kill. A heavily annotated copy of Clancy's novel was later found in Escobar's apartment, with the scene relating to the phone call underlined. On the day Escobar was killed, the same scene was being filmed.

Mixed Doubles

Twin sisters Debbie and Lydia Colbert have each had breast enhancement operations. The two beautiful young cabaret dancers went under the surgeon's scalpel on the same day in a north London private hospital. Roberto Viel carried out the operation on Debbie and his brother Maurizio operated on Lydia. As with the women, Roberto and Maurizio are also identical twins.

'We Have Had a Problem'

The famous understatement 'OK, Houston, we've had a problem here' may well have been uttered before the Apollo spacecraft even left Earth.

The words came from astronaut Jim Lovell when an explosion ripped apart an oxygen tank more than 200,000 miles (320,000 kilometres) from Earth. Its proposed moon landing was abandoned and for five days the world watched as it limped back to Earth, finally splashing down safely in the Pacific. The spacecraft was called Apollo 13; it had been set to take off on 13 April 1970 at 13.13 hours. NASA has never used the number 13 on one of its space flights again.

On the Skids

The accident officer of the Action Bus company is Paul Skidmore.

An Old Coincidence

A tale handed down through the ages tells of a certain Martin Guerre of the French village of Artigat who, in the autumn of 1557, returned home after eight years away fighting in wars that had culminated in August that year in the battle of St Quentin, in which the English and Spanish defeated the French.

Martin, a wealthy landowner, quickly settled back into family life with his wife and relatives. Compared with the rigours of war, his life was comfortable, with good rents coming in from his properties. To his delight his first child, a daughter, was born. But his family noticed that his years away had changed him in some way. His uncle, Pierre Guerre, finally put his finger on the problem: Martin was not the same trustworthy man he had been before departing the village.

A few years after his return a one-legged man on crutches hobbled to the front door of Martin's house, pounded on it and demanded admission. The maid who had gone to the door fainted when she saw him. Martin's wife came up behind her to see what the commotion was all about. When she set eyes on the man she let out a scream and almost collapsed. He was the image of her husband.

It did not take long for the truth to emerge. During a battle in Flanders Martin Guerre had lost his leg and been left for dead on the battlefield. Another soldier, Arnauld de Tilly, had come across Martin and, realizing they looked so much alike, down to having the same twisted fingernail, the same four warts on the right hand and an identical scar on the forehead, decided to take the place of the man he assumed to be dead. Tilly had walked into the village in 1557 and taken over Martin's home. Despite his survival, the real Martin Guerre had lost his memory for a time. When he had recovered it he had made his way back to his house. (Source: details supplied by Ken F. Bowden, Bacup, Lancashire)

Universal Appeal

Jeriann Sharf's life changed after attending an EST training seminar. (EST combines Eastern and Western philosophies to explore unrealized human capacities.) She writes:

> I had no previous knowledge of what this sort of mind-bending seminar was. I had no particular religious or spiritual leanings. I was an empiricist at heart. I only enrolled at the request of my then boyfriend. What came out of this 'seminar' was more than I had bargained for. I was kind of frightened and I surely didn't know that the Universe was responsive to people's thoughts.

> Twelve years later and I find I'm an old hand at this creative visualization

business. I like to experiment with visualization and 'play' with the Universe. The following is an example:

I was newly divorced and dating several men. Since I was now well aware that the Universe was responsive to my thoughts I decided that in order to know what man was in its divine plan for me I would give it code words. I 'explained' to the Universe that the man should say these words and then I would know for certain that he was chosen to be in my divine plan. My first secret words were 'Leftover Garbage'. I soon met a wonderful guy who announced to me on our second date that he had a plan to feed the world with 'Leftover Garbage'! (Now I was sure that this fellow was him.) But he wasn't. And neither was the second fellow who also said the second 'code' words (I had to keep changing codes). Each new guy in my life said the code, even though he had no conscious knowledge of the words. Finally I gave up. Then one day I met a super nice guy. No codes. No secrets. No nothing. He was a funny type of guy. One night, soon after we met, he grabbed me by the shoulders and looked me dead-on in the eye and said – not knowing anything about my 'deal' with the Universe – 'Jeri, this is the divine plan!' And this from an atheist. He still doesn't believe in a Higher Power, but I married him anyway. True story, I swear.

Jeri tells of another strange encounter full of coincidence resonances:

Not too long ago, I began a relationship via e-mail with a fellow named Jeffery Lane. We grew to be quite close, or as close as two could be who have never met. We wrote to each other at least once a day and called each other weekly. We began to notice something quite strange. Our e-mails to each other began to sound strangely similar to the dialogue between two television characters on a weekly show called Mad about You. The similarities between what we were writing to each other and what these two characters (a man and a woman who were in love and living together) were saying were uncanny and quite specific. The television character even celebrated his television birthday (19 April) on the show and the very same day that my friend Jeffrey had his. One time I was telling Jeffrey that my dog was chasing my cat, and my cat chasing a bird and the bird was killed. In the show that night they showed her dog chasing the cat, and the cat chasing a bird and her bird died too! (The synchronicities piled up and are just too numerous to mention.) Anyway, one day I took a look at the credits before the show. Guess who the Executive Producer was? A Jeffrey Lane, no kidding. Different guy, of course. I never did understand what all that was about. Not for one minute.

Jeri later told me of another incident involving her creative visualization. One morning the brilliant idea of how to avoid a car accident struck her:

I projected the thought out into the Universe that if there were some kind of danger about to befall me I could be gently warned by the Universe ten minutes preceding this event so that I might avoid it. Guess what? Ten minutes later I had a car accident! I backed up into a truck that was stationary. The back end of my car had a few hundred dollars' worth of damage, but no damage to the truck, or to me, thank God. Unfortunately, I didn't heed the warning or I would have been more careful. It was dark, rainy, and I couldn't see the truck since its backend was lower than I could see out my van's back window. Some things can't be avoided...unless we heed our guidance.

Took the Hot Tip

Chief Fire Brigade Officer W. H. Beare, who retired after 47 years, took a ticket in an office sweep and drew the horse 'Buzz Off'.

Hot Book

Frank Campbell, a sociologist and book reviewer, had his copy of *Crime Without Frontiers* stolen from him while he was making a phone call at an airport.

Minnie Comes Home

The 400 millionth visitor to Disneyland, California, home of Mickey Mouse and his girlfriend Minnie, was Minnie Pepito.

As in Life, so in Death

Bohumil Sole, one of the creators of the plastic explosive Semtex, died in an explosion at the spa of Jesenik in the Czech Republic.

Hello, Dolly!

When five-year-old Zena Snow was evacuated from Hull during World War II she took with her a gift from her mother, a rag doll she called 'Moneybags'. The mother had made it from one of her father's old jumpers, complete with a happy grin to remind her of home. But an aunt in Cambridge made the broken-hearted little girl give Moneybags away to a church jumble sale saying it would teach her the meaning of charity. Some 53 years later, on holiday from Leicester, she and her husband were browsing through stalls at a church jumble sale in Cambridge when she came across her rag doll on sale for 20p. (Source: *Daily Mail*, 18 November 1996)

chapter seventeen
Coincidence File VII

Travelling Bag

Carol Murray was given a black purse decorated with orange flowers as a 21st birthday present from her grandmother. Carol did not care for the accessory so waited until her grandmother's birthday came around and sent the bag back. Over the next ten years the bag went back and forth between the two until they decided the bag had outlived its joke value and Carol gave it to a friend. A few days later Carol's mother arrived in town with a present she had bought at a garage sale on the way in – it was the black bag with orange flowers. (Scott Ellis, *Daily Telegraph*, 28 June 1995)

Pope Predictions

Morris West's 1965 novel *The Shoes of the Fisherman* foretold the election of a Pope from Eastern Europe some 15 years before it happened. On the day the novel was published, Pope John XXIII died.

Late Night Memories

Whenever and wherever people gather and discuss coincidences, stories that are strange, amusing, extraordinary – in fact the whole gamut of superlatives – emerge. I have made many appearances on talkback radio where the switchboard has been jammed – not by listeners wanting to argue or just to talk with me about the subject, but rather wanting to tell their own story of an incident or incidents that have somehow impressed, amused or otherwise entrenched themselves in their psyches. On one show, I said only four words for the whole time. The first two were 'good afternoon' to the presenter, then half an hour later at the end of the programme I spoke again to say 'good afternoon'. In between the switchboard of the local radio station was overloaded, and many callers were still waiting as the show came to an end. This   is not an infrequent occurrence when the subject for discussion is coincidences. In short, coincidences make great talkback radio, at any hour of the day or night.

Several years ago I appeared on Louise Cooper's *Beyond Midnight* on the ABC national network. As the title suggests the show goes out in the hours when most of us have long since gone to bed. It is a time when many talkback hosts are plagued by callers who have had a night out and want to set the world to rights or vent their spleen, when insomniacs are looking not so much to say something pertinent, but for company, for someone to listen, for confirmation that they are not alone in their insomnia, and when those with an agenda to push know late night radio jocks will listen, if only to fill in air time. Given this I did not know what to expect when Louise, who had obviously done her research, finished her incisive questioning of me and opened the lines for callers. Here are some of the stories told in the remaining 15 minutes of the half-hour segment, all by callers who were sober, upright, intelligent and interested. None was asked to give a surname.

A Story to Dine Out with

Flora, a well-spoken, articulate women, related the following Small World story to me. It began during World War II when she was in Britain on a train journey. She fell into a conversation with another woman passenger. When Flora mentioned she was from Australia, the woman remarked that she had a nephew living there, Nigel. (Flora could not remember Nigel's surname after so many years.) He was in Adelaide, the woman went on, did Flora by any chance know him? (The city at that time had a population of more than half a million.) Flora did know him. She explained that she too was from the South Australian capital. Along with other girls from her college she had attended dances at St Peter's Boys' College and Nigel, a Saints college student, had become her regular dancing partner. Many years after this encounter, Flora and her husband were flying back to Adelaide from a business trip to Sydney. She sat between her husband, who was reading a newspaper, and a man reading a book. Some way through the journey, the man, who was on her right, closed the book turned to her and, in the manner of the woman on the train many years before, engaged her in polite conversation. Somehow the subject of coincidences came up and Flora found herself telling her war-time story. The man appeared to enjoy it immensely, laughing quite loudly, much to Flora's discomfort; she did not think the story was *that* amusing. Finally the man calmed and turning to her said, 'Don't you recognize me – I'm Nigel.'

The story has a final twist. Some years later, Flora attended a formal dinner at her husband's 'men only' club. Making small talk with the man opposite her whom she had not met before, she found herself recalling the two 'Nigel' encounters. As with Nigel on the plane, her dinner companion also found it highly amusing. Calming he leaned across the table and said, 'And I'm Nigel's brother.' The population of Adelaide was at that time about a million.

Life Cycle

Julia is a primary school teacher. When one of her young pupils was suffering a life-threatening illness she taught a lesson on the life cycle of tadpoles and butterflies to show the other six- and seven-year-olds in the class that all creatures die at the end of their time. To help her, the school librarian gave her a book called *The Dead Bird* which tells the story of some children who find a bird, dead but still warm, and how they react to it and, in the end, bury the creature. Julia felt that the children were not quite ready to deal with that so put the book on the shelf. A few days later when she entered the classroom after a recess she found lying on the floor a dead bird. It had flown in along the corridor, past three other classrooms and into her room where it had hit the window and fallen to the floor. The children were upset and as she tried to calm them she thought of the book she had set aside. She read it to the class before they all trooped out to bury the bird. 'I can't recall a personal coincidence as strong as that,' Julie commented.

The morning after writing this I opened a newspaper and saw under the heading 'Be frank, teachers told' a comment by Associate Professor Sue Dockman, an education expert, that teachers could not assume children were unaware of or immune to violence and trauma: 'It is often tempting to sanitize the curriculum, that is to gloss over all the injustices, the unfairness and the trauma, rather than to confront these and treat them seriously.'

Dislocated Journey

On a visit to the Philippines Colin was leaning on the rail of a night ferry as it left harbour in Sebu for Mindanao watching the activity in the harbour around him. He had his arm in a sling because he had dislocated his shoulder. Aware of a presence he turned and found another man had joined him at the rail. He was from Germany. Colin told him he was from Wangaratta in Australia. They spent some time chatting amiably as the ferry ploughed through the black night before parting.

Three years later Colin was on a ferry on its way from Mindanao to Sebu, again leaning on the rail, when he was joined by a man. The conversation opened on similar lines. When Colin said he was from Wangaratta, the man replied that he had met someone else from there. Then the two turned to look at one another. 'You met me,' said Colin. The two of them had not been back to the Philippines since their last meeting and the German had had trouble recognizing him because this time he was not wearing a sling. 'We were ships that pass in the night,' Colin mused.

Unlisted Number

Todd was at the Australian Rules Football Grand Final in 1990. Around him were young fans who had brought phone books stolen from phone boxes on the way to the ground for the purpose of tearing them to shreds and tossing them into the air when a goal was scored. A shredded strip landed on Todd's lap. He was about to brush it away when he realized he was looking at his own name, address and phone number.

Return to Eden

Anne's family moved from Palestine to Australia, and they lived there for some years before returning home. During World War I a group of Australian soldiers arrived in their village. Anne's aunt was the only one in the village who could speak English so was deputized to welcome the soldiers and make them feel at home. She asked one of the young men where he came from. 'A little town called Eden,' he responded. 'Was your father's name Fred?' she asked. The soldier looked at her open-mouthed. 'How did you know that?' 'Because,' she said, 'I went to school with him.'

Day of Prayer

Beulah's aunt died on 25 April 1923. Her younger sister was born on 25 April 1933. Her daughter was born on 25 April. She prays for their souls on that day.

House was a Home

Kerry's father rented out the family house in Townsville, Queensland, after moving to another town. Years later, Kerry, a trained nurse, and her husband were meeting the newly married wife of a friend for the first time. Discussing their backgrounds, the woman said she had grown up in Townsville. Kerry pressed her further to find out what suburb and what street, and was amazed to find that they were the same. Intrigued she also asked after the house number. The newlywed's family had been tenants in the house where she too had grown up.

Took the Tip

Tony married shortly after he was demobbed from the British army at the end of World War II. Soon he and his wife had a child, whom they called Sheila. Looking for accommodation, which at that time was hard to find, they were finally offered a cottage. On the Saturday they moved in, Tony noticed a horse called Sheila's Cottage was running in the Grand National. He put half a crown on its nose. It won.

Shark Arm Case

One of the strangest criminal coincidences began in 1935 when professional fisherman Bert Hobson caught a tiger shark weighing more than a tonne. He decided to save the huge creature for the aquarium owned by his brother Charlie and it was billed as the first tiger shark in captivity. It attracted large crowds over the following week. Then, late one afternoon, to the horror of spectators it went into a frenzy and regurgitated a bird, a rat and the arm of a man with a tattoo of two boxers shaping up to one another. Thus began the Shark Arm Case. Police, who at first treated it as a hoax, were able to take fingerprints from the arm and it was established it had not been bitten off by the shark, but removed from the body with a sharp instrument. The arm's owner had been murdered. The victim was eventually identified as James Smith, a man who had operated on the fringes of the law. Three men were charged with the murder of Smith but none was ever convicted. The case remains a true crime mystery, one that began with an extraordinary coincidence when the only shark that carried the evidence of the deed out of hundreds off the Sydney coast was caught and saved for public display.

Judge's Judgement Day

Another case of life imitating art. Retired Supreme Court Judge David Yeldham committed suicide a few days after being linked by Parliament with paedophilia. The father of three had emphatically denied he was a paedophile. However, a note he left revealed he had been depressed at receiving a subpoena to appear before a Royal Commission into the New South Wales Police Force on the day he was named in Parliament. The judge gassed himself in his car that was sitting in the garage of his home – as did two people in a movie about paedophilia. The movie, *Whipping Boy*, was written by his screenwriter brother Peter. It tells the story of corruption involving paedophilia and the protection of offenders by the police and other legal authorities. The film, based on a book of the same title by Gabrielle Lord, has a Supreme Court Judge and a headmaster as its central characters and had been scheduled many months beforehand by the TEN Network to go out five days after the judge's death.

Christmas Presents

Cherry Miller, 36, of Downend, Bristol, gave birth to two sons on Christmas Day – but six years apart. The latest was born on 25 December 1997.

A Single Life

Bachelor twins Bill and John Bloomfield were as inseparable as, well, Siamese twins. They lived together throughout their lives, dressed alike, wore the same type of glasses and kept their hair cut in the same short style. As they grew older they took to carrying the same type of walking stick after both had hip replacements. In May 1996, the twins, then aged 61, attended a body building competition. Suddenly one of them collapsed. Officials quickly went to his aid and called an ambulance. The call was logged at 12.14 a.m. At 12.16 a.m. the emergency phone rang again. The other twin had also collapsed. Neither man recovered. A police spokesman said there was no evidence to suggest their deaths were anything other than a tragic coincidence. They had come into the world together and this was the way they left.

Royal Blood

In every American presidential election since George Washington, the winner has been the candidate who has had the greatest number of ties to Royal blood.

Law Suit

Belgian prosecutor Marc Florens thought there was something familiar about the burglar he was about to prosecute...then it clicked: the man was wearing his jacket, stolen when Florens's home was burgled. Florens got his jacket back, but as a suddenly interested party had to be replaced by another lawyer before the prosecution could proceed.

Nuisance Call

Tongan national Maliu Mafua was on the run in San Francisco after breaking out of a Californian prison. He used a public phone to call directory assistance. Within minutes police had him surrounded. Instead of dialling the 411 assistance number he had dialled by mistake 911, the emergency number. The cops knew they had their man. Mafua was wearing a shirt that had 'Property of San Mateo County Jail' stamped on it in large letters.

Charmed Win

One evening in January 1996, a retired woman, feeling low and despondent about her future, remembered the Tiki (a small Kiwi carved image representing an ancestor and used as a good luck charm) her niece had brought her from New Zealand. The niece had advised her to rub the charm's stomach to invoke its lucky powers. She did so, saying a quick prayer at the same time. A moment later the phone rang. It was the Lottery office to say she had just won $A100,000 in a $2-Lottery.

Wet Weekend

A regional radio station in Australia organized a 'Drought Breaker Weekend' of festivities for the Queensland town of Dalby where it had not rained for almost five years. The event had to be cancelled because of rain.

Plague on Both Houses

A film starring Dustin Hoffman about the outbreak of a deadly virus, based on a true story about an outbreak in a Washington quarantine unit, was released just as an Ebola epidemic hit the city of Kikwit in Zaire killing more than 170 people.

Kicking for Ouch

The Canberra Raiders Rugby League Club claimed that their No. 13 jersey was jinxed when four of their top players were all injured when wearing it.

Real Life Plot

Shortly before the opening night of the musical *42nd Street*, entertainer Jan Adele slipped and tore the ligaments in her left ankle. The plot of the show concerns a Broadway director looking for one more hit before he retires. His hopes are dashed when his leading lady twists her ankle just before the opening night.

Deadly Novel

Welsh writer Gordon Thomas's novel *Deadly Perfume* inadvertently foretold the planting of a nerve gas in Tokyo's underground rail system, including the gas used, Sarin.

Twins Share

Identical twins Josie Beatson and Kath Oliver, from Wincobank, South Yorkshire, gave birth to daughters in adjoining beds in a Sheffield hospital in 1994. In another case of twin sharing, in 1996 Liam and Aaron Lynch broke their collarbones in separate and unrelated accidents within an hour of each other.

Right Position

The television show *Sex Files* came in at 69 in the Australian ratings in September 1996.

Hot Plate

A crook in Perth, Western Australia, stole a Mazda 121 from outside a house then doctored the number plate. Police became suspicious and arrested the man when they recognized the number as one that had been allocated to the state police.

Star Heroes

Within a week in early 1997, several famous actors came to the rescue of trapped children. In the first case, five-year-old Lauren Bailey was buried under snow when an avalanche tore through the remote valley where screen-hero Robert Redford's Sundance ski resort is located, snapping trees and destroying chalets. Lauren, the daughter of resort manager Matt Bailey, was in the family home, next to Redford's, when the avalanche struck. The force of the snow caved in part of the roof and tore doors from their hinges. Snow piled up to the ceiling. Mrs Bailey scrambled out through a window and raced to Redford's house for help. The star and Matt Bailey dug frantically with their bare hands for ten minutes and found the little girl, who was bruised but otherwise okay. But for snowstorms in the area, Redford would have been attending the Sundance Film Festival. As it was he was the only neighbour who could have reached the Baileys' house in time to help.

A week later, the mother of Dan Cassil, aged 17, of Florida had turned on the television in the presence of her son who had been in a coma following a car accident nearly two months earlier. As the sound of the theme music that introduced the show reached his ears the teenager turned his head and his eyes opened. With a startled, surprised expression on his face, he stared at the television set, then watched the half-hour comedy show intently. After it ended he turned to his mother and spoke his first words since the crash, 'Where am I?' He had been brought back to consciousness by a Seinfield episode – the one revolving around comas.

Dopey Deal

A German drug dealer in Bayreuth called a mobile number to arrange a 25-gram supply of amphetamines. Having placed the order he arranged a meeting place. When he arrived police were waiting. He had called a police number by mistake.

Family Car

While working as a car dealer in 1985, Bob Rider was given a new station wagon as a company car. He returned it when he left the company. In 1994 his son came home with a second-hand car. When Bob looked at it closely he realized it was the same car he had handed back nearly a decade before, although a little the worse for wear. (Source: Scott Ellis, *Daily Telegraph*)

SRENCBLDAM RWOD

Readers of the *Sydney Morning Herald* word game on 14 May 1997 had to unscramble ATSEUHRS to form a word. However, they only had to look at the comic strip beside it, where a character was saying, 'Bring us two cups of coffee and a *Thesaurus*.'

Six of the Worst

Cricketer Andrew Symonds hit a ball over the fence for six runs while playing for Gloucestershire against Sussex in June 1995. The applause was muted by the fact that the ball had hit spectator Paddy Gardner, giving her a black eye. Symonds kept on batting while Paddy was treated with an ice pack. Some ten minutes later she was once again while watching the match when Symonds hit another six – and struck her on the leg. The Australian-born batsman bought her flowers at the end of the game.

Wake on the Wildside

Scenes from the ABC's television series *Wildside* were filmed with the Blackmarket Café in a Sydney inner-city district as a backdrop. In the scene two bikie gangs are involved in a gunfight. Days later, a real-life shoot-out at the club involving bikie gangs claimed three lives. In an effort at authenticity the ABC filmmakers had borrowed motor-bikes from one of the gangs involved in the real shoot-out.

New Found Love

Ever since she was three years old and fell in love with her neighbour's Newfoundland pup, Rhonda believed it was her destiny to own one of the breed. One night many years later a friend rang and asked Rhonda if she would like to adopt a Newfoundland cross Malamute, 11 months old. It was not quite what she had desired – a cross-breed –

but it was near enough. Excitedly she checked with her husband.

The friend who had rung so unexpectedly went on to explain that the pup was a bit wild as he had lived most of his life tied to a chain. He needed a lot of love and discipline. Rhonda soon found that her friend had been quite frank with her. She put a great deal of effort into giving it both tender loving care and discipline, but one morning she went into the backyard to find that the dog had destroyed it. Her husband insisted the dog had to go. Heartbroken she rang its previous owner to come and take it back. Still upset she rang another old friend looking for sympathy. But before she had told even a small part of her sad tale, the friend interrupted. 'Rhonda, you won't believe this, but I'm at this moment reading the *Trading Post* and I'm looking at an advertisement for Newfoundland pups for sale.' She passed on the contact number and Rhonda and her husband were soon at the kennels in time to buy the last bitch of the litter. The breeder appeared interested in how they came to hear about the pups. When they mentioned her advertisement in the *Trading Post*, she said they usually advertised in the dog magazines, but for some reason she could not explain she had decided to use the *Trading Post*, for the very first time. 'I vowed to own a Nefy one day and now I do,' Rhonda commented. 'This is my coincidence and my destiny.'

Point Taken

Author and feminist Dale Spender told a conference on the 'Politics of Cyberfeminism' that women were socialized into believing that boys were good at technology and girls were not. As the audience was nodding in agreement the proceedings were interrupted when two women attempting to fasten a video camera to a tripod dropped it with a resounding crash.

Sneezy but no Cold

Six of the dwarfs appearing in a London production of *Snow White and the Seven Dwarfs* came down with bad colds. The only one not affected was Sneezy.

The Lincoln–Kennedy Assassinations

History repeats itself.

Nineteenth-century proverb

The assassinations of presidents Lincoln and Kennedy a century apart are possibly the best-documented historical coincidences. As an example of the phenomenon the similarities revealed are at times almost breathtaking. They suggest that many incidents may repeat themselves throughout history, but most go unnoticed because they lack the amount of documented evidence we find in the two great American tragedies.

However, academics and other researchers do not appear to look kindly on historical coincidence as a productive line of research. This reluctance is understandable, as it is the role of historians to attempt only to make sense of the past. It is the role of other observers to analyse the present and to forecast humankind's future course. Past, present and future remain three separate areas of study, and are never examined as a cohesive whole.

Although it is axiomatic that we should learn from the past, there is much evidence to show we do not – otherwise we would not keep making the same mistakes over and over, and war, plague and pestilence would not continue to haunt the planet.

The way we treat our leaders is a good example of our failure to learn. It takes only a superficial knowledge of history to accept that a nation's leaders of both the present and the future are at risk from would-be assassins, especially in times of turmoil. The risk is even higher when the leader chooses to walk among their people, as the Israelis learned to their sorrow in 1995 when their Prime Minister, Yitzhak Rabin, was shot in the back in a street, supposedly surrounded by his people, just as President Kennedy was shot in Dallas, and Lincoln was shot in Ford's Theatre. These were also the circumstances in the later assassination of Indira Gandhi in 1984, to be followed by the death of her son, Rajiv, some years later.

Coincidences are not by any means the major reason why the killings of two of the best-known American presidents have survived as individual cases of interest. All sorts of conspiracy theories surround both deaths. The Lincoln Commission set out – unsuccessfully as it proved – to show that John Wilkes Booth and his accomplices had conspired with Confederate President Jefferson Davis to murder Lincoln and other members of his Cabinet; the Warren Commission, with the help of the FBI, set out to find that Kennedy's murder was not a conspiracy but the act of one man, Lee Harvey Oswald. In both cases, however, there was – and still is – a belief in the high-level involvement of US government officials. The relevance of this in the context of this book is that some of the coincidences surrounding each case were seen as supporting evidence for conspiracy.

Paradoxically, when the spectre of 'coincidence conspiracy' is allowed to take hold in a population, the outcome can be dramatic. This may be a good reason why such connections have always been played down among officials. This can be seen in a different sequence of events which took place in Prague on 17 November 1989. With the communist regime collapsing, reports swept through the tense Czech capital that police had slain a protesting student. Angry citizens surged into the streets, their emotions inflamed by the fact that it was 50 years to the day since the German army had entered Prague and shot dead nine people, including students, while placing many others under arrest. The country was brought under the rule of Nazis. The symbolism was overwhelming and, within a matter of days, the regime, whose leaders were still protesting their innocence over the student's death, collapsed. Later evidence disclosed that the 'student' who was supposed to have been killed was, in fact, Ludek Zifcak, a young lieutenant in the Czechoslovak Secret Police, the StB. In fact, the StB had staged the affair. It had been working with the Russian KGB – as were secret police organizations from other Eastern bloc countries – in support of Mikhail Gorbachev's reformist approach to bring down the old conservative communist leaders. The key to the conspirators' successful plot was, of course, the 'creation' of a historical coincidence. In the swirling pattern of history, the anniversary of a day of infamy for the Czechoslovaks was so deeply etched in their psyche it took little more than a rumour of a death to bring out the citizens demanding the restoration of the freedoms that were so cruelly taken from them in the first place by the Germans exactly 50 years before. The conspirators had taken full advantage of the chance coincidence provided.

Examination of this affair may then lead us to ask the question – was the Kennedy assassination another coincidence 'creation'?

Another coincidence that has survived the fate of being forgotten in the welter of history took place in England, and involved two murders 157 years apart. The two victims were young women of the same age; according to some reports they shared the same birthday and were murdered on the same day of the year. I was intrigued to know how and why this case, involving two minor players in history, should have survived.

The facts are as follows. In the first case, on 27 May 1817, Mary Ashford, 20, was found dead at Erdington, a village about five miles (8 kilometres) from Birmingham. On 27 May 1974, Barbara Forrest, 20, was strangled and her body left near a children's home at Erdington, by then a suburb of Birmingham. In both cases the previous day had been a Whit Monday holiday. Their bodies were discovered in spots approximately 300 yards (350 metres) apart. They had both died at about the same time of night. The pattern of the women's movements just before their deaths had been similar: both had visited friends earlier in the evening where they had changed their dresses to go to a dance. Investigators of both murders thought the murder scene suggested their killers had tried to hide their bodies. Following both murders a man was arrested. In each case his name was Thornton. Both men were charged with murder – and both were acquitted.

When I started my research into this, my first discovery was that initial newspaper reports of the second murder did not link it with the first, just as reports of Kennedy's death seldom mention Lincoln's. Further research showed that the first case had not dissolved into the musty annals of crime because the ensuing trial had made British legal history. Its importance came about as a result of the acquittal verdict of the first accused, Abraham Thornton. Encouraged by lawyers who were angry at this decision, Ashford's brother William had a new trial ordered under an ancient law, called the Appeal of Murder. The law had not been invoked in England for more than a century and a half – and was never to be used again.

The appeal trial went before Lord Ellenborough of the King's Bench on 17 November 1817. It ended almost as soon as it had begun when Thornton responded to the charge by throwing down a leather gauntlet and saying, 'Not guilty; and I am ready to defend the same with my body.' The well-built Thornton had invoked a concomitant old law, Trial by Battle. Under it Thornton and the much lighter and meeker William Ashford were required to fight until sunset using staves as weapons. If Thornton could hold out until dark he would go free. If he lost he would be hanged on the spot. If either man killed the other he would go free. If Ashford gave in he would be declared an outlaw. Ashford's counsel argued that Trial by Battle was an obsolete practice and the case should proceed normally. But Lord Ellenborough responded, 'It is the law of England, we must not call it murder.' The hearing was adjourned. On 21 April 1818 the Attorney General introduced a Bill into Parliament which abolished both Trial by Battle and Appeal of Murder laws. On the same day Thornton was formally discharged.

The *Birmingham Post* ran stories in 1987 announcing the formation of a Mary Ashford Project. It reported the project's aim was to bring together people interested in the nineteenth-century case, to share material of interest with historians, writers, amateur sleuths and students, and to plan activities around the mystery and build up an archive. Commemorative postcards were issued some years ago in Birmingham showing scenes of the place where Ashford died. Other cards show buildings connected with the case, much as postcards of the Kennedy assassination scene are available. The project makes no mention of the later victim, Barbara Forrest, whose death formed the historical coincidence. It appears that just as we forget the past, we sometimes choose to forget the present, if it suits us.

Academic John Allen Paulos argues that coincidentally generated conspiracy theories can easily be constructed and urges people to prove it for themselves by dreaming up their own and supporting them with as much circumstantial and adventitious evidence as they can by, for example, searching through newspaper data bases.[1] Unfortunately there are people who choose to do just this. Their 'discoveries' can most often be found in the more obscure journals, usually those promoting extreme causes. However, such an exercise might also be carried out in search not of paranoiac-inspired coincidence conspiracies, but of other, perhaps more constructive, forces that are at work on a subtle level shaping society and that are also touched on in this book.

When we look at the fact that every 20 years since 1840 a president has died in office, we can either dismiss it as a chance coincidence, or wonder at the circumstances that bring this repetition about – and whether the president whose term begins in the year 2000 should receive extra security, an idea that will most probably be dismissed by officials as scaremongering.

The Warren Commission, which investigated the Kennedy death, noted, in one of its few retrospective comments on Lincoln's assassination, that it revealed the total inadequacy of security, and that a Congressional committee at the time had conducted an extensive investigation, but, 'with traditional reluctance', called for no action to provide better security in the future:

> This lack of concern for the protection of the president may have derived also from the tendency of the time to regard Lincoln's assassination as part of a unique crisis that was not likely to happen to a future Chief Executive.[2]

But happen it did. Attempts have been made on the lives of every five US presidents. One of every nine has been killed. Yet at the time of Lincoln's death a future assassination was regarded as too much of a coincidence to be a possibility.

The failure of the Warren Commission to look more deeply into the comparisons of the two assassinations, and perhaps even to form some opinion on them, may not be seen in the long run as critically as its finding of no conspiracy. By not affirming that there are coincidences which in some way support a conspiracy theory, the Warren Commission is left open to strong criticism for its perceived and proven inadequacies that have left the report itself in a permanent state of limbo.

Medical practitioner John K. Lattimer argues that many of the coincidences have to do with the fact that the two men were shot almost exactly 100 years apart (98 years) and have no magical significance beyond that fact.[3] Lattimer further comments that the similar personal characteristics of these two distinguished families, the Lincolns and the Kennedys, probably reflect only the traditional direction which politically oriented, well-motivated, highly successful young Americans went to fulfil their traditional roles in a society that obviously has not changed all that much in a century. He admits the similarity in the numbers of births and deaths of the various Lincoln and Kennedy children is a 'little surprising' considering the advances in living conditions in the interim, but says there would not appear to be any magical influence at work. (Author's note: each had three children and each lost a child through death while they were in the White House.[4]) Lattimer, however, concludes that the events at Dallas were such an impressive replay of the events at Ford's Theatre that it is almost startling.[5]

Roy P. Basler finds 'unfortunate' coincidences in the rumours and suspicions that abounded following both assassinations, saying those that surfaced following 'Black Friday', 14 April 1865, in many respects paralleled, if they did not entirely duplicate, those of the period following arguably the most tragic Friday in the modern era (both presidents died on a Friday). Basler, the author of a number of scholarly works on Lincoln, cites as an example the widespread belief that, instead of Lincoln's assassination being the work of one unbalanced mind, it must have been plotted and directed by an organization dedicated to the overthrow of the Federal government.[6]

Drawing a further parallel between the two deaths, Basler says that by reading Anderson's contemporaneous account of Lincoln's assassination readers may effectively participate with their forebears as spectators of that great national tragedy, in the same way as they participated in the events of Kennedy's death, as reported in newspapers and portrayed on television.[7] As with Lattimer's comments, there appears to be an unwitting suggestion of morphic resonance at play, of the past living in the present, of minds capable of sharing the feelings of similar events although separated by nearly a century.

Gerald Posner argues against the constant interpretation of coincidences in the Kennedy assassination as evidence of conspiracy. He gives as a prime example the fact that Oswald obtained a job at the Texas School Book Depository, thus giving him a clear shot at the presidential motorcade. Conspiracists, such as New Orleans District Attorney Jim Garrison, say that Oswald was manipulated into the job. (Author's note: as with Booth at Ford's Theatre, the assassination base was Oswald's place of work.) Posner says, however, that this argument ignores the fact that a motorcade route had not even been proposed by the date Oswald was hired by the Texas School Book Depository. Moreover, such a theory means that Linnie Mae Randle, who suggested to Ruth Paine that Oswald should try for the job, and Paine herself, who passed on the suggestion to Oswald, were part of the conspiracy. It would also mean that Roy Truly, who hired him, and the employees who had rejected him for other jobs were co-conspirators.[8]

Posner's book seeks to repudiate any argument of a conspiracy surrounding Kennedy's death and one of the ways he does so is to examine the apparent coincidences critically, an interesting exercise in itself. Our concern is to present the facts relating to the coincidences between Kennedy and Lincoln; whether or not they add to or subtract from either conspiracy theory is largely up to the reader and the perspective they bring to the subject.

A cursory study of history in the 1860s and 1960s shows that American society was going through very similar crises and problems in each era. In the 1960s the division between North and South had not been greater than since Lincoln's presidency and the dividing issue was similar: the civil rights of black Americans. It is possible to argue that the Americans of the 1960s were tuned into a morphic field that had been laid down by the Americans of the previous century, and that the thoughts, feelings, anger and frustration had all emerged as in the

1860s template. This is most strikingly illustrated by the coincidences that link the two presidents' deaths. It suggests a vast mass of coincidences was at work in and between these decades.

Furthermore the morphic resonance theory offers an explanation for the behaviour of the principals involved. There is no escaping the fact Oswald displayed many of Booth's attributes, to the extent it was almost as though Booth was guiding Oswald. The morphic resonance theory (see Chapter Two) argues that it is easier to learn an action once it has been carried out by others. It is accepted that Booth and Oswald were driven by dark and unreasonable forces that are still not explicable to the modern mind. Neither man in his diaries and other writings compares himself with other assassins – a striking trait in such people, who tend to regard their actions as unique and bold, and cowardly though they are, believe they will be regarded as heroes, a Cassius come to slay Caesar. How does one learn to adopt an assassin's persona while consciously believing one's actions to be unique?

We now come to brief outlines of some of the coincidences between the assassinations of Lincoln and Kennedy. There were striking coincidences concerning each tragedy alone, but, unlike Posner, I have chosen to ignore them, compelling though some of them are, for our central thesis.

The strands of what are conventionally accepted as unrelated events began to weave themselves into patterns of coincidence the moment Oswald on the sixth floor of the Texas School Book Depository, on that November day in Dallas, lifted his gun and aimed it at Kennedy passing below him in the motorcade...

Bad Friday

Kennedy was killed on 22 November 1963. It was the Friday before Thanksgiving, the start of a holiday weekend. Booth shot Lincoln on Good Friday, 14 April 1865, also the start of a holiday weekend.

Fatal Shots

If we accept that Oswald *was* Kennedy's assassin – and for the purpose of this exercise we must – then both Oswald and Booth shot at the head of their victims, effectively destroying their brains and thus ensuring death. As Oswald's shot rang out, Kennedy's head jerked back sharply. One bullet smashed into the back of his head, blowing away a section of skull and brain. By the time Kennedy was admitted to Parkland Hospital, according to 28-year-old surgical resident Dr Charles J. Carrico, 'his colour was blue white, ashen. He had slow, agonal respiration, spasmodic respirations without any co-ordination. He was making no voluntary movements. His eyes were open, pupils were seen to be dilated and later were seen not to react to light…He had no palpable pulse.' The president, Dr Carrico concluded, was clearly 'a terminal patient'.[9]

Just over 100 years earlier Booth had entered the State Box at Ford's Theatre, pointed his single-shot derringer pistol at the back of Lincoln's head and pulled the trigger. There was a flash and a loud report and the half-inch Britannia metal ball crashed into Lincoln's skull, destroying his brain.

Dr Charles Leale, another young surgeon, was, like Carrico, the first to examine the president and his initial conclusion was similar: 'He appeared to be dead.' He too found no pulse and, lifting Lincoln's eyelids, found evidence of brain injury.[10] Dr Leale was employed in an army hospital and was familiar with gunshot wounds.[11]

With the help of another young surgeon assisting, Dr Charles Taft (both men were exactly the same age, 23), who had clambered onto the stage from his seat in the audience, Leale applied artificial respiration and closed chest cardiac massage.[12]

Surgeons at Parkdale applied exactly the same emergency treatment in an attempt to revive Kennedy. Lattimer, a former military surgeon, familiar with gunshot wounds, points out that in each case experienced and highly skilled medical personnel were quickly at the side of the dying presidents. However, in each case the men concerned just as quickly concluded nothing could be done, because one side of the brain had been hopelessly and irretrievably damaged by the assassins' bullets. 'There was no hope that either Lincoln or Kennedy could have been saved by modern neurosurgical and support methods,' Lattimer writes.[13]

Assassins in public places tend to aim at the heart or other vulnerable body parts when using a gun, especially in America: for example, Charles Guiteau, whose bullet struck President James Garfield in the pancreas on 2 July 1881, and Arthur Bremer, who shot Alabama governor George Wallace on 15 May 1972 five times in the body, crippling him. In Israel, Yigar Amir, the 1995 assassin of the country's Prime Minister, Yitzhak Rabin, was, like Booth, directly behind his victim and at similar close range and could as easily have aimed at Rabin's head, instead of firing into his back as he did. Even in officially sanctioned executions the heart is the target, with a possible *coup de grâce* to the head. If death by gunshot is part of popular American culture, promoted by gangster movies and Westerns, then we must accept that the myth-makers seldom show a victim dying as a result of a bullet to the head. Aesthetic reasons may explain this, especially in film, but that is to say that Oswald, in particular, was either not effected by the myth or had not aimed one of his shots at the head and hit it by accident, or chance – or had some unconscious memory of how Lincoln met his death.

Where Did the Shots Come From?

In both cases doubts were raised about the direction of the shots that killed the presidents. Because the bullet entered Lincoln's head on the left side, it was suggested that the shot may not have come from Booth's gun but from another assassin in the audience. The State Box in which Lincoln was sitting overlooked the stage on the right side of the theatre, so the audience was to Lincoln's left. When Booth entered the box, Lincoln was to his left. To shoot him on the left side it seems he would have had to waste valuable seconds to position himself. However, it is argued at the sound of Booth's entrance Lincoln may have turned his head first to his right, then his left, as he sought to see who it was. As he was turning his head to look over his left shoulder Booth fired from behind without having to move from his entry position.

The dispute over the direction of the shots that killed Kennedy continues. The conspiracists most favoured spot for an alternative shooting position is the grassy knoll area that runs off Elm Street which the presidential limousine was passing when the shots were fired. Another possibility suggested is the triple underpass towards which the vehicle was heading and/or other buildings in the vicinity. At the sound of the shots, pigeons on the roof of the Texas School Book Depository building fluttered up in confusion. The grassy knoll site contains trees in which birds were almost certainly present, but no witness has come forward to say they saw birds fluttering out from its limbs at the sound of firing.

Pre-arrangements

Both Booth and Oswald had read newspaper accounts that gave them the information needed to show their assassinations could be carried out from their places of work.

On the morning 14 April 1865, Booth read in a Washington newspaper the following announcement:

> Lieut-General Grant, President and Mrs Lincoln, have secured the State
> Box at Ford's Theatre TO NIGHT [sic] to witness Miss Laura Keen's American
> Cousin.

Booth knew the theatre intimately and even used it as his postal address in Washington. A century later Oswald read in *The Dallas*

Times that President Kennedy was to pass along Elm Street beneath the window from where he fired. He had by then come to know the Texas School Book Depository building very well, in particular the sixth floor.

Booth and Oswald planned how they would go about the shooting by making some changes to the areas from which they would fire to ensure they would not be observed or hindered. Booth hid a strong stick behind the door of the State Box and burrowed a hole in the plaster behind the entrance door into which he could wedge the stick, thereby preventing the door from being opened from the outside without either breaking or removing the stick. He then drilled a hole through the second door in the anteroom of the box so that once inside he would be able to peep into the box to see exactly where the president was seated.

For his part, Oswald piled up boxes to form a barrier which hid him from anyone else on the sixth floor. Just before the shooting he jammed the lift on the sixth floor.

Work in Progress

In both cases the working places of the two assassins were in disrepair, thus helping them greatly in carrying out their assassinations. It is doubtful whether the assassinations could have been attempted had the sites from which the two men fired the fatal shots been in their normal state.

With Lincoln's assassination the lock which could have secured the door to the State Box from inside had been broken by Thomas Raybold, a ticket seller at Ford's Theatre, more than a month before the night of the assassination. Raybold told the military trial of Booth's accomplices that it came about because on the night of 7 March, he had sold four orchestra tickets in advance to a man named Merrick whose party failed to arrive by the time the show started so the seats were given to other customers. When Merrick and party came later, Raybold showed them to the State Box, which was unoccupied. But he could not find the doorkey, so he broke the lock with a kick and 'never thought of having it fixed'.

Roscoe sees grounds for suspicion in Raybold's story, pointing out that Merrick was a day clerk at the National Hotel (where Booth was staying prior to the assassination), and in the same party was a Mrs Bunker, who bore the name of the night clerk at the hotel. He asks, was it coincidence that people who knew Booth were involved in the lock-breaking episode?[14] At any rate all locks to the State Box at Ford's Theatre were useless on 14 April. Had Lincoln or any member of his party wished to close the door for security or privacy reasons from the inside they could not have done so. This enabled Booth to freely open the door, step into the box, aim his derringer at the back of Lincoln's head and fire.

In Kennedy's case, the sixth floor of the Texas School Book Depository building was being relaid with a plywood floor by workers who had moved many of the book cartons to the side of the large room and the workers who were usually on the floor were absent. One of the floor layers, along with two other employees, decided to watch the parade from the fifth floor.[15] Another employee, Bonnie Ray Williams, 19, had gone to the sixth floor where he ate his lunch shortly before the president was due and, since nobody had joined him to watch the parade, he went down to the fifth floor to be with the others,[16] leaving the unseen Oswald, hidden behind the disturbed book cartons, to prepare the firing position.

The Texas School Book Depository provided the deadliest sniper's roost on the presidential route, because the motorcade was scheduled to first zig and then zag directly beneath the windows. A gunman could size up the president's car as it approached the building from the front, wait while it pivoted sharply at his feet and fire as it crept slowly out of the turn to his right.[17]

Security Risk

Neither Lincoln nor Kennedy liked the idea of guards surrounding them, nor the thought they could not travel openly in their own country. At Dallas Love Field Airport, Kennedy ordered the bubbletop to be removed from his Lincoln Continental so that he, and his beautiful wife, Jackie, could be more easily seen during the cavalcade through the Texas city. There was to be criticism of the lack of Secret Service bodyguards on and around his vehicle, but, following the assassination, one of them told Charles Roberts, the noted White House correspondent who had travelled in the press bus with the motorcade, that Kennedy had also ordered the bodyguards off the retractable footholds on the side of the car where they normally rode when moving through a crowd. 'He wanted to be seen,' the bodyguard explained to Roberts.[18]

In another breach of Secret Service regulations, the president and the vice-president were permitted to be in close proximity in the same city, in the same motorcade and both in open slow-moving vehicles. This procedure was, it is claimed, unheard of until that day.

As for Lincoln's security, when Booth entered the theatre through the main entrance he found the presidential box unguarded. John Parker, the White House policeman charged with protecting the president, was not to be seen. He had reportedly left his post out-side the State Box entrance door at least once to get a drink and, on another occasion, to move to a position where he could see the performance.

Discarding conspiracy theories, both men acted in a manner that made them easy targets for their assassins. What impulse drove them to such apparent foolishness? Washington was a town riddled with Confederate agents and violent enemies of Lincoln, a town where 'the furies unleashed by military conflict put Lincoln's life, like the nation's, squarely at stake'.[19] Similarly, Dallas was full of right-wing zealots where, warned Southern lawyer Byron Skelton, a Kennedy supporter, the atmosphere had become so highly charged that an unstable, sug-gestible individual might easily be incited. He suggested Kennedy cross Dallas off his Texas itinerary.[20]

The Wounded

Both presidents were in the presence of another couple and in each case the other man was also wounded by the assassin. John Connally, the Governor of Texas, was riding in the jump seat with his wife directly in front of Kennedy. A bullet passed through Connally's body and emerged to hit him in the wrist, before going on to smash into his thigh. He survived his wounds, and died on 15 June 1993 of a lung ail-ment.

Lincoln told his wife that he had invited roughly a dozen people to accompany them to Ford's Theatre. Most for various reasons (a sixth sense?) declined, except for 28-year-old Major Henry Reed Rathbone and his fiancée, 20-year-old Clara Harris, the daughter of New York Senator Ira Harris.

Major Rathbone and Miss Harris were together on a settee to the right of the president that was set against the wall nearest the stage when Booth stepped into the box at 10.15 p.m. After shooting the president, Booth threw down his gun and turned to deal with Rathbone, who had leapt up to tackle him. Producing a razor-sharp hunting knife he inflicted an eight-inch cut on the soldier's upper arm which bled profusely and was to hamper his removing the bar Booth had used to wedge the door shut.

There was initial confusion when doctors reached the box where Lincoln was slumped in his rocking chair. Noting Rathbone's severe injury, Dr Charles Leale assumed that the president had also been stabbed. When the president's upper clothing was cut away, however, Leale could find no wound, It was only then that he lifted the eyelids and saw evidence of brain injury. Confusion also came about as a result of the presence of another man as to who Oswald's target actually was. Oswald had written to Connally, who until recently had been Secretary of the Navy, after learning the Marine Corps had downgraded his discharge from honourable to undesirable in view of his defection to the Soviet Union. He had asked Connally to have the ruling overturned.[21]

Hidden Evidence

Roscoe claims that perhaps the most important single item of evidence concerning the conspiracy surrounding Lincoln's assassination was in Booth's diary. It was taken from his body at Garret's farm (where Booth was shot and killed by troops) and rushed to Washington by Lieutenant Colonel Everton Conger (who was present at the farm). Conger delivered the diary to Lafayette Baker, who carried the little red book in person to War Secretary Edwin Stanton. According to his own subsequent admission, Stanton received the book from Baker. 'I examined it... with great care,' Stanton recalled, 'and read over all the entries in it.' So far as is known, Stanton, Baker and Conger were the only Federal leaders who ever saw all the entries in Booth's diary. In spite of its obvious importance the diary was not produced as evidence, nor ever mentioned, during the 1865 conspiracy trial.[22] In his book Roscoe asks: did it list conspiracy leaders? Did it mention certain accomplices, or exonerate persons held under suspicion?[23] The book disappeared and when it was 'rediscovered' in a forgotten War Department file two years later, 18 pages were missing, cut from the section leading up to Lincoln's murder. Baker claimed it was intact when he gave it to Stanton. Stanton declared the excised pages were always missing. Roscoe concludes that, if nothing else, the mutilated diary bore evidence to War Department or Secret Service skulduggery.[24]

On 12 November 1963 Oswald walked into the FBI office at 1,114 Commerce Street, near the Texas School Book Depository, and asked for Agent James Hosty. When the receptionist told him the agent was at lunch he gave her an unsealed envelope with 'Hosty' written across the front. According to Hosty, inside was an undated note that read, 'If you have anything you want to learn about me, come talk to me directly. If you don't cease bothering my wife, I will take appropriate action and report this to the proper authorities.' According to Hosty, two days after the assassination, he was called into the office of the Dallas Special-Agent-in-Charge, J. Gordon Shanklin, who told him to destroy the note as 'Oswald is dead now.'[25] Hosty then destroyed the note. The FBI hid the existence of the note from the Warren Commission.[26] Despite extensive examination before the Commission, Hosty never mentioned it. In later testimony before the Senate Intelligence

Committee, Shanklin said that he never knew about the note until 1975.[27]

The destruction of Oswald's note leaves open the FBI's overall role and relationship to him. (Just as in the earlier case the diary brought questions about the relationship between the Secretary of War and his staff and Booth.) Oliver Stone, in his 1991 film *JFK*, implies that the Oswald note may have been a warning to the FBI of a plot to kill the president. Stone based his film on Jim Garrison, the New Orleans District Attorney, who conducted his own investigation into the assassination in which he claims Oswald was a spy and Hosty his secret FBI contact. But, argues Posner, it requires a leap of faith to accept that Oswald, armed with information of a plot to kill Kennedy, would drop it off in an unsealed envelope.[28] Many years later Hosty revealed that he was one of the interrogators who had taken notes of their interview with Oswald at Dallas police station shortly after Oswald had been arrested. Notes taken by another interrogator, Dallas Police Captain 'Will' Fritz, turned up in 1984. The captain's notes included comments such as 'Denies shooting Pres…Denies owning rifle…says nothing against Pres…' Neither of these notes were produced for the Warren Commission.

Eluding Capture

Shortly after the shootings, both Oswald and Booth were stopped, questioned and allowed to proceed. In Oswald's case this was carried out by a police officer, in Booth's by a sentry.

Oswald was briefly apprehended in the Texas School Book Depository by Dallas motorcycle policeman Marion Baker. As the first shot was fired Baker looked up and saw pigeons scattering from the roof of the Book Depository building. Gun in hand, he ran to its entrance where he met Supervisor Roy Truly. Together they headed for the lifts but found they were jammed on the fifth floor. The two men took to the stairs. On the second floor they saw a man through the window door of the employees lunchroom, known as the Domino Room. Waving his pistol, Baker ordered the man to walk towards him. Oswald did so without saying a word. Baker recalled, 'In fact, he didn't change his expression one bit. He didn't seem to be excited.'[28] This was despite the fact that the officer's gun was almost touching Oswald's midriff. Truly identified him as an employee and they moved on. Moments after that Oswald left the building through the main entrance.

After fleeing Ford's Theatre, Booth mounted his horse and rode onto Pennsylvania Avenue, around the Capitol building and then to the

Navy Yard Bridge, which spans the Anacostia river. At the bridge, the armed guard ordered him to stop. As with Oswald, at this early period after the shooting, the hue and cry had not yet gone up. Booth, as Oswald had done with Baker, gave his own name to the guard. Normally the bridge was closed to civilians at 9 p.m. each day. As he was talking to the guard, David Harrold, one of Booth's accomplices, rode up. Both men claimed they were residents of the area on the opposite side of the bridge and, having satisfied the guard, were allowed to proceed.

Booth and Oswald

The assassins themselves share many similarities. The names of John Wilkes Booth and Lee Harvey Oswald each contain fifteen letters. Both assassins were nearly the same age: Booth was born in 1838 and Oswald in 1939. Both were Southerners. Oswald's father was Robert E. Lee Oswald. Oswald's first name was handed down from that of the Confederate general who was the 'commander' of Booth.

Booth was born into a family of actors. His father, a famous tragedian, died when he was ten (Oswald's father also died when he was a child). Booth's father, Junius Brutus, was named after Caesar's assassin.[29] Both John Wilkes and his father made their stage debuts in *Richard III*. Junius at Covent Garden, London, in 1814, John in 1855 at Richmond, Virginia.

Early in his career Booth used a stage name, J. Wilkes, because he had been subject to some bad reviews and believed he might tarnish the famous family name. Oswald too used aliases, including A. Hidell, to buy his guns by mail order and as the 'president' he invented for his 'Fair Go for Cuba' committee.

The fraternal links of the two assassins were somewhat similar. Booth's brothers, Junius Brutus Jr. and Edwin, were already highly successful actors when Booth first trod the boards. One hundred years later Oswald's two brothers, John and Robert, were both well into successful careers in the military before Oswald set out to make his mark on life: John was a Marine and Robert a member of the Coast Guard. Both killers had a burning ambition for recognition and were desperate to 'catch up' with their brothers.

In July 1952, three months after his 18th birthday, Oswald enlisted in the Marines. Booth made his stage debut when he was 18.

Both men regarded themselves, at least for some stage of their lives, as enemies of the US. Oswald claimed he was a Marxist and a supporter of the USSR and the communist regime in Cuba. Booth's support was for the Confederacy.

Both men were accused of consorting with the enemy. Booth in Canada with the Confederates based at their 'embassy'. Whether Oswald 'consorted' with the USSR by discussing or revealing plans for the assassination of Kennedy at the Soviet Embassy in Mexico City in October 1963 is still not known. A few years ago a news report claimed the CIA had tapes of everything Oswald discussed inside the embassy building, picked up by bugs which had been planted with the help of the Mexican government. The report says the CIA was fighting to stop the declassification of the tapes based on the grounds that the material could still damage American national security.[30]

Both men had suffered gunshot wounds. Booth had been wounded in 1860 when a pistol owned by a theatre manager had accidentally discharged, the ball hitting Booth either – accounts of the matter differ – in the side of his torso, or in the thigh.[31]

On 27 October 1957, while serving in the Marines in Japan, Oswald was wounded in one elbow when he dropped a .22-calibre derringer pocket pistol he'd secretly obtained from the States by mail order. 'I believe I shot myself,' he declared solemnly to his agitated comrades. Both the suspicion that the wound was self-inflicted and possession of a private firearm meant he had to face a court-martial.[32]

Similar claims were made by two people close to the assassins that they were admirers of the men they shot. 'Booth always liked Mr Lincoln and was very fond of his jokes,' said an accomplice, David Harrold, after he had been arrested.[33]

Marina Oswald pointed out in a 1988 interview that Oswald 'admired and liked' Kennedy. 'Lee even said he was good for the country,' she said of her husband, adding, 'I'll go to the grave believing that Lee adored John Kennedy. Lee always took pride in the country's young president.'[34]

The Murder Weapons

In both cases the assassin conveniently left the gun at the scene of the crime. Booth's derringer pistol was found later the same night when William T. Kent, one of the first to enter the box after the shooting, returned to look for his latchkey, which he realized must have fallen from his pocket when he loaned surgeon Leale his knife to cut open Lincoln's coat, vest and shirt. While searching on the floor of the box, his foot struck an object which turned out to be the murderer's derringer.[35]

A rifle was discovered on the sixth floor of the Texas School Book Depository at 1.22 p.m. on 22 November. The finders were Deputy Constable Seymour Weitzman and Deputy Sheriff Eugene Boone.

Carbine Slings

Both men carried carbines, Oswald a Carcano, the murder weapon, and Booth a Spencer for his escape from the murder scene. The gunslings look almost identical. Both are flat and narrow. Lattimer says that Booth's sling was made of a strip of fabric resembling heavy cloth-tape or flattened rope, while Oswald's was made of a leather belt for a pistol holster.

The Boarding Houses

Booth and Oswald each plotted their assassinations and kept their weapons in a boarding house. Booth and his fellow plotters held regular meetings at a boarding house at 541 H Street, Washington, owned by Mrs Mary E. Surratt (who was hanged for her part in the plot). The plotters were also said to have kept their guns and other weapons there.

Shortly after the shooting of Kennedy, Dallas police arrived at the boarding house at 1,026 North Beckley, kept by Mrs Earlene Roberts. In Oswald's room they found a pistol holster.

The Captures

Oswald fired at Kennedy from a warehouse and was shortly afterwards captured in a Texas theatre in the Oak Cliff section of Dallas. Booth shot Lincoln in Ford's Theatre and was captured in an old tobacco warehouse which was being used as a corn barn on the Garret farm off Bowling Green Road, near Port Royal, Virginia. Although both were armed they surrendered without firing a shot.

As he was secured at the theatre Oswald yelled, 'I protest this police brutality.' As he was being taken into Dallas police headquarters he was asked if he wanted to conceal his face. 'Why should I cover my face?' he retorted. 'I haven't done anything to be ashamed of.' While being interrogated he continued to protest his innocence.[36]

Booth, 'when challenged [by troops surrounding the old warehouse] to come out and surrender, in a very wild and excited tone demanded to know who they supposed him to be and by what authority, desiring to know of what crime he was charged, and evincing the greatest excitement...'[37]

South of the Border

Mexico appears to have been the destination to which each assassin intended to flee following the shootings. As he lay dying, Booth told his captors, 'You, gentlemen, have spoiled my fun in Mexico.'[38]

Although Oswald's intentions as he fled from the scene are still

215

uncertain, a draft of Chapter 6 of the Warren Report says that when police patrolman Jefferson Tippit stopped Oswald just over an hour after the shooting he was only four blocks away from catching a Route 55 bus due to arrive at 1.40 p.m. that would have taken him to a point on Lancaster Road where a Greyhound bus was scheduled to leave at 3.30 p.m. This southbound bus would have, with connections, taken him to Monterey, Mexico. Earlier Oswald had taken a transfer ticket on the bus he boarded at the corner of St Paul and Elm after leaving the Texas School Book Depository. That morning in an uncharacteristically generous gesture, he had left his wife, Marina, $170 – most of his savings. He had on him at the time of his arrest $13.87, just enough to pay for the bus trip to Mexico.[39] Oswald was a non-driver and the only way he could afford to get out of town was by bus. A final fact: Oswald had travelled to Mexico by bus in September and was seen to enter both the Cuban and Soviet Embassies in Mexico City.

Deaths of the Assassins

Both Oswald and Booth were murdered in similar circumstances. Both were surrounded by their captors, under a blaze of lights and constricted in their movements. Their assassins were Jack Ruby and Boston Corbett respectively, and each used a Colt revolver and fired only one bullet – both lethal.

Oswald was murdered on the morning of 24 November 1963 in the basement of the Dallas police and courts building in the presence of more than 70 local police officers. The scene was highly illuminated by television and newsreel camera lights. As he was being led to a waiting police car while handcuffed to a detective, Jack Ruby pushed through the crowd, pistol in hand, and placed the muzzle against Oswald's stomach. Oswald tried to protect himself by bringing up his hands, but he was to all intents and purposes defenceless. Ruby shot him once in the stomach.

Booth was illuminated by the flames of the burning barn with the armed cavalry troops surrounding it. He was also constrained in his movements by the fact he could only walk with the aid of a crutch as a result of having broken a bone in his leg when he had leapt from the State Box to the stage after shooting Lincoln. The shot fired by Corbett entered Booth's head in almost precisely the same spot that Lincoln was shot[40] and he died at almost the same hour of the day that Lincoln had died.[41]

Oswald and Booth each lived for only a few hours after they had been shot. Booth died a few minutes after 7 a.m. and Oswald about 1.20 p.m. According to Lattimer this is extraordinary in itself, since a single pistol bullet rarely kills its victim.[42] As a consequence neither was brought to trial and, of course, the reasoning behind their actions could never be fully examined.

An autopsy was done on each man, but persistent and recurring suggestions were made in each case that the bodies should be exhumed to satisfy doubts raised that the bodies were, in fact, those of the two assassins.

In Booth's case they still wanted to see if the body really had a broken leg and in Oswald's case whether there was evidence of a childhood mastoid infection and a scar from the self-inflicted pistol wound incurred while he was in Japan as a member of the US Marines.[43]

Jack Ruby and Boston Corbett

The men who killed the assassins were strange tortured souls. The contemporaneous writer Dwight Anderson, in flush of hyperbole, called Boston Corbett 'the hero of Booth's capture', while the initial reaction of the several hundred people gathered outside the Dallas police headquarters to the news that Oswald had been shot indicated that Ruby was for a brief period in history treated also as a hero – when word spread about what he had done the crowd spontaneously broke into cheers and applause.

Thomas Corbett was born in England and brought to New York by his father, aged eight. In 1858, when working as a hat-maker, he was confronted by two prostitutes in the street and, as a penance, went home and castrated himself using a large pair of scissors. He subsequently went to Boston where he changed his first name and was baptized in a Methodist church under his new name – Boston. As he aimed his gun at Booth, Corbett claimed he prayed fervently for Booth that God would have mercy on his soul.[44]

Later in life, when he was on the Kansas State legislative chamber staff, he shot at some pageboys because he believed they were laughing at the chamber's chaplain who was giving the blessing at an opening of a session. As a result he was declared insane and committed to a mental institution.[45]

Both Boston and Ruby were unmarried at the time they carried out their shootings.

Ruby had also changed his name. Born Jacob Rubenstein, in Chicago in 1911, he moved from his place of birth to Texas in 1947. Ruby had a reputation for attacking patrons of his nightclub. Once he ran after another nightclub owner shooting at him several times, but missing.[46]

Posner says that after Ruby's arrest he underwent a steady mental deterioration.[47] His sister, Eva, told the Warren Commission that he was 'mentally deranged' in prison.[48] Rabbi Silverman, who also visited him in prison, found him to be demented, schizophrenic and psychotic.[49] Quite clearly, had he not already been incarcerated, these are strong indications he would have been placed in a mental institution, as was Corbett.

Each assassin's assassin had an earlier opportunity to shoot his man down at close range. Two days before he killed Oswald, Ruby found himself right next to the man as he was being pulled through the packed crowd on the third floor of the Dallas police headquarters on his way to a press conference. Ruby said that as Oswald walked past, 'I was standing about two or three feet away.' He went on to deny he was armed at the time.[50]

Corbett also said he had had an earlier opportunity to shoot Booth. Corbett testified: 'As the flames rose, we could distinguish [Booth] about the middle of the barn turning towards the fire, either to put the fire out or to shoot the one who started it...he was coming towards me...I could have shot him then much easier than when I afterwards did.'[51]

The Paines

Two people named Paine played critical roles in the assassinations. In the Lincoln case, the original name of the Paine concerned was Lewis Thornton Powell, an ex-Confederate soldier and son of a Baptist minister in Florida. He was a well-built, handsome, clean-cut and fearless young man. Wounded and captured at the battle of Gettysburg, he escaped from hospital in Baltimore and joined John Singleton Mosby's Confederate Guerrilla Rangers.[52] In January 1865, he deserted Mosby and went back to Baltimore where he was arrested for assault, then released after signing an oath of allegiance and a statement, using the name L. Paine, that he would not engage in activities against the Union. Paine became Booth's dutiful accomplice. He managed to carry out a deception that got him into the house of the Secretary of State, William H. Seward, whom he critically injured. This attack took place about the time Booth was shooting Lincoln. Paine was hanged with three other conspirators in Washington on 7 July 1865.

Oswald's wife, Marina, and the couple's child were living with Mrs Ruth Paine in the Dallas suburb of Irving at the time of the assassination. Oswald visited them from Dallas at the weekends and, unknown to Paine, kept his carbine among his and Marina's personal possessions that were stored in her garage. According to the Warren Commission he removed it on the morning of the assassination. Thus, Paine had unwittingly been involved in the tragedy. Her predecessor, Lewis Paine, had stored weapons for Booth in various boarding houses.

Author Colin Davies claims that the day before Oswald started work at the Texas School Book Depository, the Texas Employment Commission had contacted Paine to advise Oswald of a vacancy as a baggage handler at Dallas airport. But that information was inexplicably not passed on to Oswald despite the fact that the airport position paid $100 a month more than the Book Depository job. Davies concludes from this that only one answer is possible – Paine wanted Oswald to work at the Depository.[53] However, the Warren Commission report says: 'It seems clear that Oswald was hired by the Depository Co. before the higher paying job was available.'[54]

The Hearings

A military commission of inquiry into Lincoln's assassination was appointed by President Andrew Johnson, just as President Lyndon Johnson was to appoint the Warren Commission of inquiry on 29 November 1963. According to Henry Kyd Douglas, the commission into Lincoln's assassination 'had been organized to convict'.[55] The entire proceedings would turn out to be just what the Army Judge Advocate or the War Department chose to make of it.[56]

(Author's note: in the situation in which President Lyndon Johnson found himself, we have a fine example of the lessons of history – not to say those of coincidence – being ignored. The Lincoln commission, while a trial, found itself having to inquire into the circumstances surrounding the death of the president. Yet when it came to the Warren Commission, the circumstances were considered to be unique even though it too was dealing with the assassination of an American president by a lone gunman. Writing just a few years after Kennedy's death, Edward Jay Epstein says in his book *Inquest* that the Warren Commission operated under virtually unprecedented circumstances.[57] Epstein's book began as a thesis: how does a government organization function in an extraordinary situation in which there are no rules or precedents to guide it? In the book's introduction, Richard H. Rovere goes further, saying that Johnson could find little 'guidance in American history' for the Warren Commission. It was a view shared by many, even though it too was dealing with the assassination of an American president.)

The Lincoln inquiry was reopened in 1867 for the trial of John H. Surrat. He had also been charged with conspiracy to murder the president but had fled overseas where he had been captured and brought back to trial. The jury were unable to agree on a verdict, and he was freed. The trial was reopened again during the attempt to impeach President Johnson.

The Kennedy assassination inquiry was reopened in 1975 as part of the Senate Select Committee on Intelligence inquiry headed by Vice-President Nelson Rockefeller and again in 1978 by a House of Representatives Select Committee on Assassinations. Norman Mailer writes:

> The Warren Commission has been heavily criticized for its appearance of bias, of being set up with but one purpose – to convict. If the seven august men who presided were out to blur every possibility but one – that Oswald was a twisted and lonely killer – then one has to assume the opposite. As inquiry, the Warren Commission's work resembles a dead whale decomposing on a beach.[58]

Historian Hugh Trevor-Roper, one of the Warren Commission's early critics, claims the Commissioners 'insensibly and progressively' emphasized the evidence which appeared to support the conclusion of Oswald's guilt. 'We lack confidence in the evidence submitted by the Commission and the Commission's handling of it. This is undoubtedly a serious omission,' he wrote.[59]

Despite the similar criticism of the two inquiries, they set out in diametrically opposite directions, Lincoln's to prove there was a conspiracy, Kennedy's to prove there was not a conspiracy. However, in their findings both left doubts in the public's mind that have lasted to this day.

The Wives

At the time of the slayings both men were seated by their wives. Despite this proximity neither wife was injured. Moments after each shooting both women cradled their husbands' heads in their hands and only let go when doctors took over. Each underwent an agonizing wait as doctors made futile attempts to save the lives of their husbands.

Both women married at the same age, 24, men who were in their thirties. They came from socially prominent families. Both women spoke fluent French. Each had three children. Each woman lost a child through death while they were in the White House – Patrick Kennedy and William Lincoln. In each case their children rode ponies in the White House grounds.

Kennedy and Lincoln

The names Lincoln and Kennedy each contain seven letters. Both men were second children. They grew into tall, lean men. Kennedy had a lazy muscle in one eye which would sometimes permit it to deviate and a portrait of Lincoln suggests a possible similar lazy eye.[60]

They each had sisters who died before their election as president.

Lincoln was related to General Isaac Barnard, who in 1827 became a US Senator for Pennsylvania. Kennedy's younger brother Edward was elected US Senator for Massachusetts in 1962.

Both men had been skippers. Lincoln was the co-captain of a Mississippi river boat and Kennedy of Torpedo Boat 109. Both served in the armed forces. Lincoln was a captain in the Black Hawk Indian War and Kennedy, a Navy Lieutenant in the South Pacific in World War II.

In each case a relative had been a long-term mayor of Boston. F. W. Lincoln, a cousin, was mayor for seven terms. J. F. Fitzgerald, Kennedy's grandfather, was elected mayor of Boston for five terms.

Both had relatives who were Harvard graduates and who went on to become US Attorneys-General in Democratic administrations: Levi Lincoln Sr, under President Thomas Jefferson, and Robert F. Kennedy was appointed by his brother.

Both presidents became friends with a Billy Graham. For Lincoln this was William Mentor Graham, a New Salem, Illinois, a schoolmaster who helped Lincoln with his studies; Kennedy was friends with the well-known evangelist.

Kennedy knew a Dr Charles Taft, the son of President William Howard Taft, 27th president of the US, 1909–13. Lincoln knew Dr Charles Taft, who, in fact, was the second doctor to reach him at Ford's Theatre and who fought valiantly to save his life.

Each president had a next of kin who had been ambassador to the court of St James. Robert Todd Lincoln, the oldest son of the president, was US Ambassador from 1889 to 1893. Kennedy's father, Joseph P. Kennedy, was US Ambassador from 1938 (1893 transposed) to 1940.

Both were elected first to the House of Representatives, Lincoln in 1847 and Kennedy in 1947. They were runners-up for vice-presidential nominations of their parties, Lincoln in 1856 and Kennedy in 1956.

The first public proposal that Lincoln be the Republican candidate for president came in a letter to the *Cincinnati Gazette* (6 November 1858) which also endorsed a John Kennedy for Vice-President (John P. Kennedy, formerly Secretary of the Navy).[61]

In their presidential campaigns they outpointed in public debate their rivals for office, Senator Stephen A. Douglas and Vice-President Richard Nixon respectively.

Kennedy took office in 1960 and Lincoln in 1860.

Both presidents were fatalistic and used bodyguards only reluctantly; they both believed they should be able to move freely in public anywhere in the USA.

Both men were noted for their writing and speaking abilities and for words that have become immortal. In his Gettysburg address, Lincoln said: '...this nation, under God, shall have a new birth of freedom and that government of the people, by the people and for the people, shall not perish from the earth.' Kennedy in his inaugural address declared: 'Let every nation know, whether it wishes us well or ill, that we shall pay any price, bear any burden, meet any hardship, support any friends, oppose any foe to assure the survival and success of liberty... ask not what your country can do for you – ask what you can do for your country.'

Both presidents had the legality of their elections contested.

Lincoln fought against slavery and kept the USA from being split. Kennedy fought for the civil rights of the descendants of those blacks who had supposedly been given their freedom 100 years before. As Kennedy came to power the nation was more divided over the issue than it had been since the Civil War. Kennedy delivered his civil rights message to Congress in 1963 and Lincoln freed all slaves with his 1863 Emancipation Proclamation.

In 1963 two authors published books with surprisingly similar titles. William O. Douglas wrote *Mr Lincoln and the Negroes* and Harry Goldin wrote *Mr Kennedy and the Negroes.*

Kennedy's secretary, whose name was Mrs Evelyn Lincoln, had a husband known as Abe. She advised her boss not to make the trip to Dallas. It has been claimed in more recent years that Lincoln had a secretary named John Kennedy who advised Lincoln not to go to Ford's Theatre. This person appears to be New York Police Superintendent, John A. Kennedy, who, Lattimer says, was an adviser to Lincoln.[62] If so, it was only a part-time job as he was still a member of the New York Police at the time of the assassination and investigated some aspects of the case in that city for the War Department. Whether he specifically warned Lincoln against a visit to the theatre is uncertain. But the fact that the War Department approached this New York policeman to carry out post-assassination investigations could indicate some prior connection.

Kennedy was shot dead while riding in a Ford car – a Lincoln – and Lincoln was shot dead in Ford's Theatre.

Both presidents were shot in the back of the head.

In each case, partial autopsies were carried out. A member from both Cabinets banned the use by the press of photographs of the bodies.

Both presidents lay in state in the east room of the White House. The catafalque base on which Kennedy's body lay had been used for Lincoln's body. Mrs Kennedy had read about the funeral of Lincoln and asked that the same type of bier be used for her husband. This is one of the few instance in which the shock of Kennedy's death had brought to the mind of somebody involved the death of Lincoln. Mrs Kennedy in fact requested the same funeral parade be arranged as for Lincoln, including the use of muffled drums. Her request, and the reasons for it, went largely unheeded by commentators; certainly few, if any, saw it as acknowledging the symbolic link between the men or how much their deaths had in common. It is doubtful that Mrs Kennedy's decision was based on any feeling for historical perspective, or historical coincidence.

Both presidents used rocking chairs. Kennedy claimed it eased the pain of his bad back. When he attended a show, Lincoln's rocking chair was taken to the theatre beforehand. He was sitting in it when Booth shot him. Lincoln's chair is kept in the National Archives. A reliable witness reported seeing Kennedy's rocking chair at the Dallas Trade Mart where he was on his way to give a speech before being killed.

Premonitions and Predictions

Premonitions and predictions foreshadowed the deaths of the presidents. A story in the 13 May 1956 edition of *Parade* magazine carries this paragraph: 'As for the 1960 elections, Mrs Dixon [Jean Dixon, the famed Washington seer] thinks it will be dominated by Labor and won by a Democrat. But he will be assassinated, or die in office.' As the assassination date approached dozens of people had similar visions. Arthur Ford, one of America's best-known mediums, saw Kennedy 'falling forward in a moving vehicle and dying'.[63]

On the morning of the assassination Kennedy, in his Fort Worth Hotel suite, was shown that day's copy of the *Dallas News* which carried an advertisement made to look like an obituary notice, complete with a heavy black border, that basically accused him of being a communist supporter. Clearly upset, he told his wife, 'You know we're heading into nut country today.' After a pause, he went on: 'Last night would have been a hell of a night to assassinate a president...we were getting jostled. Suppose a man had a pistol in a briefcase...'[64]

On the afternoon before he was assassinated, Lincoln spoke to one of his White House guards, William Crook. 'I believe there are men who want to take my life and I have no doubt they will do it...if it is to be done, it is impossible to prevent it.' Lincoln went on to say he did not want to go to the theatre that night, but he did not want to disappoint the people by cancelling when his visit had been advertised. The president's comments upset Crook, who would never forget that in parting that afternoon the president said 'goodbye' to him instead of the usual 'good night'.[65]

Some time before (accounts differ on the actual time) Lincoln had a nightmare in which he heard deep sobbing. As the dream unfolded, he left his bed and wandered through the White House until he came to the east wing where he met with a sickening surprise:

> Before me was a catafalque, on which rested a corpse wrapped in funeral vestments. Around it were stationed soldiers who were acting as guards and there was a throng of people, some gazing mournfully upon the corpse, whose face was covered. 'Who is dead in the White House?' he demanded of one of the soldiers. 'The President,' was his answer. 'He was killed by an assassin.'[66]

The Two Johnsons

Lincoln and Kennedy were succeeded by vice-presidents Johnson. Both were large men, Southern Democrats who had been Senators. Andrew Johnson was born in 1808 and Lyndon Johnson (LBJ) in 1908.

The names Andrew Johnson and Lyndon Johnson each contain thirteen letters. Both Johnsons had been the only two vice-presidents from the South in the 100 years between the assassinations.

Both were the fathers of two daughters.

Education was an important influence in the early adult years of both men, but, ironically, for opposite reasons: one was self-taught, the other the teacher. LBJ received a B.S. from Southwest Texas State Teachers College in San Marcos, and then taught for a year in Houston before going to Washington in 1931.

They entered their presidencies in their mid-fifties and each was opposed for re-election by a man whose name started with G: Grant in the case of AJ and Goldwater in the case of LBJ.

In office, the major tasks confronting the Johnsons were dealing with the problems of a nation divided by war, the American Civil War for AJ, and in LBJ's case the Vietnam war, the freedom of black slaves and civil rights for blacks.

Both were born into poor white Southern families, AJ in a wooden shack in Raleigh, North Carolina, and LBJ in a small farmhouse in Texas. AJ's father was a janitor; LBJ's father also worked for a time as a janitor.

As a Southern Democrat, AJ defended slavery throughout the 1840s and 50s, just as LBJ was a consistent opponent of civil rights legislation throughout the 1940s and much of the 50s before having a change of heart.

When the Southern States began to leave the Union to form the Confederacy, AJ argued that secession was illegal. By then a US Senator for Tennessee, he fought to keep the state in the Union. He was the only Southern Senator to remain loyal to the United States in the ensuing civil war.

In recognition of his loyalty to the Union, the Republicans chose the Democrat AJ to run as vice-president with their man Lincoln in the 1864 presidential campaign.

Soon after stepping into the presidency, AJ ran into trouble with a powerful Northern group in Congress known as the Radical Republicans who pushed through a sweeping civil rights Bill for the Southern Blacks. AJ vetoed the measure on the grounds of state rights and also his belief that whites should rule by right. Congress overrode the veto and passed a series of Acts establishing suffrage for the freed slaves and guaranteeing them civil rights. The Bill also established military rule in the Southern States and harsh conditions on their readmission to the Union. Johnson vetoed all these measures but each time Congress overrode him.

The struggle reached a climax in 1868 when the president was tried on impeachment charges. The Senate found AJ not guilty. However, his power had been broken and he spent the remainder of his term in impotent frustration. AJ died of a stroke in 1875.

LBJ feared he too would be tried on impeachment charges over what became known as the Bobby Baker Scandal. Baker was secretary for the Majority. The Majority leader traditionally makes the appointment and in this case it was LBJ in that position and he appointed Baker in 1955. The two men were close. LBJ, when he became vice-president, asked Baker to stay on in the role. Baker was reputedly involved in a call girl racket, providing them for Senators and Congressmen. Also, in a clear conflict of interests, he had amassed a fortune in deals involving government contracts. If Baker went down in disgrace, LBJ feared he would take him with him. The possibility of impeachment disappeared, however, on 1 April 1964, when the House Baker Hearing was permanently discontinued.

With Kennedy gone, LBJ was left to deal with the growing campaign for civil rights among the Blacks the likes of which the nation had not seen since AJ's presidency. Acting as though he wanted to make up for his Southern namesake's entrenched white supremacist stance, in 1957 LBJ, then a Senator, helped engineer the first national civil rights legislation since the Civil War.

As president, LBJ began a rapid escalation of the war in Vietnam. While AJ had been against the use of military force in the conquered Southern States, Johnson saw its use as a solution against North Vietnam.

Just as the 1866 Congressional elections had shown the dwindling support for AJ, the New Hampshire presidential primary of 1968 revealed the dwindling support for LBJ and his war policies.

After stepping down from the presidency in January 1969, like his predecessor, frustrated that he had been unable to complete many of his goals, LBJ returned to his ranch in Texas where he died in January the following year.

History regards the two men as among the most colourful of American presidents. But each suffered under the handicap of dealing with a nation divided by war and being overshadowed from the outset by the comparisons with the two most impressive presidents in American history.

Strange Deaths

Sylvia Meagher claims that 18 'material witnesses' to the Kennedy assassination had died by early 1967, five of them of natural causes, while 13 were the victims of accidents, suicide or murder. There were six murders, one manslaughter, two suicides, three motor vehicle accidents and one person who died from falling through a plate-glass window.[67] These were persons who could have been called on to give evidence had Oswald lived to stand trial. By 1975 up to 50 witnesses had met untimely deaths.[68] The implication is that the deaths were part of a still-unexplained conspiracy surrounding the assassination. The deaths do not include George de Mohrenschildt, who in 1977 put a gun into his mouth and blew his head away hours after he had been located by Gaeton Fonzi, an investigator for the House Select Committee on Assassinations. De Mohrenschildt had befriended Oswald and many saw him as a central figure in the conspiracy. Indeed, Fonzi describes him as 'one of the most important witnesses – perhaps the most important witness – in the Kennedy saga'.[69]

Similarly, Roscoe writes of a series of murders, suicides and strange disappearances of central characters in the Lincoln saga. Among them, Edwin Stanton, the War Secretary, widely believed to have cut his own throat in 1869. His strange behaviour following the assassination has left historians groping for plausible explanations. For example, although Booth had been readily identified as Lincoln's killer his name was left off the initial dispatches sent out by Stanton ordering the hue and cry. Stanton also, as we have seen, withheld Booth's diary from the military hearing into the assassination. Stanton is also accused of being reluctant to bring alleged conspirator John Surratt to trial. He was the son of Mary Surratt, who had been hanged as a conspirator: 'Did the dictator in the War Department fear an exposure by John Surratt of "others unknown"?' asks Roscoe, adding, 'Whatever Stanton's motives they were never divulged.'[70]

The mysterious deaths may be considered on the basis of probability calculus or as a clustering effect. Charles Roberts estimates that 1,000 adult persons were related to the Kennedy case. He argues that if, as Meagher claims, 18 of them had died by 1967, then some must have had unexpected longevity. According to the Metropolitan Life Insurance Company, in a group of 1,000 persons 20 years of age and older in the US population at large, a total of 43 persons should have died in the three-year period following Kennedy's death.[71] Sceptics, therefore, can dismiss the issue of the deaths of the principals in both cases as a matter of randomness.

But there could be some argument for these deaths to be seen as evidence of the clustering or converging effect (see p. 58), i.e. it never rains but it pours.

Early Editions

On the afternoon of 14 April, the *Whig* newspaper in Middletown, New York, announced that Lincoln had been killed by an assassin – hours before the assassination took place.[72] Roscoe opines that this and other incidents in which word of the killing appeared to have spread before any official announcement – even to places without a telegraph office – appears to suggest some underground agent advised what was coming.[73]

On the day of Kennedy's assassination Fletcher Prouty, then Chief Pentagon liaison officer to the CIA, was in New Zealand. Prouty claimed a local newspaper, *The Christchurch Star*, published an 'extra' edition containing Oswald's life story before he was even charged with any crime in Dallas.[74] The implication of Prouty's claim is that an intelligence agency released an early pre-written story about the assassin to the press.

As with many others matters to do with the assassinations it appears that neither claim was ever officially investigated.

In presenting this material I did not set out to find evidence either for or against a conspiracy or conspiracies. Many, perhaps too many, books have sought to do that, so far none of them conclusively either way.

There are so many points in the conspiracy arguments for both deaths where the answer has to be either conspiracy or coincidence that the similarities between the two have become mired. For example, what were the FBI Chief, J. Edgar Hoover, and Kennedy's rival for the presidency, Richard Nixon, doing in Dallas the day before the assassination – conspiracy or coincidence? Why was Booth not identified as the assassin in the initial dispatches on Lincoln's shooting?

There is, in mythology, a figure known variously as the Trickster or Cosmic Joker whose task, it appears, is to mock the human condition and one of the ways this figure chooses to do so is through coincidence – apply this possibility to many of the unlikely anecdotes recorded in this book and it does appear to offer an explanation. In the case of the coincidences between the two assassinations, can we see the work of our mischievous figure, who enjoys a prank, especially on a grand scale? At the very least, this should remind us that we are not Masters of the Universe, but simply an indivisible part of it.

The coincidences cannot tell us when the next presidential assassination attempt will come, but then, neither can probability analysis. We will have to leave that to the Cosmic Joker.

appendix

Psychology and Coincidences

By Dr Caroline Watt

(Author's note: Dr Caroline Watt began working as a Research Associate with the Koestler Chair of Parapsychology in 1987. In 1993 she completed a part-time PhD on the topic 'The Relationship Between Performance on a Prototype Measure of Perceptual Defence / Vigilance and Psi Performance'. This work, which she hopes to continue, consists of a conceptual replication and extension of successful parapsychological research that has found a consistent relationship between performance on the Defence Mechanism Test and psi performance [most of this DMT research has been conducted by Erlendur Haraldsson]. Her first degree is in Psychology from St Andrews University [Scotland], which probably explains why her main interest is in psychological aspects of ESP performance. She is also heavily involved in producing the *European Journal of Parapsychology*. Her interests have been divided between part-time parapsychology and motherhood.)

The first large-scale survey of coincidences experiences was begun on Christmas Eve 1989 in a questionnaire that appeared in the *Observer Review*. Just over a thousand people responded. Men and women were equally represented. 84 per cent of the respondents felt they had experienced coincidences that were in some way meaningful.[1] Of course this is likely to be an exaggerated percentage, due to the fact that the respondents were not a random sample of the population and that the questionnaire was accompanied by an article on coincidences. We can only guess at the true incident of coincidence experiences.

Here is a typical account of a coincidence. A woman went to a small local town which she had not done for months. She goes on:

> On impulse I went to a newsagents and bought only a local newspaper,
> which I never normally do. I opened the paper on a page and my eyes were
> drawn immediately to a small item detailing a granted planning permission

(again I do not normally read these). This item turned out to be crucial evidence needed for my impending divorce settlement. Without this chance happening I would have had no other means of discovering this vital information. I had no idea of its existence.[2]

We see here some of the characteristics that can make coincidence so striking: we do something out of our usual character or habit, perhaps on an impulse, and we discover information or meet someone that fulfils a personal need. A coincidence may be defined as a surprising concurrence of events, perceived as meaningfully related with no apparent causal connection.[3]

In the above example one possible normal cause – that of pure chance – is made less plausible because the woman's actions were unusual for her. Had she been in the regular habit of visiting that small town, buying the local newspaper and scanning the classified advertisements, then we can see that there would be a much higher likelihood of her coming across the information that turned out to be so important for her. One kind of information that can be useful, therefore, in evaluating the likelihood of striking coincidences being due merely to chance is information about the frequency of events.

In the inexact world of everyday life, it is often difficult to clearly establish the frequency of the components of a coincidence, However, public lotteries involve a known number of players and a known probability of winning. Consider the likelihood of winning the jackpot in the Lottery twice. On 14 February 1986, *The New York Times* carried a story about a woman who won the New Jersey Lottery twice in a short time period. *The Times* claimed that the odds of one person winning the top prize twice were about one in 17 trillion. That looks like an amazing coincidence. However, the odds are misleading because they refer to the likelihood that a specific individual who plays the New Jersey Lottery exactly twice will win both times. Actually millions of people play the Lottery every day. Someone, somewhere, some day, is certain to win twice. Professor Stephen Samuels and George McCabe calculated that in the United States, there was at least a one in 30 chance of a double winner in a four-month period and more than a 50/50 chance of a double winner in a seven-year period.[4] Incidentally I live in Linlithgow, Scotland, in the area that has become known as the Golden Triangle due to the apparently high number of Lottery jackpot winners. I'm still waiting for my big win, but the part of me that is a scientist reminds me that, with any random distribution of events, you can get clusters that, to the untrained eye (and the wishful thinker), appear non-random. An incredible coincidence happens daily to only one person in a million. This appears quite rare, but the population of Britain is 55 million, so each day there are likely to be 55 amazing coincidences. That makes 20,075 incredible coincidences per year. As statisticians Persi Diaconis and Frederick Mosteller put it: with a large enough sample any outrageous thing is likely to happen.[5] It's when that statistically predictable coincidence happens to you or someone you know that it feels spooky and you may attribute meaningfulness to it.

It's all very well talking about frequencies and probabilities, but often in everyday life it is difficult if not impossible to estimate frequency and therefore the actual probability of a coincidence occurring. We often have to rely on our intuitions when judging likelihood and psychologists have shown that these can be quite misleading. In the rest of this chapter, I will describe some of the findings from psychological research on people's intuitive judgements.

This research suggests that we should be cautious in how we interpret coincidence anecdotes. While there may well remain a core of coincidences that suggest some paranormal factor was involved, many apparently meaningful coincidences become somewhat diluted when normal psychological factors are taken into account. The problem and the joy of being human are that we are subjective beings. As we go about our everyday lives, we are constantly bombarded with snippets and fragments of information. A half-heard conversation, a partially obscured sign, a glimpse of a newspaper as it is read by someone else on a bus, a distant memory that is evoked by a fragrance. The wonder of the brain is that it is able to construct a comprehensible world out of this chaos. Part of the reason for this is that, over our lives, we have built up expectations of how the world works. For instance, we know that a chair has four legs. Even if we can only see the top of the chair behind a table, we expect it is resting on four legs. For a baby, the world is more chaotic – perhaps it perceives the top of the chair to be floating off the ground, for it can see no means of support. A large part of our cognitive development is geared towards learning how the world works and our experiences and memories help us to have expectations that, usually, are correct. Precisely how much we take for granted the continual inferences made by our brains was found out by artificial intelligence scientists when they started to develop robots to do routine tasks, such as avoiding obstacles when we walk. It was found that this was no simple matter and a large amount of computational power, together with many sensors, was required in order even to crudely simulate human abilities.

So, our brains are expert at rapidly drawing inferences based on incomplete information. Usually this is perfectly adequate for us to go about our daily business effectively. However, we can sometimes be misled by our expectations and recollections. For instance, when having a phone conversation on a noisy line, it is easy to talk at cross-purposes when we interpret an ambiguous word or phrase according to our expectations.

Conjurors are expert at exploiting our expectations of how the world works in order to surprise and amaze us. Even conjurors may easily be fooled if an apparently familiar trick is done in a way different to their expectations.

First of all, let us consider how we judge *likelihood*, since this is an important aspect to the 'surprisingness' of coincidences.

The Intuitive Statistician

Most coincidences only seem improbable. We have already seen that, with a large number of people and a large number of experiences, the likelihood of something unusual happening to someone somewhere some day is actually very high. When we personally experience that unusual happening it is very striking indeed.

Overlooking Non-Coincidence. We do not notice the multitude of non-coincidences that are happening to us most of the time: when we go on holiday and don't bump into anyone we know; when we board a bus and don't meet a friend unexpectedly; when we read a newspaper and don't come across any personally relevant information. This neglect of non-coincidence contributes to the seeming improbability of coincidences.

Example: Psychic phone calls. Many of us may have had experiences of receiving a phone call from someone of whom we have just been thinking. Could this be extrasensory perception? In order to evaluate that question, we would need to know the number of times that we think about individuals, the number of times these individuals phone us, and we would need to take into account common factors that might increase the likelihood of a coincidence between our thoughts of a friend and their phoning us. For instance, a television programme might evoke common memories and associations for us and our friend. This could lead to the urge to make a call, even though we might not be conscious of the source of the impulse. At the same time the non-events, the non-coincidences, of our thoughts and phone calls, the failures of the phone to ring, get overlooked. Thus it is easy to overestimate the frequency of coincidences because they are so much more memorable than non-coincidences.

Actual events that are vivid and easily brought to mind seem to exercise a disproportionate influence on our frequency judgements. This is known as judgement by availability, otherwise termed the *availability heuristic*.[6] A coincidence can be very impressive if it is very specific. Often, however, a 'close' coincidence is also regarded as impressive, although the chances of a 'close' coincidence happening are that much greater than are the chances of an exact or specific coincidence.

To return to the phone calls example. We might be thinking of Great Aunt Maude, to whom we have not spoken for months, and we would probably consider it to be a striking coincidence if Maude's husband Bert or their daughter Sue phoned us. If a prediction has multiple endpoints, several different outcomes could still be impressive to us. With hindsight, we can even fudge the original prediction so that in our memories it becomes more specific than it actually was. Statisticians Dianconis and Mosteller have provided simple formulae to calculate the likelihood of close coincidences.

In Edinburgh we often get people calling in who think they are having psychic experiences, such as precognitive dreams. People may be wanting to confirm their abilities or to get rid of them. As a first step we need to get a good description of what is going on, so we may ask people to keep a diary, noting every possible precognitive dream and whether or not it 'came true'. Doing this, people often find that they have been overestimating the frequency of their success rate, presumably because successes are so memorable. Recording actual performance can circumvent the availability heuristic to some extent and make the non-coincidences less easy to ignore.

The Gambler's Fallacy. Another aspect of our statistical intuitions is that we often think of random events as self-correcting. For instance, if we toss a coin and get a sequence of 'heads', we expect that the next toss is more than likely to be 'tails'. While this is true in the long run, in any random sequence it is quite normal to get runs of 'heads', runs of 'tails', and patterns in the data that appear non-random. Remember that our brain is expert at drawing meaning from chaotic and often ambiguous information, but the coin has no 'memory' of the outcome of the previous toss. Each toss will be independent of the previous one, and if it is a fair coin then there is a 50/50 chance that the next toss will be heads. So it would be a brave and foolish man who would confidently bet on the outcome of the next toss based on the previous one.

Example: The 'hot hand' in basketball.[7] To illustrate the gambler's fallacy, let us consider the phenomenon often experienced by basketball fans and players – the 'hot hand' – where a player has a run of successful shots at goal. Psychologists Tversky and Gilovich compared the reality contained in the records of basketball shooting with the fans' impressions of 'streak shooting'. They found that people tended to think there were streaks when there were not. Almost two-thirds of fans judged the probability of a hit to be higher after a hit had just been scored. When the researchers examined the actual scoring records they found no evidence of streak shooting. To sum up, our strength in being able to make rapid judgements based on incomplete information can also prove to be a weakness when it comes to making estimations of likelihood. We do not excel as intuitive statisticians and this may lead to us underestimating the likelihood of coincidences.

There are other psychological factors that affect our experience of coincidences. One of the most important is the influence of our expectations and beliefs on perceptions and recollections. Let us consider this in more detail.

The Influence of Beliefs. Psychologists have shown that memory does not work like a tape-recorder. Instead our memories can alter over time. Not only does memory tend to fade over time – we have all experienced this – but also memory changes over time. Memory is a construction based partly on our perceptions and partly on our interpretations. It appears that when we remember coincidences that we have heard described by other people, or have been involved in ourselves in the past, our memory may blur some details and strengthen others so as to make the coincidence seem more impressive than it was to begin with. This is a process of which we may be wholly unaware.

Example: Eyewitness testimony. Work in this area has shown how easy it is to alter recollections simply by altering the phrasing of questions about an incident in the past.[8] In a typical experiment subjects were shown a film of a traffic accident. Soon after that, they were asked questions about their memory of the accident. One of these questions, about the speed of the cars, was asked in two different ways. Half of the subjects were asked, 'How fast were the cars going when they smashed into each other?'; the other half were asked, 'How fast were the cars going when they hit each other?' A week later subjects were given a memory test, where they were asked, 'Did you see any broken glass?' Apparently, subjects used the different inferences suggested by the words 'smash' or 'hit' to alter their memory of the accident. 'Smash' implies a more destructive collision than 'hit'. Although there was no broken glass in the original film, those subjects who had been asked the 'smash' question were more likely to say, mistakenly, that they remembered seeing broken glass.[9]

The implication of research such as this on eyewitness testimony is, of course, that we must be very careful when relying on memory alone. In a review of the literature Hall, McFeaters and Loftus[10] describe how new information can be absorbed and interpreted as an original memory. New information might be embedded in a misleading message, or in a biasing question, or in a sketch or photograph. Private remembering of the event, discussion with friends or family, or questioning by a careless investigator can be a source of misleading recollections. When we experience a coincidence, we can to some extent circumvent the weaknesses in our memory by thoroughly documenting the event as soon as possible after it happens. Thus there is an unchanging record in existence against which our changing memories may be continually compared.

Biased perceptions. Not only can memory alter over time according to our beliefs and expectations, our initial perceptions, too, can be heavily influenced by our beliefs and expectations. Information that is consistent with our expectations is readily assimilated to strengthen our beliefs. On the other hand information that does not fit with our expectations may be distorted to make it fit, selectively ignored or forgotten so that our prior expectations or interpretations of an event or a coincidence are not challenged.[11] Psychologists Nisbett and Ross identified three factors that increased the likelihood of erroneous bias based on *a priori* beliefs.[12]

1. Confidence. If confidence in one's beliefs is based on emotional commitment rather than on a solid factual foundation then it is more likely that we will selectively process information so as to strengthen our beliefs.

2. Availability. The likelihood that our beliefs will influence how we interpret information depends on its availability – that is, how readily our beliefs can be brought to mind. For instance, if we have just completed a course on the fallibility of human judgement, then this perspective will be more available and will tend to be used to interpret and judge a coincidence. Alternatively, if our recent course was on Jung's ideas of synchronicity, then this will be the more available perspective against which we will judge a coincidence.

3. Ambiguity. If an event is clear and unambiguous then it may be more difficult (though not impossible) for us to put our own interpretation on that information, based on our preconceptions. If, on the other hand, the event is

experienced in an ambiguous way – say in poor light or confusing circumstances – then it is much easier for us to interpret it so as to fit our expectations. Fading of memory and the operation of the various 'rules of thumb' that we use to process information can render initially clear information ambiguous.

Belief Cuts Both Ways. Before I move on to the final section, I wish to make an important point about the emphasis in the paragraphs above. I have been focusing on the influence of beliefs on our perceptions and recollections specifically, as this reflects how we may be mistaken about the details of a striking coincidence. Just as a person who is open to the idea that coincidences may have paranormal interpretations may selectively interpret events so as to strengthen this belief, so can a person who is closed to the possible paranormal interpretations of coincidences selectively interpret events so as to strengthen this belief. All too often I find in the so-called 'sceptical' literature (sceptical should mean questioning, not counter-advocacy) examples of passionately held beliefs (in the non-existence of paranormal phenomena) that are dressed up as objective and rationally held positions. Hence I find myself just as cautious when considering 'anti-paranormal' arguments and rhetoric as I am when considering 'pro-paranormal' positions. There is no substitute for careful scientific inquiry on this matter, and a familiarity with the literature is essential before passing judgement.

The final factor I would like to consider with regard to psychological aspects of coincidences is that of the impact of personal involvement in coincidences.

The 'egocentric bias'. People are not ignorant of the fact that amazing coincidences can occur purely by chance, as only one of many possible events that could have happened. Falk[13] asked subjects to rate the surprisingness of coincidences that had happened to others. The subjects were not very surprised by the others' accounts. When, however, they compare coincidences that have happened to themselves with those that others have experienced, the self-coincidences are consistently described as more surprising, even though others do not find these coincidences particularly surprising. Falk then went on to make some of the coincidences meaningful (that involved personal names or birthdays) and some other coincidences trivial (that involved random numbers that were arbitrarily assigned). She found that the more meaningful a self-coincidence is to the person involved, the more surprising it is rated as being.

The 'egocentric bias' suggest that personal involvement in a coincidence makes it seem subjectively less likely. Although we can appreciate that coincidences happening to others represent only one of a large range of possible events, when coincidences occur to us personally we do not see ourselves as 'parts of the statistics'. This is a powerful effect: Falk describes how, when telling academic colleagues of the increased surprise for self-coincidences, she was often interrupted with, 'But you should hear what happened to me...' Thus, personal involvement is one important consideration in explaining why some concurrences of events are seen as remarkable while others are not.

A similar egocentric bias may explain why, although they may be perfectly aware of the statistics of the risk of death in car accidents or from smoking-related disease, individuals consistently underestimate the likelihood that they personally will become victims.[14]

Summary

People will continue to experience striking coincidences. I have pointed out certain important factors that should be considered when evaluating coincidences: the flaws in our intuitive statistical reasoning; the ways in which our perceptions and recollections may be influenced by our beliefs and expectations; and the particular impact of being personally involved in a coincidence. These factors clearly play a large role in our amazement at coincidences. Once they are taken into account there may yet remain a core of experiences that will pose some interesting questions for parapsychologists.

Notes to Text

Introduction

1 Diaconis, P., and Mosteller, F., 'Methods for studying coincidences', *Journal of the American Statistical Association*, No. 84, pp. 853–61

2 Lou Caracciolo, 'Synchronicity – Creation of Meaningful Coincidence', unpublished manuscript

chapter one

1 Mansfield, Victor, *Synchronicity, Science and Soul-making* (Open Court, Chicago, and La Salle, Illinois, 1995), pp. 232–3; reproduced with permission of the author.

2 *Reality Change* (January–February 1992, Vol. 9, No. 1); Mrs Kaboolian has added to the material from the article for this book

3 Mansfield, op. cit., pp. 38–40

4 Burroughs, William S., *Adding Machine Collected Essays* (John Calder, London, 1985), pp. 101–2

5 Vaughan, Alan, *Incredible Coincidences* (Corgi, Transworld, London, 1981), p. 357; Vaughan cites as his sources:
   Gaddis, Vincent, *Invisible Horizons: The Mysteries of the Sea* (Radnor, Chilton, 1965), pp. 40–1
   – *The Unexplained: Mysteries of Mind, Space and Time* (Orbis Publishing, London, 1981), p. 640

chapter two

1 Sheldrake, Rupert, *The Presence of the Past* (Fontana/Collins, London, 1988), p. 196

2 Ibid., pp. 177–81

3 Combs, Allan, and Holland, Mark, *Synchronicity, Science, Myth and the Trickster* (Floris Books, New York, 1990), p. 24

4 Sheldrake, op. cit., p. 221

5 Combs and Holland, op. cit., p. 25

6 Sheldrake, op. cit., p. 269

7 Scottao@sonic.net

chapter three

1 Cohen, Jack, and Stewart, Ian, 'That's Amazing Isn't It?', *New Scientist* (17 January 1998, No. 2117)

2 Weaver, Warren, *Lady Luck and the Theory of Probability* (Heinemann, London, 1963), p. 361

3 Anderson, Ken, *Coincidences: Chance or Fate?* (Blandford, London, 1995), pp. 8–9

4 Paulos, John Allen, *Skeptical Inquirer* (Summer 1991, Vol. 15), pp. 382–5

5 Ibid., p. 384

6 Weaver, op. cit., p. 293

7 Submitted by Ron Doon of Orchardstown, Waterford, Ireland; see also *Independent on Sunday* (8 February 1998), UK

8 Borel, Emile, *Probabilities and Life* (Dover Publications, New York, 1962), p. 4

9 Diaconis, P., and Mostellar, F., 'Methods for studying coincidences', *Journal of the American Statistical Association* (1989, No. 84), pp. 853–61

10 Shallis, Michael, *On Time* (Penguin, Harmondsworth, 1982), pp. 144–6

11 Combs, Allan, and Holland, Mark, *Synchronicity, Science, Myth and the Trickster* (Floris Books, New York, 1990), p. 24

12 Jung, Carl, *Synchronicity: An Acausal Connecting Principle* (Princeton University Press, New Jersey, 1973), pp. 40–1

13 Koestler, Arthur, *The Challenge of Chance* (Hutchinson, London, 1973), p. 208; Kammerer's work was never translated into English

14 Combs and Holland, op. cit., p. 77

15 Fordham, Frieda, *An Introduction to Jung's Psychology* (Pelican Books, Harmondsworth, 1953), p. 28

16 Jung, Carl, *Collected Works, Vol. 7* (Pantheon Books, New York, 1954), par.119, p. 82

chapter four

1 Saionji, Masami, *Infinite Happiness* (Element Books, Rockport, MA, 1996), pp. 24–5

2 Slater, Philip, *The Wayward Gate* (Beacon Press, Boston, 1997), p. 106

3 Based on interview with author

4 Saionji, op. cit., pp. 24–35

5 Koestler, Arthur, *The Roots of Coincidence* (Random House, New York, 1972), p. 64

6 Mansfield Victor, *Synchronicity, Science and Soul-making* (Open Court, Chicago, and La Salle, Illinois, 1995), pp. 153–4

chapter five

1 West, John Anthony, and Toonder, Jan Gerhard, *The Case for Astrology* (Macdonald, London, 1970), p. 221

2 Jung, Carl, *Synchronicity* (Princeton University Press, Bollingen Series, New Jersey, 1960), p. 111

3 Jung, Carl, 'The Spiritual Problem of Modern Man', *Civilization in Transition*, Collected Works, Vol. 10 (1964), p. 516

4 Anderson, Ken, *Hitler and the Occult* (Prometheus, New York, 1995), p. 178

5 Extract from Mansfield, Victor, *Synchronicity, Science and Soul-making* (Open Court, Chicago, and La Salle, Illinois, 1995), pp. 108–10; reproduced with permission of the author

chapter six

1 Shallis, Michael, *On Time* (Penguin, Harmondsworth, 1982), pp. 140–1

2 *Raja Yoga*, first published in 1970 by Swani Budhananda, President Advaita Ashrama, Mayavati, Atlmora, Himalayas. Hudson's book was first published in 1893. Haywood's copy is the 1970 edition, published by the Hudson-Cohan Publishing and Communications Company, 20 Carmel Avenue, Salinas, California, USA

3 Dunne, J. W., *An Experiment with Time* (A & C Black, London, 1927), p. 17

4 Hutton, J. Bernard, *On the Other Side of Reality* (Howard Baker, London, 1969), pp. 171–6

5 Lambert, R. S., *Exploring the Supernatural: The Weird in Canadian Folklore* (Arthur Baker Ltd, London, undated), pp. 165–6

6 Hall, Angus, *Signs of Things to Come* (Aldus Books, London, 1975), p. 17

7 Dossey, Larry, *Space, Time & Medicine* (Shambhala, Colorado, 1982), p. 163

chapter seven

1 Reprinted with permission of MaryEllen Angelscrib, who may be reached at: angelscrib@aol.com

2 From audio-cassette home study course *The Silva Method*, 1989

chapter eight

1 Reprinted with permission of the *Washington Post* (21 April 1978)

chapter nine

1 Porter, Jonathan, 'Between the Lines', *Daily Telegraph*, 20 February 1998

2 *The Times*, 4 February 1998, p. 4; *Independent on Sunday*, 8 February 1998, p. 24

3 *That's Life*, No. 13 (1 April 1995); reprinted with permission of the publisher

chapter ten

1 Pritt, D. N., *Must the War Spread* (Penguin, Harmondsworth, 1940), p. 25

chapter eighteen

1 Paulos, John Allen, *A Mathematician Reads the Newspaper* (Basic Books, New York, 1995), p. 51

2 Warren Commission Report, pp. 506–7

3 Lattimer, John, *Kennedy and Lincoln, Medical and Ballistic Comparisons of their Assassinations* (Harcourt Brace Jovanovich, New York, 1980), pp. 363–4

4 Ibid.

5 Ibid., p. 364

6 Anderson, Dwight, *The Assassination and History of Conspiracy* (J. R. Hawley & Co., Cincinnati, 1865), p. viii

7 Ibid.

8 Posner, Gerald, *Case Closed: Lee Harvey Oswald and the Assassination of JFK* (Warner Books, London, 1993), p. 202

9 Warren Commission Hearing, Vol. III, p. 359

10 From an account written by Dr Leale in 1909 and quoted in Lattimer, op. cit., p. 28

11 Clark, Champ, *The Assassination* (Time-Life books, Virginia, 1987), p. 86

12 Lattimer, op. cit., p. 350

13 Ibid.

14 Roscoe, Theodore, *The Web of Conspiracy* (Prentice-Hall Inc., New Jersey, 1959), p. 458

15 Warren Commission Report, p. 250

16 Ibid.

17 Manchester, William, *The Death of a President* (Penguin, Harmondsworth, 1977), p. 32

18 Roberts, Charles, *The Truth about the Assassination* (Grosset & Dunlap, New York, 1967), p. 12

19 Roscoe, op. cit., p.10

20 Manchester, op. cit., p. 34

21 Clark, op. cit., pp. 22–3

22 Johnson Impeachment Investigation, p. 281; quoted in Roscoe, op. cit., p. 505

23 Ibid., p. 506

24 Ibid.

25 Posner, op. cit., p. 215

26 Ibid., pp. 215–16

27 *The Daily Telegraph,* 22 November, p.11

28 Warren Commission Report, p. 152

29 Clark, op. cit., p. 86

30 *The Daily Telegraph Mirror,* 25 September 1995, p. 25

31 Clark, op. cit., p. 86

32 Ibid., p. 14

33 Anderson, op. cit., p. 65

34 *Good Weekend Magazine,* 1 October 1988, pp. 50, 53

35 Lattimer, op. cit., p. 48

36 Clark, op. cit., p. 44

37 Anderson, op. cit., p. 61

38 Ibid., p. 65

39 Posner, op. cit., p. 267 and fn 273

40 Anderson, op. cit., p. 65

41 Roscoe, op. cit., p. 398

42 Lattimer, op. cit., p. 363

43 Ibid.

44 Anderson, op. cit., p. 62

45 Lattimer, op. cit., p. 64

46 Warren Commission Exhibit 1502, p. 355, WC Vol. IX

47 Posner, op. cit., p. 400

48 Testimony of Eva Grant, WC Vol IV, p. 471

49 Posner, op. cit., p. 402

50 Warren Commission Report, p. 811

51 Lattimer, op. cit., p. 64

52 Ibid., p. 6

53 Davies, Colin, *Named* (Bookman Press, Melbourne, Australia, 1993), pp. 74–5

54 Warren Commission Report, p. 247

55 Douglas, Henry Kyd, *I Rode with Stonewall* (University of North Carolina, 1940), pp. 341–3; quoted in Roscoe, op. cit., p. 445

56 Benn, Pitman, *The Assassination of President Lincoln and Trial of the Conspirators* (Moore, Wilstrach and Baldwin, Cincinnati, 1865); quoted in Roscoe, op. cit., p. 446

57 Epstein, Edward Jay, *Inquest* (Hutchinson, London, 1996), pp. x–xvi

58 Mailer, Norman, *Oswald's Tale* (Little Brown & Co., London, 1995), p. 551

59 Lane, Mark, *Rush to Judgement* (Penguin, Harmondsworth, 1966), Introduction, p. xxiv

60 Lattimer, op. cit., pp. 350–1

61 Quoted in *Mysteries of the Unexplained* (Reader's Digest Inc., New York, 1982), p. 66

62 Mentioned in testimony given by Wesley Wise, a newsman at Jack Ruby's trial, CE 2413, p. 500, WC Vol. XXV; quoted in Posner, op. cit., p. 386

63 Greenhouse, Herbert B., *Premonitions: A Leap into the Future* (Turnstone Press, London, 1972), p. 79

64 Manchester, op. cit., pp. 109, 121

65 Roscoe, op. cit., pp. 19–22

66 Zohar, Danan, *Through the Time Barrier* (Paladin, London, 1983), p. 27

67 Meagher, Sylvia, *Accessories after the Fact* (Vintage Books, Random House, New York, 1966), p. 302

68 Shaw, Garry, with Harris, Larry R., *Cover-Up* (published by Gary Shaw, Texas, 1976), p. 113

69 Fonzi, Gaeton, *The Last Investigation* (Thunder's Mouth Press, New York, 1993), p. 190

70 Roscoe, op. cit., p. 511

71 Roberts, op cit., p. 93

72 Bishop, Jim, *The Day Lincoln was Shot* (Harper & Brothers, New York, 1955), p. 145

73 Roscoe, op. cit., p. 280

74 Prouty, Fletcher, *JFK* (Birch Lane Press, New York, 1992), p. 306

appendix

1 The survey was organized by Ruth West, Brian Inglis and Jane Henry under the auspices of the Koestler Foundation. The formal report of the results of the survey is by Jane Henry, 'Coincidence experience survey', *Journal of the Society for Psychical Research* (1989, No. 59), pp. 97–108

2 Inglis, Brian, *Coincidence: A Matter of Chance or Synchronicity?* (Hutchinson, London, 1990)

3 Diaconis, P., and Mosteller, F., 'Methods for studying coincidences', *Journal of the American Statistical Association* (1989 No. 84), pp. 853–61

4 Utts, Jessica, *Seeing Through Statistics* (International Thomson Publishing, London, 1996)

5 Ibid.

6 The 'representative heuristic' proposed by Tversky, A., and Kahneman, D., 'Judgment under Uncertainty: Heuristics and Biases', *Science* (1974, No. 185), pp. 1124–31

7 Tversky, A., and Gilovich, T., 'The cold facts about the "hot hand" in basketball', *Chance* (1989, No. 2), pp. 16–21

8 See for example Wells, G. L., and Loftus, E. F. (eds), *Eyewitness Testimony: Psychological Perspectives* (Cambridge University Press, 1984)

9 Loftus, G. R., and Loftus, E. F., *Human Memory: The Processing of Information* (Halstead Press, New York, 1975)

10 Hall, D. F., McFeaters, S. J., and Loftus, E. F., 'Alteration in recollections of unusual and unexpected events', *Journal of Scientific Exploration* (1987, No, 1), pp. 3–10

11 For recent reviews of this and related topics see Plous, S., *The Psychology of Judgment and Decision Making* (McGraw Hill, New York, 1993); and Gilovich, T., *How We Know What Isn't So: The Fallibility of Human Reason in Everyday Life* (Free Press, New York, 1991)

12 Nisbett, R. E., and Ross, L., *Human Inference: Strategies and Shortcomings of Social Judgment* (Prentice-Hall, New Jersey, 1980)

13 Falk, R., 'Judgment of coincidences; Mine versus Yours', *American Journal of Psychology* (1989, No. 102), pp. 477–93

14 Slovic, P., Fischoff, B., and Lichtenstein, S., 'Facts versus fear: understanding perceived risk', in Kahneman, D., Slovic, P., and Tversky, A. (eds), *Judgment Under Uncertainty: Heuristics and Biases* (Cambridge University Press, 1982)

Further Reading

Anderson, Dwight, *The Assassination and History of the Conspiracy* (originally printed by J. R. Hawley & Co., Cincinnati, 1865; republished by Hobbs, Dorman and Co., New York, 1965)

Anderson, Ken, *Coincidences: Accident or Design?* (Collins Angus & Robertson, Sydney, 1991)
— *Extraordinary Coincidences* (HarperCollins, Sydney, 1993)
— *Coincidences: Chance or Fate?* (Blandford, London, 1995)
— *Hitler and the Occult* (Prometheus, New York, 1995)

Assassination of JFK by Coincidence or Conspiracy, produced by the Committee to Investigate Assassinations under the direction of Bernard Fensterwald Jr and compiled by Michael Ewing (Zebra Books, New York, 1973)

Bishop, Jim, *The Day Lincoln Was Shot* (Harper & Brothers, New York, 1955)

Borel, Emile, *Space and Time* (Blackie and Son, London, 1926)
— *Probabilities and Life* (Dover Publications, New York, 1962)

Born, Max, *Natural Philosophy of Cause and Chance* (Oxford University Press, Oxford, 1949)

Bowman, John S. (General Editor), *Chronicle of 20th Century History* (Bison Group, London, 1989)

Clark, Champ, *The Assassination* (Time-Life Books, Alexandria, Virginia, 1987)

Combs, Allan, and Holland, Mark, *Synchronicity, Science, Myth and the Trickster* (Floris Books, New York, 1990)

Davies, Colin, *Named* (Bookman Press, Melbourne, Australia, 1993)

Dossey, Larry, *Space, Time and Medicine* (Shambhala, Boulder, Colorado, and London, 1982)

Duffy, James P., and Ricci, Vincent L., *The Assassination of John F. Kennedy: A Complete Book of Facts* (Thunder's Mouth Press, New York, 1992)

Dunne, J.W., *An Experiment with Time* (A & C Black, London, 1927)

Epstein, *Inquest: The Warren Commission and the Establishment of Truth* (Hutchinson, London, 1966)

Fonzi, Gaeton, *The Last Investigation* (Thunder's Mouth Press, New York, 1993)

Fordham, Freida, *An Introduction to Jung's Psychology* (Pelican Books, Harmondsworth, 1953)

Four Days: The Historical Record of the Death of President Kennedy, compiled by United Press International and *American Heritage* magazine (American Heritage Publishing, 1964)

Gilmore, Christopher Cook, *Hoover vs. the Kennedys: The Second Civil War* (St. Martin's Press, New York, 1987)

Gould, Rupert T., *Enigmas: Another Book of Unexplained Facts* (University Books, New York, 1965)

Greenhouse, Herbert B., *Premonitions: A Leap into the Future* (Turnstone Press, London, 1972)

Huff, Darrell, *How to Take a Chance* (Pelican Books, Harmondsworth, 1959)

Hutton, J. Bernard, *On the Other Side of Reality* (Howard Baker, London, 1969)

Inglis, Brian, *Coincidence: A Matter of Chance – or Synchronicity?* (Hutchinson, London, 1990)

Jung, Carl, *Synchronicity* (Princeton University Press, New Jersey, 1960)

Kammerer, Paul, *Das Gesetz der Serie (The Law of the Series)* (Deutsche Verlag-Anstalt, Stuttgart and Berlin, 1919)

Kennedy Assassinated! Oswald Murdered, compiled by Ian Griggs (self-published, Waltham Abbey, UK, 1994)

Koestler, Arthur, *The Invisible Writing* (Collins & Hamish Hamilton, London, 1954)
— *The Roots of Coincidence* (Random House, New York, 1972)
— *The Challenge of Chance* (Hutchinson, London, 1973)

Lambert, R. S., *Exploring the Supernatural: The Weird in Canadian Folklore* (Arthur Baker Ltd, London, undated)

Lane, Mark, *Rush to Judgment* (Penguin Books, Harmondsworth, UK, 1966)
— *Plausible Denial* (Thunder's Mouth Press, New York, 1991)

Laplace, P. S., *A Philosophical Essay on Probabilities* (Paris, 1812)

Lattimer, John, *Kennedy and Lincoln: Medical and Ballistic Comparisons of their Assassinations* (Harcourt Brace Jovanovich, New York, 1980)

Lindop, Edmund, *Presidents by Accident* (Franklin Watts, New York, 1991)

McDonald, Hugh, and Moore, Robin, *LBJ and the JFK Conspiracy* (Condor, Westport, Connecticut, 1979)

McMillan, Priscilla, *Johnson, Marina and Lee* (Harper and Row, New York, 1977)

Mailer, Norman, *Oswald's Tale* (Little Brown and Co., London, 1995)

Manchester, William, *The Death of a President* (Penguin Books, Harmondsworth, 1977)

Mansfield, Victor, *Synchronicity, Science and Soul-making* (Open Court, Chicago, and La Salle, Illinois, 1995)

Meagher, Sylvia, *Accessories after the Fact* (Vintage Books, Random House, New York, 1966)

Mysteries of the Unexplained (Reader's Digest Inc., Pleasantville, New York, 1982)

Oglesby, Carl, *The JFK Assassination: The Facts and Theories* (Signet, Harmondsworth, 1992)

Paulos, John Allen, *A Mathematician Reads the Newspaper* (Basic Books, New York, 1995)

Posner, Gerald, *Case Closed: Lee Harvey Oswald and the Assassination of JFK* (Warner Books, London, 1993)

Proctor, Richard, *Chance and Luck* (Longman, Green and Co., London, 1887)

Progoff, Ira, *Jung, Synchronicity and Human Destiny* (Dell, New York, 1973)

Prouty, Fletcher, *JFK* (Birch Lane Press, New York, 1992)

Redfield, James, *The Celestine Prophecy* (Bantam, Sydney, 1994)

Richards, Steve, *Luck, Chance and Coincidence* (Aquarian Press, Wellingborough, 1985)

Roberts, Charles, *The Truth about the Assassination* (Grosset & Dunlap, New York, 1967)

Roscoe, Theodore, *The Web of Conspiracy* (Prentice-Hall Inc., New Jersey, 1960)

Saionji, Masami, *Infinite Happiness* (Element, Dorset, 1996)

Scott, Peter Dale, *Deep Politics: The New Revelations in US Government Files, 1994–1995* (Green Archive, Skokie, Illinois, 1995)

Shallis, Michael, *On Time* (Penguin Books, Harmondsworth, 1982)

Shaw, Garry, with Larry R. Harris, *Cover-Up* (Gary Shaw, Cleburne, Texas, 1976)

Sheldrake, Rupert, *A New Science of Life: The Hypothesis of Formative Causation* (Blond and Briggs, London, 1981)
— *The Presence of the Past* (Fontana/Collins, London, 1988)

Silva, José, and Miele, Philip, *The Silva Mind Control Method* (Pocket Books, New York, 1977)

Stern, Philip Van Doren, *The Man Who Killed Lincoln* (The Literary Guild of America, New York, 1939)

Sullivan, William C., *The Bureau: My Thirty Years in Hoover's FBI* (W. W. Norton & Co., New York, 1979)

The Highlights and Hearings Before the Warren Commission. The Witnesses, by *The New York Times* (McGraw Hill, New York 1964)

The President's Commission on the Assassination of President John F. Kennedy (the Warren Commission Report) (United States Government Printing Office, Washington, DC, 1964)

Vaughan, Alan, *Incredible Coincidences: The Baffling World of Synchronicity* (Corgi, London, 1981)

Weaver, Warren, *Lady Luck and the Theory of Probability* (Heinemann, London, 1963)

Weisberg, Harold, *Whitewash: The Report on the Warren Report* (Adell Books, New York, 1967)

West, John Anthony, and Toonder, Jan Gerhard, *The Case for Astrology* (Macdonald, London, 1970)

Zohar, Dana, *Through the Time Barrier* (Paladin, London, 1983)

Index

accidents
  car crashes 139, 141, 173, 187–8
  plane crashes 59, 72–4, 80, 161–3
actors 128–9, 135–6, 196
Adcock, Pat 126–7
aircraft accidents 59, 72–4, 80, 161–3
airships 173
Alyn, Kirk 128
American presidents 194, 199–201,
  202–28
Amir, Yigar 206
amputees 28–9
Anderson, Dwight 217
angels 84, 89–90, 131–2, 152, 155
Anzacs 184–5
Apollo spacecraft 185
Ashford, Mary 201–2
assassination 199–201, 202–28
Assisi 163
Astrid, Queen of Sweden 157
astrology 64, 70–5, 184
astronauts 185
Auckland 178–9
Austin, Audrey 57–8, 98
availability heuristic 233
Awad, Tony 64
awareness 20–42
Azuonye, Dr Ikechukwu 89

Baker, Lafayette 211
Baker, Marion 212
Ball, David 7–8, 159
basketball, 'hot hand' 234

Basler, Roy P. 203–4
Bay Fortune, Prince Edward Island 40,
  41, 42
Beame, Robert 169–70
Beard, Emily 164
beliefs, influence of 234–6
Belushi, John 61
Benedict, June 161, 165–6
Bible 7, 138–9
birds 47–8, 147, 163, 180–2
birthdays 37, 38, 55, 151
Blair, Tony 129
bluetits, and milk bottles 47–8
boars, wild 152
Bono, Sonny 60
Booth, John Wilkes 200, 204, 205,
  206, 207–10, 211, 212–18, 226, 228
Borel, Emile 56
Bowden, Ken F. 171–2
Bowman, Arthur 64
brain 231–2, 233
'brain in vat' theory 30
Brando, Marlon 128–9
Brandt, Joachim 78
Bremer, Arthur 206
Brisbane 178–9
Brunson, Catherine 180–2
Brunson, Judith 180–2
Bryson, Bill 140
burglars 194
Burnett, Dr Macfarlane 150–1
Burroughs, William 33, 35
Butler, David Henry 11

Butler, Frederick Henry 11
Butts, Robert 26

Cabrera, Suni G. 9–10, 173–4
cancer 30–1, 86–7
Caracciolo, Lou 22, 26, 65
Carden, Greg 10, 28–31
Carrico, Dr Charles J. 205–6
cars 79, 197
  accidents 139, 141, 173, 187–8
Carson, Johnny 55
cats 48–9
Chalker, Bill 115–16
channelling 109
Chesterton, G. K. 10
Christie, Agatha 129
Christmas 81–3
Christopher, Gerard 128
CIA 214, 227
Clancy, Tom 185
Cline, Catherine 149–50, 170–1
Clinton, Bill 177
clustering effect 58–62, 134, 227
Cobain, Kurt 60
Cochrane, Martin 56
Coghlan, Charles 39–42
Cohen, Jack 54
collective memory 43–53
Colomb, Charles 124–5
Colville, Kim 152
Combs, Allan 50, 51, 56–7, 62
Conger, Colonel Everton 211
Connally, John 210, 211
conspiracy theories 200, 202, 203–4,
  227–8
Cooper, Glenn 68–9
Cooper, Louise 190
Corbett, Boston 216, 217–18
Coyote 28–9
creative visualization 85, 186–8
cricket 164, 197
crosswords 44
crows 147
Czechoslovakia 200–1

Darwin, Charles 50

Davies, C. E. 7
Davies, Colin 219
Davis, Jefferson 200
Deans, Esther 112
Defence Mechanism Test 229
Deigan, Jackie 144–5
Descartes, René 85
Diaconis, Persi 56, 231
Diana, Princess of Wales 134–5
diary keeping 104–21
Dickinson, Caroline 148
dogs 48, 117–18, 127, 197–8
Dossey, Dr Larry 80
dreams 57, 156
Drury, Nevill(e) 115–16
Dunne, J.W. 77–8
Dwyer, Professor John 85–8, 89

'egocentric bias' 236–7
Egypt, ancient 70
Einstein, Albert 64, 85
Eisenberg, Linda 174
electoral rolls 136
Elizabeth II, Queen 134–5
Ellenborough, Lord 201–2
Ellis, Scott 133
Epstein, Edward Jay 219
Escobar, Pablo 185
Eugenie 45–7
Eves, Colin 124
eyewitness testimony 234–5
Eyre, Peter J. 96–7
Eyre, Tony 177

Farley, Chris 61
FBI 211–12, 227
Fischer, Kerstin 49–50
fish 193
Fleming, Kere 58, 155–6
Flentjar, Sue 8–9
Flockton, Charles P. 40, 42
floods 136
Florens, Marc 194
Forbes-Robertson, Sir Johnston 41
Ford, Steve 127
Fordham, Frieda 62

Forrest, Barbara 201, 202
The Fortean Times 111
Foster, Jon 160–1, 180
Francis of Assisi, St 163
Fraser, Eugenie 178
Fraser, Mary 79
Frentzen, Heinz-Harold 54
frequency theory 56
Fryer, Cathy 165
future, 'knowing' 49, 78–80, 155–6

Gaardner, Jostein 116
Galileo 13
Gallipoli 184–5
Galveston, Texas 39–40
gambler's fallacy 233–4
Gandhi, Indira 200
Gandhi, Rajiv 200
Garcia, John 127
Garfield, James 206
Gauntlett, Frank 148
Geraghty, Daniel 155
Germany 71, 78, 200
ghosts 131–3, 154–5
Gilman, Isaac 66
Givens, Edgar G. 95–6
Givens, Edward R. 95–6
God 14–15, 139
Goddard, Air Marshal Sir Robert
    79–80
Gould, Bryan 129
Grand Prix 54
Grant, Jenny 52
Greenwood, Eileen 10–11
Griffiths, Wyn 8
Grigg, Grace 102–3
guardian angels 84, 89–90, 131–2,
    152, 155
Guerre, Martin 186
Guildford, Sydney (Australia) 153
Guillemet, Christine 140
Guiteau, Charles 206

Hamburg 78
Hamilton, Tom 161–3
Hancock, Tony 9

Haraldsson, Erlendur 229
Harrison-Ford, Carl 145
Harsveld, Bill 143–4, 174
Hawkshaw, Clair 155
Haywood, Maurice 76–7
Heathcote, Ian 164
Hedderwick, Mairi 158
Herron, Dorothy 137
Holland, Mark 50, 51, 56–7, 62
Holland, Teresa 9, 151
Holland, Wayne 151
Hoover, J. Edgar 227–8
Hopcke, Robert H. 15
horoscopes 64, 70–1
Hosty, James 211–12
'hot hand', basketball 234
Howard, Nick 129
Hudson, Thomas Jay 77
Hunter, Guy Jr 174
Hurley, Jade 145
Hutchence, Michael 60
Hutton, J. Bernard 78–9

Iacono, Stephen 156–7
intuition 63–9
Iyer, Hari Haran 151–2

John XXIII, Pope 146, 189
Johnson, Andrew 219, 224–6
Johnson, Lyndon 219, 224–6
Johnson, Wanda Marie 92
Jung, Carl 14, 16, 44, 57, 62, 70–1

Kaboolian, Ute 24–8
Kammerer, Paul 58–9, 61–2
Keller, Helen 23
Kennedy, John F. 60–1, 153, 199–201,
    202–28
Kennedy, Robert 61, 102
Kennedy family 60–1
Kepler, Johannes 13
Kesavan, Scarlet 7
Kidder, Margot 128
Kijanowski, Kimberley 138
Koestler, Arthur 68
Kubrick, Stanley 128

Langtry, Lillie 40, 41
Lashley, Andrea H. 90–1
Lattimer, John K. 203, 204, 206, 215, 216–17
Lawrence, Carole 89–90, 154–5, 175
Le Fanu, Dr James 131
Leale, Dr Charles 206, 210, 215
Leibniz, G. W. 50
Lennon, John 10
likelihood 232–3
Lincoln, Abraham 27, 199–200, 202–28
lost property 139–40
Lottery 64, 130, 133, 141, 142, 147, 156, 164, 167, 195, 230
Luck, Peter 135–6

Mackay, Mary 39–42
Magritte, René 27, 28
Maguire, Ruth 152–3
Mahoney, Lilian 14–15
Mailer, Norman 220
Malcolm, Scott D. 52–3
Maloney, Jean 155
Mansfield, Victor 20–1, 68
marijuana 167
Marshall, Bruce 116
Martens, Sharon 175–6
Martin, James 138–9
MaryEllen 81–4
Matthews, Ted 184–5
Mayes, Bruce 97–8
medical miracles 85–9
mediums 109
meetings, unexpected 99–103
Meir, Golda 24
memory 234–5
  collective memory 43–53
Mercieca, Juliet 147
milk bottles, blue tits and 47–8
Mills, Tony 10, 122, 149, 178
miracles 81–91
Mitchum, Robert 136
Mohrenschildt, George de 226
money 159, 176
Monroe, Marilyn 172
morphic resonance 43–53, 204–5

Mosteller, Frederick 56, 231
Mullington, Neridah 183–4
Munro, Matt 165
murder 50–1, 59, 201–2
Murray, Carol 189
music 24–5, 60

names 92–8, 136, 148
NASA 185
New Age 15
Newton, Sir Isaac 13, 50
Newton, John Haynes 128
Nixon, Richard 227–8
Nottingham University 44
Nova Scotia 79
Nugent, David 144, 173
numbers 27, 38, 57–8, 183–4
Nussbaumer, Roger 177

Observer Review 229
Oksuka, Fujiko 137
Oliver, Judith 138
Oswald, Lee Harvey 200, 204, 205, 206–9, 211–20, 226, 227
owls 180–2

Paine, Lewis 218
Paine, Ruth 218–19
Patton, General George 47
Pauli, Wolfgang 14
Paulos, John Allen 55, 202
pearls 167
Peck, John 167
Peregrine Investment Bank 163–4
Perry, Belinda Lee 92–4
Pierce, Katie 183
Pitkin, Margot 157, 177
plane crashes 59, 72–4, 80, 161–3
poetry 148–9, 161
police 177
Pombeiro, Dulce 33–6
pop music 60
Posner, Gerald 204, 205, 212, 217
Poundstone, William 30
power failures 178–9
Pratchett, Terry 10

pregnancy 142, 183–4
premonitions 49, 78–80, 155–6
presidents, American 194, 199–201, 202–28
Prince Edward Island 39–41
probability theory 13, 15, 54–7
Prouty, Fletcher 227
Pryor, Richard 129
psychology and coincidences 229–37

Rabin, Yitzhak 199, 206
radio 24–5, 189–90
railways 79, 123
Raja Yoga 77
Rama, Swami 124
Rathbone, Major Henry Reed 210
Redfield, James 8, 15, 16
Redford, Robert 135–6, 196
Reeve, Christopher 128
Reeves, George 128
Reif, Joseph A. 57, 125–6
rings 32, 139–40, 173
Ripley's Believe It or Not 40–1
Roberts, Jane 26
Romans 45–7
Roscoe 211, 226–7
Rowley, Colin 144
Ruby, Jack 216, 217–18
Russell, Rhonda 182–3

Saionji, Masami 64, 67–8
sample spaces 54
Sampson, Deana 156
Savage, Joanne 176
Schumacher, Michael 54
scientific discoveries 50
seances 172
Serafino, Domenico 123
Seth concepts 26
Setlowe, Karen 22–4
Seward, William H. 218
Shackleton, Sir Ernest 131
Shakespeare, William 118
Shallis, Michael 56, 76
Sharf, Alyssa 102
Sharf, Jeriann 16, 85, 186–8

sharks 193
Sheldrake, Dr Rupert 8, 43–5, 47–8, 50, 51
Shuster, Joe 128
Siegel, Jerry 128
Silva, José 88
Silver, Kathleen 168
Silvio, Salvatore and Maria 130
Singh, Onkar 127–8
Slater, Philip, 66
Sloat, Rev. John W. 100–2
Slocum, Joshua 131–3
Small, Rodney 94–5
Small World Effect (SWE) 99–103
Smith, Mona 99
Smith, Stevie 43
Snow, Arthur 141
soldiers 45–7
Sothern, Andy 124
Souter, Wendy 139
Spencer, Barbara 183
Spender, Dale 198
Springer, Michael 131
Stanton, Edwin 211, 226–7
Stead, Joanne 104–10, 113
Stewart, Ian 54
Stewart, James 136
Stiles, Danny 25
suicide 60, 154, 193–4
Sullivan, Annie 23–4
Sumner, Hilary 174–5
Superman 128–9
Surrat, John H. 219, 226–7
synchronicity 14, 15–16, 20–1, 62

Taft, Dr Charles 206, 221
teddy bears 158
telepathy 51
telephone calls 23, 64–5, 133, 180, 182–3, 185, 194, 232–3
television 168, 174–5, 232
Thomas, Dylan 43
Thomas, Jill 146
Thompson, Stan 137–8
Thornton, Abraham 201–2
Tilker, Dr Karen 63–4, 65, 66–7

time 76–80
Toonder, Jan Gerhard 70
Trevor-Roper, Hugh 220
twins 185, 194, 195–6

umbrellas 167
Universe 16, 186–8

Van der Rest, John 143–4
Venecek, Suzanne 37–9, 172
Veroni, Vittorio 123
Vidal, Gore 117
Vietnam 140–1
Villeneuve, Jacques 54
viruses 195
visualization 85, 186–8
vultures 48

Waite, Terry 33–4

Wallace, Alfred Russel 50
Wallace, George 206
Waratah Rugby Union team 123
Warren Commission 200, 202–3, 211,
    217–18, 219–20
watches 160
Watt, Dr Caroline 18–19, 105, 229–37
Weaver, Warren 55
West, John Anthony 70
West, Morris 189
whist players 55–6
Whiteley, Emily 155
Woodward, Dean 135
World War I 131, 184–5, 192
World War II 78, 143, 174–5
Wright, Eve 158
Wurst, Adeline 100, 101, 102

Yeldham, Judge David 193–4